Foolproof Recipes for Beginne

THE FIRST-TIME COOKBOOK

Janet and Sayeed Rizvi

HarperCollins *Publishers* India
a joint venture with

New Delhi

For
Jamal, Adil and Gillian
Katherine, James and Andrew
Atiya and Akbar
Grant and Myles
and all the other aspiring cooks for whom
this book is written

HarperCollins *Publishers* India
a joint venture with
The India Today Group

First published in India in 2003 by
HarperCollins *Publishers* India

Second impression 2006

ISBN 13: 978 817223 491 1
ISBN 10: 81 7223 491 0

HarperCollins *Publishers*
1A Hamilton House Connaught Place, New Delhi 110001, India
77-85 Fulham Palace Road, London W6 8JB, United Kingdom
Hazelton Lanes, 55 Avenue Road, Suite 2900, Toronto, Ontario M5R 3L2
and 1995 Markham Road, Scarborough, Ontario M1B 5M8, Canada
25 Ryde Road, Pymble, Sydney, NSW 2073, Australia
31 View Road, Glenfield, Auckland 10, New Zealand
10 East 53rd Street, New York NY 10022, USA
Typeset in 11/14 Classical Garamond
Printed and bound at Thomson Press (India) Ltd.

Contents

Acknowledgments

We want to thank all the people who have along the way shared with us particular recipes or generalised culinary expertise, or both.

For a start, our mothers, Margaret Clarke and the late Qamrunnissa Rizvi, who gave us our first lessons in good food and good living.

The friends and relatives who have shared their expertise with us, or whose recipes are included: Raufan Bua, Asiya Hussain, Manjari Khan, Hariveen Nain, Edith Imam, Fariba Thomson, Rahmat Salahuddin, Beera Mitra, Mahasweta Ghosh, Prema Devi and Usha Ramakrishnan. We didn't manage to profit adequately from the crash course Usha and her friends gave us in south Indian cookery, but a little of it stuck, and we're grateful to them for trying anyhow.

Uma Khan was, so to speak, the original young professional in our life, whose success with some of our early recipes encouraged us to persevere. Shamshu Rizvi, James Clarke, Andrew Clarke and Gabriele Reifenberg also gave us useful feedback.

Sherna Wadia chopped, sliced, diced and stirred our raw text till it emerged in its present form.

And of course special thanks to the immediate family. Our daughter-in-law Gillian, though her appetite is as slender as her form, is unfailingly polite about the food in her *sasural;* she has even, she claims, tried our recipes with success. Of our two sons, Adil wolfs down happily whatever we give him, provided it isn't baingan, tinda, toori, lauki, shalgam, or various other unmentionable foods. Jamal eats even those, and everything else besides, with appreciation but also discrimination and a helpfully critical palate.

We are grateful to them all.

Preface

It's a jungle out there. It's the big world, every man for himself. And every year they're let loose in it—young women and men, fresh from college or training institutions, ready to earn their own livelihood and stand on their own feet. They've spent the best years of their lives so far preparing for this moment; they've had the classiest education and training their parents could afford, and now they're embarking on careers as airline pilots, lawyers, bankers, computer programmers, business executives, teachers, chartered accountants, publishers, editors, pharmacists, environmentalists, journalists, you name it.

They have the skills to survive in the jungle. They opt for sleeper class in the train, when travelling at their own expense, and with equal aplomb fly business class, when their employers are footing the bill. They have credit cards and mobile phones and they're computer literate. They know how to operate a bank account, and what investments they should make to minimise their tax liability. They can deal with estate agents and potential landlords, to say nothing of cranky colleagues and demanding bosses.

But can they cook?

In previous generations women—men rarely—learnt to cook and manage a household standing by their mothers' sides. Now the world has changed. For many of the present generation, the chain of orally transmitted culinary culture has been summarily broken. In a highly competitive environment, girls as much as boys have from their adolescence had their poor little noses kept close to the grindstone, their sole and constant objective being the 90 per cent or better marks that they need to make the grade, and they simply haven't had the time or the interest to learn cooking.

And now here they are, boys or girls—perhaps on their own, perhaps sharing with a friend, perhaps indeed newly married—with no culinary knowledge or experience to fall back on. They've just moved into a small flat (in Delhi, typically a barsati or flatlet-on-the-roof), and on top of the stress of taking their initial steps in the adult world, they find themselves in a situation where they have no alternative but to get down to their own housekeeping and cooking, and they don't have a clue where to begin.

Hundreds and thousands before them have been there, done that and survived. If you have to do it, you can—no doubt at all about it. Still, we thought perhaps we could help a little.

In an attempt to ease things for them, we've compiled a selection of the recipes of the dishes we cook more or less regularly at home. None of them are difficult, yet we think they comprise enough variety to make both the cooking and the eating reasonably interesting, and we've tried to express them in a way that assumes little or no previous experience.

To the recipes, we've added chapters on the basics—how to equip the kitchen, stock it and manage it; the processing of various standard ingredients; and some of the basic methods of Indian cookery.

Since one of us was brought up in the very different culinary tradition of the UK, is rather keen to demolish the myth that the British live exclusively on boiled food, and has a passion for the food of the eastern Mediterranean and the Arab world, we've included a small selection of Videshi dishes, which we hope our readers will enjoy.

The world of cooking is one of infinite variety, of which we can explore only a tiny corner. Our readers should consider our recipes and suggestions not as the last word, but as guidelines to be followed till they acquire enough interest and confidence to branch out on their own.

In the meantime, we hope that our efforts will help you—young, professionally ambitious and raring to go—to enjoy taking your first steps in the kitchen; and that before long you'll come to regard cooking not as a chore, but as relaxation and pleasure.

1

The Kitchen, the Fridge and the Store Cupboard

So here you are in your little flat, and probably quite dismayed at the thought of having to cook and manage for yourself. Don't worry, generations of young people before you have learnt to cope; so can you. You should feel free to cut every corner in sight, and to simplify things at every turn. No grinding of spices for you—what's the need, when everything you want is available in packets? Similarly, there is no need for elaborate equipment. When you set yourself up, get the basics, always buying the best quality stuff you can afford, and add to them as you feel the need according to your cooking style, as it evolves.

Cooking style? we hear you ask. You whose culinary skills don't go beyond making a cup of tea or frying an egg, if that? Oh sure. In precisely the same way as you've got your own individual style of studying or working, writing prose or poetry, playing football, painting pictures, making spreadsheets, or handling a difficult boss, and have evolved this style with the hands-on experience of just doing it, exactly the same thing is going to happen in the kitchen.

As a novice cook you'll probably want to follow the recipes closely; but gradually as you get the feel of it, you may like to start experimenting; then you may start feeling comfortable doing things rather differently from the way we suggest. Sometimes your experiments will work, sometimes they won't, but it's not by following our suggestions slavishly that you're going to learn cooking; it's by trial and error, and what we hope to do is to give you a basis from which to start the process.

The kitchen: Young people at the outset of their careers typically find themselves in relatively inexpensive lodgings, in which the kitchen may be tiny, or makeshift, or both. Accordingly, it's going to take a bit of ingenuity to fit yourself and your stuff into it, let alone getting any work done. The secret is to make the best use of the space available, and if possible to create space.

Many kitchens have been designed with no thought for the convenience of the cook, and often the working surface is too low. This puts a lot of strain on your back and arms. A possible solution is to get your friendly neighbourhood carpenter to make a platform with an easy-to-clean surface, about 6-10 cm high and 30 x 45 cm in area. You can place your chopping-board on that, and you will find it much more comfortable. In the less likely event of the working surface being too high, get a platform of suitable dimensions to stand on.

Assuming you'll be using gas, consider buying a **four-burner cooker.** As you gain experience and want to have several dishes cooking at one time, you'll find having four burners, instead of the standard two, an enormous saving in time and convenience. Place your cooker away from draughts, and on an easy-to-clean surface. The wall behind the cooker should also be easy to clean of splashes and spatters from the frying pan. Tiles are the best option; otherwise consider tacking up a square of oilcloth that can be wiped clean. You also need enough working-space close to the stove. An **exhaust fan** will help to minimise the spread of cooking smells through your living space.

Many people today consider a **microwave oven** less a luxury than a necessity. Its reheating function does make a lot of difference to life, especially for those who don't reckon to cook every day; rather who cook in bursts and sit back four days out

'If you can't stand the heat', says the old saying, 'stay out of the kitchen.' If only it were that easy! The summer heat can be killing in the kitchen, and if you're cooking on gas, you can't use a ceiling fan. One partial solution is to keep a table fan on the floor, where it won't affect the flame, but will give you some relief.

of seven, confident that there's enough in the fridge to keep body and soul together for a couple of days more. Cooking in the microwave is a completely different scene, and if you want to go in for it in a big way, buy a specialised microwave cookbook.

Before you go in for a rice cooker, consider adopting our simple-minded technique of cooking rice in a blanket (no kidding, see box on p. 39). It's a saving in both space and expense.

To make the best use of limited storage space, **pans without handles,** which fit into one another, are the best. They should have a heavy base to spread and retain the heat, and reduce the risk of burning. Start with a couple of medium-sized and a couple of smaller ones. We recommend you get them in heavy aluminium, with perhaps one in stainless steel. Stainless steel is better than aluminium for heating water and making tea, because aluminium turns blackish when you boil water in it, especially if the water is hard; but stainless steel heats up faster, which makes it much easier to burn the food. You could substitute **cook-and-serve casseroles** for a couple of the aluminium pans; they help to cut down the labour of washing dishes. You must have at least one **pressure cooker.** Get a good-sized one—at least five litres. Buy **separators** along with the cooker; they are invaluable also for such tasks as cleaning dal or rice, or washing vegetables. A couple of different sized **kadhais (woks)** in heavy-gauge aluminium, and a heavy **frying pan** are essential. A good non-stick or stick-resistant finish on your kadhais/frying pans is a help but not essential. To hold the pans steady on the heat as you stir the cooking food, you'll also need **tongs (pakad).** A couple of **long-handled spoons/spatulas** for stirring—**wooden spoons** are good because they don't get too hot to hold; a **slotted spoon** in metal, for taking solid items out of hot cooking liquid; **a tin opener; a whisk** (useful for whipping curd and cream and some dals, but not essential, you can always use a fork); a **vegetable peeler; ladle;** and **spatula** (for frying). Buy several **strainers** of different sizes—a small one for tea, and a large one for draining soaked rice, dal and washed vegetables. If you're

> *It's not supposed to be healthy to store food in aluminium, especially sour items which can cause a chemical reaction. Best to decant from the pan into some other container before refrigerating.*

going to make rotis, you'll need a **griddle (tava), rolling pin (belan)** and **flat-bladed tongs (chimta).**

Some appliances, like **gas lighters**, come with their own wall brackets. For the rest, affix to the wall one or two wooden batons, say a metre-and-a-half to two metres long, into which you hammer nails at intervals. Hang all spoons, spatulas, etc, not forgetting kadhais and frying pans, on the nails. See what we mean about creating space?

A **dish rack** that can hang securely on the wall is another useful space-saver. Have it fixed next to the sink, and dishes can be put to drip immediately.

Your **knives**—three or four of different sizes, some serrated, some plain—should be good and sharp. You're actually more likely to cut yourself with a blunt knife as you vainly try to wrestle it through whatever you're cutting. Keep one smallish one for onions and garlic—you can use it for other vegetables too, and even for trimming meat or chicken, but the onion smell may cling, so be careful not to cut fruit with it. In addition, you must have a wooden or plastic **chopping board**, or you'll ruin your knives as well as whatever surface you try to chop on; two or three **bowls** of different sizes that fit into each other for marinating, mixing, stirring and beating; a **colander** for draining and drying fruit and vegetables after washing them, and also for draining noodles/spaghetti. There's no shortcut to peeling garlic, but a **garlic crusher** takes the pain out of grinding it. A good-quality **hand grater** is a must—for ginger and nutmeg, also some vegetable-grating jobs; and a **lemon squeezer** for extracting lime juice.

A basic **electric blender-grinder** increases your scope quite a bit and saves you enormous time and effort. If you want a full-fledged **food processor** with a dozen different attachments, that's fine, as long as you have room for it, and can afford it. Otherwise, a small compact unit with interchangeable bowls for grinding and blending is essential. A small **pestle and mortar** for minor grinding jobs is a convenience.

Miscellaneous items include a large **vacuum flask** for storing cold water, so that in summer you don't have to open the fridge every time someone feels thirsty; **kitchen scales; a measuring cup;**

measuring spoons; and a **garbage bin** or **bucket. Insulated casseroles,** if your lifestyle is such that food is often kept waiting on the table; they can also be used to keep chapattis warm. A **timer,** which you can set to sound an alarm at the end of the cooking time, is something that will save you a lot of tension.

Items in constant use should be handy to the workspace. If possible, keep spices a short arm's length from the stove (ideally in a wall cabinet above the workspace), so that the containers don't get mucky. To store spices, use for preference screw-topped glass containers that are airtight, and clearly labelled. (Or there are a variety of spice-boxes available in the market.) Be careful with oil in plastic bottles; you want to keep them near the stove, but remember the plastic will melt at the touch of a hot cooking vessel. Stand oil bottles on a pad of folded newspaper to absorb drips, and change the newspaper often.

The fridge: The real point about the fridge is that it absolves you from having to shop and cook every day. With a fridge, cooking for just one meal at a time is a waste of effort. Whenever you cook, make double quantities, and serve the dals and vegetables over the next couple of days in different combinations.

It follows that you should have as big a fridge as you can afford and have room for. (You may find it an economy in the long run, as you may not have to go in for a bigger model too soon.)

Small or big, there will be times when you're using the available space and cooling power to their limit. To maximise capacity, think carefully about the arrangement of the movable shelves to avoid wasting space vertically. Use square bottles for water. You can actually fit five square bottles into the space occupied by four round ones. By the same token, you'll be able to fit more into the body of the fridge if you use square containers than if you use round ones. This is worth remembering when you first set yourself up and are shopping for household items.

Defrost regularly; heavy frosting reduces the fridge's effectiveness. (The cheat for defrosting in a hurry is to disconnect the fridge from the electricity supply, and put a pan of boiling water straight off the stove into the freezer.) Clean the fridge at least once a month, and be sure to clean up any spills as they occur. It's much harder once they dry out.

As far as possible, avoid putting anything hot in the fridge. If you're rushing out and have to put in a hot pan, cover it with a lid to trap the steam. Strong-smelling items like chopped onions must be stored in airtight containers. Cooked food should be covered to prevent it drying out. Make sure that fruit and vegetables are dry before putting them in the fridge; they may go bad if stored wet. We all know, with every politically correct and ecologically conscious fibre in our bodies, that there's nothing under the sun as environment-unfriendly as a plastic bag. But the ones that come into the kitchen containing vegetables and other purchases can usefully be recycled for storing vegetables and fruit. This will prevent these from drying out; on the other hand the wrapping shouldn't be airtight, which might encourage the growth of mould. Use plastic too, for wrapping meat or chicken. These items will keep for several days in the chiller-tray just below the freezer. But don't keep mince or fish for more than a day without freezing.

You can freeze meat, chicken or fish in the freezer quite satisfactorily, and they keep for a couple of weeks (but beware of power-cuts which will cause them to defrost untimely; it's not safe for food to freeze, thaw and re-freeze repeatedly). Wrap in two to three layers of plastic, and place in a bowl or on a plate to prevent the juices running disgustingly into the frost, as the meat contracts while freezing. When it is frozen, you can remove the bowl. We don't advise the freezing of cooked foods in the freezer compartment of a domestic fridge. The temperature isn't low enough, and it fluctuates too much with the frequent opening and closing of the fridge door.

Remember when serving cooked food that's been in the fridge for several days—or even only for one day—to heat it through thoroughly. Let the dal or vegetable bubble hard on high heat for a couple of minutes; add half a cup of water to a dry vegetable so that you can stir it over high heat and by the time the water evaporates it will be piping hot. The object of the exercise is to clobber the occasional bacterium that may have found its way into the food, and which at a comfortably lukewarm temperature will be happy to multiply and play merry hell with your digestive system.

No one puts anything into the fridge with the express purpose of letting it sit there for a fortnight; but your programme may change, there are a couple of unexpected meals out and what you expected to eat the day before yesterday is discovered languishing in the back of the top shelf the week after next. What to do? To eat or to throw? There are two rules to govern your decision in such a situation.

- If it looks OK and smells OK, it is OK.
- If in doubt, chuck it out.

In general, you have to be more careful with cooked than uncooked food, and with meat than with vegetable dishes. If by some oversight your ingredients for a dish aren't as fresh as they once were, you will of course take extra care in cutting and cleaning them to ensure that nothing goes in that's the least bit dicey. In the end, the worst that can happen is that the result won't taste as good as it should. And you should avoid using even slightly un-fresh materials for salad or any other uncooked preparation. But cooked food that's gone off, especially non-vegetarian stuff, even if it's thoroughly heated through before being eaten, may have developed toxins that can make you really ill. It's not worth taking a chance.

The store cupboard: This contains the dry ingredients you use on a day-to-day basis, of which you can lay in several days' or weeks' supplies at one time. These include rice, flour (if you're a roti freak, and can bear the thought of making your own rotis), cooking oils, dals and spices.

If you organise yourself properly, you may be able to reduce major shopping expeditions to about one a month. For this, you might look around to find whether there's a government-run or consumer cooperative store nearby, where quality and prices are more or less guaranteed. For everyday needs, sample the various shops in your nearest market, decide which ones

You will be tempted, and why not, to buy convenience foods, like the ready-cooked dals and vegetables in sealed packets, that keep for months and only need to be heated up. Some of them are really good. Keep a few packets in your store cupboard—nothing like them in an emergency.

seem best in terms of being well-stocked with a good variety of items, and having friendly, polite and pleasant people behind the counter (very important for our money), and stick mainly to those. Once the people in a particular shop get to know you, they'll start giving you a little consideration; towards the end of the month, or on a day when you've gone shopping in a rush and left your purse at home, they'll probably allow you to sign for what you've bought. Find out if they deliver—this can be an enormous convenience.

For cooking a reasonable variety of simple Indian dishes, your store cupboard is going to need supplies of most of the following items:

Cooking oil or ghee: Your choice will depend on your taste and what you're used to. Whether or not you go in for any of the heavier more traditional oils, you may also like to keep one of the blander varieties for frying, pulaos, etc. (see p. 10).

Rice and atta: The premium rice in north India is **basmati**, which can cost up to five times as much as more plebeian varieties. You don't, however, have to buy the most expensive variety of basmati. For everyday use, try **parmal** or the local equivalent. For the roti freaks, you can of course locate the nearest chakki and get your flour warm from the grinding, with nothing added and nothing taken away, which no doubt gives you the maximum food value; or you can trot along to your friendly neighbourhood provision shop, and buy it in pre-packed plastic bags.

Dals and other pulses come in a number of varieties that you may find confusing at first (see p. 78). Start by identifying two to three that you like and, as you gain confidence, you can start experimenting with others.

Spices: Obviously you're not going to be grinding your own spices; but to be sure you get the real stuff, buy them from reliable outlets, and get them in sealed and branded packets, preferably with the Agmark. Don't buy enormous amounts; and store them in airtight containers, remembering to close them firmly after use.

Don't be over-ambitious at first. Get a few basic spices, and add to them as you learn the character of each and want to add new dishes to your repertoire. Start with **chilli (lal mirch), turmeric (haldi), cummin (jeera), coriander (dhania),** and **mixed spice (garam masala)** powders. Of whole spices, you may like to have **dried red chillies, cummin, cloves (laung), green cardamom (chhoti ilaichi), black cardamom (badi ilaichi), cinnamon (dalchini), bay leaves (tej patta)** and **black pepper (kali mirch** or **gol mirch).**

Ginger (adrak), garlic (lahsun), green chilli (hari mirch) and **tamarind (imli)** now come in ready-made pastes, separate or combined, in various brands. Purists may frown, but for the likes of you and us, they're an enormous convenience.

As you gain experience, you may want to give more zing and subtlety to your cooking. You will then experiment with **fennel** or **aniseed (saunf), ginger powder (saunth), asafoetida (hing), mango powder (aamchur).** Also the following whole spices: **coriander seeds, mustard seeds (rai** or **sarson), sesame (til), fenugreek (methi), poppy seeds (khus-khus), nigella (kalaunji** or **mangrela), ajwain, nutmeg (jaiphal), mace (javitri)** and **saffron (zafran** or **kesar).**

Items that you may need as you extend your culinary repertoire are **gram flour (besan), semolina (sooji** or **rava), sultanas (kishmish), almonds (badam), vinegar (sirka).** Hold out for the real thing, labelled 'malt vinegar' or 'molasses vinegar' and don't touch synthetic vinegar.

That leaves the perishables that you have to shop for once or twice a week: **bread, eggs, butter, meat, fish, chicken** and **vegetables.** You should always try to have **onions** and **potatoes,** both of which keep for several days even out of the fridge. So does **garlic,** another standby. **Ginger, lime (nimbu)** and **tomatoes,** other items that may be in constant use, are best refrigerated.

So there you are, with your kitchen set up and stocked. The next step is to learn what to do with all this stuff...

2

Ingredients and Their Preparation

Apart from main ingredients like meat, chicken, fish, dal and particular vegetables, the processing of which is described in the relevant chapters, some of the standard ingredients also need preliminary processing. We have devoted a certain amount of time and thought to the cutting of corners, but take our methods as guidelines, and modify them later in the light of your own increasing experience and evolving style.

Oil and ghee: Although many cookery books specify which kind of cooking medium to use for which recipe, as a beginner you can to a great extent choose whichever you prefer. The disadvantage with **ghee,** especially in winter, is that as the food cools on the plate it starts to congeal. Used on a regular basis it is also reckoned more liable to clog the arteries and cause heart problems than oil. However, it certainly adds richness and opulence to some dishes.

As far as **oil** is concerned, you have a choice of **mustard (sarson), sesame (til or gingelly),** or **coconut (nariyal),** for traditionalists. Otherwise, lighter, blander oils derived from **groundnut, sunflower, safflower, corn,** or unspecified, probably a mixture, known simply as **refined oil.** Your choice may very likely be made according to which part of the country you come from. Gujaratis swear by sesame oil for that distinctive Gujarati flavour, and it's also used in the cooking of Tamil Nadu, while Keralites tend to prefer coconut oil. Mustard oil is standard for most north Indian dishes, including those from Kashmir and Bengal, and it's what we use when we cook most of the recipes in this book.

If you're using mustard oil, for most recipes you have to **'burn'** it, to remove the harsh rawness of its flavour. To do this, you set the pan on high heat till the oil thins and starts to smoke. When this happens, turn down the heat, to avoid burning whatever goes in next. (There are a few dishes, however, whose USP is the mustardy flavour of the unburnt oil.)

On the other hand, today more and more health-conscious people prefer to use lighter non-traditional oils, without a strong flavour of their own, many of which are claimed to be better for health than the traditional varieties. You might prefer to start with some of these. Safflower is good; a bit expensive, but it gives excellent results in Indian cooking, and failing olive oil, which is prohibitively expensive, it's probably the best for Western-style salads. In any case, bland oil is what you'll use for any frying jobs, as well as for pulaos, the occasional cold dish like a raita, which needs a baghar (see p. 25), and the Western-style dishes.

Excess oil from frying can be recycled in any other dish, though perhaps not if it has acquired a strong aroma from whatever was fried in it. From the health point of view, however, there's no harm in twice-used oil.

Onions (piaz) are basic. One important function of onions, apart from adding flavour, is to disintegrate and give body to the gravy of a meat or chicken dish. Even if you are vegetarian, you will be using them in vegetable dishes, salads and raitas.

Onions should be hard, and the outer skin not too flaky. For convenience, try not to buy them very small, otherwise you have more units to peel per given weight. They keep well, up to a week or more, even out of the fridge.

> *Cutting onions can be a real pain, because the fumes get to your eyes and make them sting and water. The best solution is to do the job in the open air, if you have a convenient veranda or terrace; otherwise under the fan in a well-ventilated place.*

To peel, cut off both ends of the onion. Make a couple of shallow slits, from one end to the other. Insert the point of the knife under the topmost papery layer, and ease it off. Sometimes the next layer may also have papery patches and you have to remove that too. The edible part is so well protected by the skin that it's hardly necessary to wash it, except that sometimes, especially during the monsoon, the first layer under the skin is covered with a black mildew, which you obviously have to wash off.

To slice, cut your peeled onion in half from pole to pole, and set each half, cut side down, on the chopping board. Cut into lengthwise slices, and the layers will fall apart. To chop the onion, hold the slices so that they don't fall apart, turn them through 90°, and cut across. If you want rings, set the onion on its side without cutting it in half, and cut round the lines of latitude.

Some Indian recipes call for onion paste. If you have a blender, put the onions, peeled and roughly chopped, into the blender goblet with a little water, and give them a whirl. The snag with this method is that the added water may make the paste a bit too wet, though you can always dry it in a pan over low heat for a few minutes. The alternative is to grate them on the coarse side of a grater, or simply slice and chop them as fine as possible.

Sliced onions **browned in oil** are the basis of many a masaledar gravy. They may also be cooked at the start, and taken out when crisp, to use as a garnish for pulaos or khichdis. To get them nice and crisp, slice them as fine and as even as possible. Heat plenty of oil till smoking, or nearly so, add the onions and fry them, stirring constantly, on high heat till they begin to take on a faint brown tinge. When this happens, immediately turn the heat to low, as it is only a small step from faintly brown to frizzled black and burnt. Continue to stir-fry for one to two minutes more till they are light golden, just a little lighter in colour than you think you want them. Turn the heat off, and stir for a further one to two minutes, till the residual heat cooks them to a rich gold. If using fried onions as a garnish, take them out, using a slotted spoon, and put them on a small plate covered with absorbent kitchen paper to blot up the excess oil.

Garlic (lahsun) adds incomparably to the richness of flavour of cooked foods, in which it can be used in very considerable quantities. Garlic comes in bulbs the size of a small onion composed of segments called, confusingly, cloves. Try to buy garlic of which the cloves are not very small, because they have to be peeled individually and tiny ones are a bit of a pain. On the other hand, the huge ones, with only about six cloves to every bulb, though convenient to work with, tend not to have the same pungency. It keeps well, a couple of weeks even out of the fridge. To loosen the papery skins so that they slip off easily, put the cloves on your work surface and bash them—but gently—with something hard like the bottom of a jar or bottle. Make a slit down the length of the convex surface, and ease off the skin. Cut lengthwise and then crosswise into tiny dice; or put several cloves in a garlic crusher to pulp them. Or, if squeezed/ground garlic is what most of your recipes call for, get a jar of garlic paste.

Ginger (adrak), like garlic, is fundamental to much Indian cooking. You can buy it already processed in paste form; in fact, to such an extent does it go together with garlic that you may be happy to settle for ginger-garlic paste.

Some recipes, however, call for diced ginger so it's not a bad idea to have some of the real stuff on hand. It comes in the form of a knobbly root. Buy it fresh and hard, not wrinkled. It keeps reasonably well in the fridge—up to ten days wrapped in plastic. Cut a piece as big as you need, peel and wash it. Slice as fine as you can, then turn the pile of slices 90°, and cut them into thin sticks (such sticks are known in cooking parlance as juliennes). Turn the juliennes another 90° and cut again into tiny dice.

Tomatoes (tamatar), although not indigenous to India, any more than chillies, have become an almost indispensable ingredient for many dishes. At certain seasons, in certain places, you can get round desi tomatoes, which tend to have a better flavour than the otherwise ubiquitous oval hybrid ones. The latter are bred for the market-oriented qualities of firmness and long keeping rather than for rich flavour. Anyhow, too bad, for most of the year they are the only ones available. Buy them firm to the touch; if they're a bit under-ripe that's OK, you can keep them out of the fridge for a couple of days to ripen. Once ripe, they keep in the fridge for three or four days.

Unless you have a really delicate digestion, or are cooking something out-of-this-world special, it's hardly necessary to peel tomatoes. What you can do, is to cut out the stalk point by inserting the point of a sharp vegetable knife close to it and rotating the tomato 360°. If you do want to peel your tomatoes, dip them one by one into boiling water, leave for twenty to thirty seconds, and remove with a slotted spoon. This is called **blanching.** Nick the skin with the point of a knife, and it will peel off easily. If you like tomatoes and use them a lot, it's worth investing in a **tomato slicer** with which you can almost effortlessly slice your tomatoes evenly for salads, or chop them small for cooking.

We have never understood the logic of recipes that tell you not only to peel but also to de-seed tomatoes. You de-seed them and what's left? Forget it.

Cucumbers (kheera), indispensable for salads and raitas, are washed, peeled, and either cut into rounds or diced. To dice, cut them into quarters lengthwise, and cut or scrape out the central portion with the seeds. Then cut into fine or medium dice.

Herbs add variety and freshness to your cooking. When you buy them, be sure to get fresh stuff; the leaves should not be wilted or damaged, and the colour should be bright green.

Fresh coriander (hara dhania) is used as a garnish on a cooked dish, ground up as a chutney, and sometimes cooked into the dish. In season (for most of the year except a few months in summer), your subziwala may add a bunch free with your purchase of vegetables. To keep fresh coriander in the fridge, put it roots and all into a cup with water (as you'd put flowers in a vase) and cover with a plastic bag. Even slightly wilted leaves revive with this treatment, and it can stay for up to a week without withering.

To prepare, cut off the roots and coarse lower stems. Before washing, pick through carefully, discarding any wilted, yellow or otherwise unpleasant looking leaves, then wash in two to three changes of water. You don't have to strip the leaves off the stems, which are usually quite tender. Shake off as much water as possible, and chop fine or coarse.

Fresh mint (pudina) is less versatile than fresh coriander, but has its uses, especially in some raitas, and vegetable dishes, or chutneys. Used more in Western cooking and salads, it blends excellently with tomato. It'll keep for a couple of days in a plastic bag in the fridge, but not as well as coriander.

Prepare it as you would coriander, but as the stems are coarser, you'll need to strip the leaves off them. Dried mint is also available, and is a useful standby for most of the year when the fresh stuff is out of season.

Dill (sua) is a lovely herb with a strong flavour, which comes in winter. Prepare as for coriander, cut off and discard the coarse lower parts of the stems, and chop the rest.

Curry leaves (kari patta) with their wonderful earthy aroma are used a lot, especially in south Indian cooking. It's easiest to wash them on the stem, shake off as much water as possible, and then strip the leaves off.

Green chillies (hari mirch) give pungency and 'heat', but they also have an agreeable flavour. You will often get a handful thrown in free with your other vegetables. They should be fresh bright green, and not look wilted or wrinkled. For convenience, better not to have them very small, though it's said that the smaller ones are more pungent, so you can use fewer of them. They will keep for several days in the fridge wrapped in plastic. For some recipes, they are to be diced—cut lengthwise, then crosswise; for others they are just slit in two. If you don't like your food very hot, you can **de-seed** them after slitting. Ease out the seeds with the point of the knife, and wash the 'shells' under running water to ensure no seeds remain. In a few recipes, they're added whole for flavour rather than heat. You can also get green chilli paste in the market, separately or in combination with ginger and/or garlic.

The annoying thing about green chillies is that, while you wash, cut and de-seed them, some of the 'heat' gets transferred to your hands; and if you inadvertently scratch your lip or your eye they start burning too. This effect takes time to wear off. Even thorough washing with soap helps only marginally. The best cure we've found is to suck or lick your fingers energetically. Your mouth will burn for a few minutes, of course, but the enzymes in the saliva seem to dissolve the 'heat' in your hands better than anything else.

Whole, dried red chillies (lal mirch) can be broken so that the seeds escape through the dish, if you like your food good and hot. Conversely, if you like it mild, slit the chillies and shake out and discard the seeds.

The most basic **spice powders** in north Indian cooking are **red chilli (lal mirch), turmeric (haldi),** and the aromatic **coriander (dhania).** If in doubt, throw in half a teaspoon each of chilli and turmeric,

To get rid of yellow turmeric stains from colourfast materials, wring out the garment in water, and rub the stain with the cut surface of half a lime. Spread it out in the sun, and as it dries the stain will fade. If it's not gone completely, repeat the treatment, the effectiveness of which depends on the strength of the sunlight. Wash as usual.

and one teaspoon of coriander, and you can't go very far wrong. If you like your food less chilli-hot, use less chilli powder, or try **kashmiri mirch,** which has the flavour and imparts a wonderful colour to the dish, but is less pungent.

Whole coriander seeds (sabut dhania) are used occasionally.

Almost as essential is **cummin (jeera).** Almost any chaunk or baghar (see p. 25) can take a teaspoon of whole cummin **(sabut jeera),** and a teaspoon of the powder never did anyone any harm. One standard combination, used especially in Gujarati and Maharashtrian cooking, is two parts coriander powder and one part cummin powder. **Caraway (siah jeera** or **kala jeera,** often called **shah jeera)** though cultivated in the West, is relatively rare in India, because it only grows wild in parts of the Himalayas, and is correspondingly expensive. It is used only occasionally, and never as far as we know in powder form.

Fennel or **aniseed (saunf)** is used a lot in Kashmiri cooking. Fennel seeds are larger, aniseed smaller, but they can be used interchangeably. The seeds look a bit like cummin seeds, but are greenish rather than greyish. Some recipes call for fennel powder, which is unfortunately not very readily available even in well-stocked shops. If you have an electric grinder, you can grind up a couple of spoonfuls of the seeds, without roasting; otherwise, you have to improvise by adding the seeds to the chaunk (see p. 25), instead of the powder as a seasoning.

Mustard seeds come in three varieties: tiny and reddish **(rai),** larger and blackish **(sarson),** and yellowy-brown (husked). We reckon they can be used interchangeably. Either way they are a lovely spice, used much in south Indian cooking. When used whole they don't taste at all like mustard, but have an intriguingly nutty flavour. In Bengali cuisine, they are ground to release their mustardy pungency. But don't try it in your electric machine, it grinds too fine and the flavour turns bitter. Assuming you're not going down on your knees to the old-fashioned grinding-stone, you can substitute mustard powder when you want the flavour.

Nigella (kalaunji or **mangrela,** sometimes referred to in English, quite incorrectly, as onion seeds) are the small black seeds you see on naan in restaurants. They are not ground, but are included in some vegetable dishes.

The roundish brown seeds of the leafy vegetable **fenugreek (methi)** are used as a spice. They have a very strong flavour, and a little goes a long way. Health-food freaks eat the seeds sprouted; they are said to be full of vitamins and other useful trace elements.

Panch-poran is a combination of one spoonful each of cummin, fennel, mustard and nigella seeds, and half a spoonful of fenugreek seeds. Put them all together in a jar, and close to keep airtight. Shake the jar well before using, to distribute the different seeds evenly.

Black pepper (kali mirch or **gol mirch)** comes in both seed and powder form. It is used mainly as a seasoning, especially for eggs and Western dishes. For this reason, it is the only spice that we would recommend the novice cook to grind at home in the electric grinder. The flavour of the home-ground stuff is incomparably better than the powder you get in the bazaar.

Sesame (til) and **poppy seeds (khus-khus),** like mustard seeds, both develop a delightfully nutty taste when dry-roasted or lightly fried. Sesame is used more in south Indian cooking, and poppy seeds in Bengali cooking. Both are oily seeds, so when ground tend to become more like a paste than a powder. (This is probably why they are not sold in powder form like other spices.) Roasted and ground sesame is the basis of **tahina,** the famous seasoning extensively used in the food of west Asia, from Iraq to Greece.

Asafoetida (hing) is a resin, but also comes conveniently in powder form. People tend either to hate or to love it for its strong aroma, and it features commonly in Kashmiri pandit cooking. Used with discretion it adds zing to many vegetable and dal and a few meat dishes. Different companies formulate the powder somewhat differently, so that some are more and some less pungent. With the pure resin, or an almost undiluted powder, a pinch is enough in a dish even for eight people; of some of the milder powders, on the other hand, you might need up to half a teaspoonful. You can gauge the strength of the formulation by a sniff at the container. The quarter-to-half teaspoonful we recommend is therefore to be taken as a basis for your own judgment, remembering always that it's best to err on the side of caution. You can add, but you can't take away.

Ajwain has a strong aromatic flavour and is used in a few dishes.

The **garam masalas—cloves (laung), cinnamon (dalchini), nutmeg (jaiphal)** and **cardamoms (ilaichi)**—are all relatively expensive spices, and are used sparingly. **Black cardamoms (badi ilaichi)** are also used whole, fairly extensively in meat dishes. Some recipes (none of ours) call for grinding different combinations of these. It's simpler to cheat by using ready-made **garam masala powder,** a blend of these and possibly other spices, which is available in every grocery shop. Different brands of garam masala will have slightly different formulations. Find the one you like best. Cinnamon powder is used occasionally in Western food, especially sweet dishes. If you need it, you may have to grind your own.

As well as garam masala, you'll notice that the shops stock a bewildering variety of mixed masala powders—meat masala, subzi masala, chaat masala, sambar masala, choley masala...you name it. You want to experiment with them, feel free.

Nutmeg comes in the form of small nuts. You need to reduce it to powder by grating it on a grater. **Mace (javitri)**—just for the record, it doesn't feature in any of our recipes—is the outer covering of the nutmeg, a lacy amber-coloured membrane.

Bay leaves (tej patta) are bought dry and are used mainly in meat and chicken dishes to impart an aromatic flavour, and cut the 'meatiness' of the meat.

Saffron (kesar, zafran) is the stamen of a particular variety of crocus that grows in temperate climates—in India, only in Kashmir. It is worth a good deal more than its weight in gold, but is used only in minuscule amounts, like six to eight stamens at a time. Because saffron is so rare and valuable, it's liable to adulteration, so you need to be very sure of your source of supply. It gives food not only a lovely yellow colour, but also an indefinable aroma. However, it's not a basic necessity. (If all you want is the colour, use a pinch of turmeric instead.) Before adding saffron to a dish, soak the stamens in a tablespoon of warm water or milk.

Souring agents are **vinegar, lime juice (nimbu), tamarind (imli)** and **aamchur** (mango powder). Limes need to be washed, cut in half around the equator, and the juice squeezed out by hand or in a squeezer.

No need to buy fresh **tamarind,** which takes a lot of processing. It's available as a ready-made **paste.** If it seems very thick, thin it down with a little water before adding it to the dish, to help it blend in evenly.

Aamchur comes as a brownish powder, ready to use. Be careful to keep the container tightly closed as it tends to cake.

Unripe mango (kutcha aam), available for most of the summer and monsoon months, as well as being used for pickles and chutneys (which you probably won't be getting into), features occasionally as flavouring in dal, etc. It is also the basis of the cooling summer sherbet, panna. To use, wash, peel and cut into chunks, discarding the stone.

Unripe papaya (kutcha papeeta) is a tenderising agent, used in some meat marinades. Wash, but do not peel, cut a piece of the specified size, and grate. But go easy. Its action can be so strong that if you use too much, or leave the meat too long in the marinade, the meat is reduced almost to halva. (The professional cook's trick is to tenderise meat using papaya that is halfway between unripe and ripe, in minimal quantities and for not more than two hours. But it's hard to find papaya at just the right stage of half-ripeness.)

Almonds (badam) are added to some meat and other dishes for flavour and consistency. Buy shelled almonds—cracking open the shells is a nuisance. Lightly fried and salted they make a delicious, though expensive, 'nibble' with drinks, but for cooking, you have to get rid of the brown skin. **Blanch** them by pouring boiling water over them in a small bowl. Let them soak for fifteen minutes and the skins will slip off easily. They may be used whole, sliced, or put through a grinder, according to the recipe.

Coconut (nariyal) and **coconut milk** are essential for many south Indian recipes, but processing the raw coconut is a cumbersome business, which we don't advise you to try. Coconut powder is readily available, likewise coconut milk in tetra packs, and coconut milk powder that can be reconstituted thick or thin.

The **milk** you get in the metropolitan cities, in plastic packets or out of machines, is pasteurised. Of the various types on offer, **full-cream milk** is nice for desserts; but even if you keep it in the fridge, be sure to boil it within twenty-four hours at the outside, or twelve to be on the safe side. Probably the most versatile and useful for other purposes is **toned milk.** It has a slightly longer shelf life, may keep in the fridge for up to thirty-six hours without boiling. There's not much to be said for **double-toned milk**—just avoid.

Milk, apart from its obvious uses in tea, coffee, milk shakes and sweet dishes, also figures in the occasional meat or chicken recipe.

> *It makes a nice change, if you need to 'loosen' the gravy of a meat or chicken curry or korma, or when reheating it, to use milk instead of water.*

We all know, only too well, the problem of milk—its regrettable tendency as it boils to froth up in the pan and spill over. Everyone who has ever worked in a kitchen must have let it boil over at least once. **The only answer is to train yourself from the start always but *always* to concentrate as you put milk on the heat so that you don't forget it; *always* to have it in a large enough pan to give room for expansion; and *never* put it on high heat unless you are giving it your undivided attention.**

The other problem with milk is its short shelf life. You can buy UHT (ultra heat-treated) milk, which is sterilised, and keeps for several months, provided the pack it comes in remains sealed. But once opened, UHT milk behaves like any other milk. If you have milk in the fridge that you think has been there long enough but don't have an immediate use for, you can extend its life by bringing it up to the boil, cooling and refrigerating it again. Obviously there's a limit to how often you want to do this. Best make curd.

Cream, available everywhere in tetra packs, is a useful ingredient for some Western desserts.

Curd (dahi) is not only eaten plain as an accompaniment to the main dish, but is also the main element in delicious raitas and is an ingredient in a lot of meat and chicken dishes, as well as some vegetable ones. Although it's freely available mass-produced in hygienic plastic tubs, making it at home is the simplest thing in the world, and something you really ought to master. Basically, it's no more than milk, boiled and cooled to a bit more than blood heat, with a little curd stirred in and kept in a warm place for three or four hours to set.

To make curd, take about half a litre of milk and bring it to the boil, exercising the usual precautions so that it doesn't boil over. If you like your curd a bit creamy, keep the milk simmering on low heat after it boils for about fifteen to twenty minutes to reduce. This is not obligatory, some don't like it that way, claiming that it gives the curd a peculiar 'over-boiled milk' taste. You can also thicken it by stirring in some cream, or a tablespoonful or two of milk powder, dissolved according to the instructions on the packet. Alternatively, you could use powdered milk, reconstituted with extra powder in proportion to your water. Either way, when it has boiled for one or twenty minutes take it off the heat and let it cool to the correct temperature. The usual prescription is that when you can just about dip your finger into it and keep it there for a leisurely count of ten, you're ready to carry on. You don't want it a lot hotter than that but there is a margin; you don't have to be all that precise. If you've sweetened the milk to make Mishti Doi, it needs to be warmer rather than cooler.

Put two teaspoons of curd into the bowl in which you plan to set your new lot. With a spoon, smear it around the base and sides of the bowl, breaking up the semi-solid curd so that it becomes a more or less homogeneous cream. Pour in a little of the warm milk and blend to the consistency of a thin cream. Pour in the rest of the milk, and stir well. Cover, and put in a warm place for two hours or a bit longer, by which time you should have a well set semi-solid curd. Put it in the fridge.

'A warm place' means somewhere that it will stay warm for a couple of hours till it sets. You can keep it in the sun; or insulate it by covering with a tea cosy, or the blanket in which you cook your rice (perhaps). Some people use insulated casseroles. Work out your own system.

Curd is not temperamental, and once you have the knack, it can be relied on to set for you every time. If, however, before you get the knack, you go back to it after four hours and find it hasn't set, the reason probably is that the milk wasn't hot enough. No matter. Take the bowl of would-be curd, set it in a larger, shallow vessel, and pour in boiling water all around it. It's magic—you'll find it setting within five minutes. If it was already showing signs of setting, let the water be well off the boil before you pour it into the outer vessel, or the curd may over-set and split. (Not that that's a disaster. Carry on regardless.) If even this treatment doesn't work, the milk was probably too hot and killed the lactobacilli, which obligingly work for you to curdle the milk. So now what you do, stir in a couple of teaspoons of homogenised curd, and repeat the hot water treatment.

For raitas, you don't want the curd to be too sour, so remember to keep a check on it, and get it into the fridge as soon as it's properly set. Some recipes, especially when the curd is to be cooked, specify **sour curd**. To sour it, just leave it out of the fridge for a couple of hours in summer or the monsoon, or overnight in winter. Or for a rush job set the bowl of curd in a larger bowl, which you then fill up with hot, not boiling, water.

To thicken curd, you can drain out some of the water. Put it in a close-meshed nylon strainer, or take a clean thin white cloth (e.g. part of an old torn kurta or shirt), spread it over a shallow vessel, and turn the curd into it. Gather up the edges of the cloth, and either tie them up and hang the bundle to drip; or, especially in warm weather, place it in a strainer over another vessel for the water to drain out, and place it in the fridge. Keep a check on it, and turn the curd into another clean bowl when it seems to have the consistency you want. Curd drained to a thick pasty consistency is an excellent base for a variety of dips and spreads, and some sweet dishes.

Although each batch of curd is set from the last one, you don't necessarily have to make it every day. It keeps well in the fridge; the lactobacilli remain active and prevent other bacteria from turning it bad. We've kept it for up to a week; the worst that happens is that it gets a bit sour by then. Even sour it's still perfectly usable for most purposes, and for starting the next batch.

Always remember, by the way, to keep a 'starter', or you'll be stumped when you want to make more.

Paneer (usually called **cottage cheese**, but not much like what your average British or American person recognises as such) is curdled milk, drained and pressed to get rid of most of the moisture. You can buy it in the bazaar. It's not worth the trouble making your own.

To fry it preliminary to adding it to a dish, cut it into pieces, which are better not very small (the smaller the pieces, and the chunkier their shape, the more the surface area which has to be browned). We suggest slices approximately one centimetre thick and three to four centimetres square. As for all frying jobs, use a bland oil, heat it till hot but not smoking in as large a frying pan as you have, and put in as many slices of paneer as will leave you a bit of room to turn them over without having them fall off the pan. (Always cook in a larger rather than a smaller pan, to leave yourself room for manoeuvre.)

In spite of all the draining and pressing that went into the making of the paneer, there is still a surprising amount of moisture left, so when you fry it, it tends to splutter and the oil goes all over the stove. This can't be helped. You could try covering with a lid till the spluttering subsides, but then you can't see properly what's going on. Cook on medium to high heat. As the paneer dries out, the spluttering subsides, and gradually the slices start turning golden on the underside. Reduce the heat, keep investigating each slice to see if it is done, and as it turns a nice rich brown, turn it over and fry the other side till evenly brown. Have beside the stove a plate lined with kitchen paper, and as each slice is ready, take it out and place it on the kitchen paper to blot up the excess oil.

3

Cooking Methods

Since you would surely like to approach the whole business of cooking and housekeeping as systematically as you approach your professional activities, it might be well to apply your mind to the matter of method, so that when you come to the recipes you know what's going on.

Cooking is the process of combining different ingredients, and applying heat to them to alter their character, and help them to fuse into something different from, and more delicious than, the sum of the parts. To facilitate this fusion, the ingredients may be cut, minced, ground, pulverised or otherwise disintegrated.

Often meat or chicken may be combined with a mixture of spices and usually curd, called a **marinade,** and left for several hours. This technique, which enhances the blending of flavours, is known as **marinating.** Marinated foods usually need to stand for at least a couple of hours. Busy office-going cooks may find it convenient to make the marinade and combine the meat, etc, with it in the morning or even the night before, and let it sit quietly in the fridge all day. Then probably there's not much to do in the evening but get it on the heat and let it cook.

There are various methods of applying heat. **Boiling** (including **poaching** which is the cooking of delicate ingredients in water at just below boiling point), **steaming** with or without pressure, **frying,** **grilling,** **roasting** and **baking**, to which, at the turn of the millennium, we have to add **microwaving.** Assuming that young first-time cooks have limited space and resources at their disposal, most of the recipes in this book can be prepared on a gas or electric stove, by boiling, steaming (mostly under pressure) and frying. These are actually the methods most applicable to Indian food, much of which is best cooked in a kadhai or pressure cooker. Sometimes you have to **baste** meat, etc, by spooning fat or gravy over it.

In a world of ideal simplicity, it might be possible just to dump all the ingredients in the pan and boil them all up together. But even in the world as it actually is, there are recipes like that and some of them are as delicious as the more elaborate ones. However, in a great many Indian dishes, richness and flavour are added by a preliminary frying, usually with whole spices, or else by adding a fried mixture of spices and other seasonings after the dish is cooked.

Baghar, chaunk and **tadka** are among the familiar terms for these two frying operations. Although the terms are commonly used more or less interchangeably, we feel that it is useful to make a distinction between the two processes. We therefore propose **chaunk** for the preliminary frying of spices, and **baghar** for what is often called **tempering,** the adding of fried seasonings at the end of the cooking process. (This is also called **tadka** in some parts of the country.)

It's true that the actual method is the same for both chaunk and baghar. Having made sure that the pan, etc., is quite dry, you heat some oil or ghee. The function of oil or ghee is not only to add richness but also to lubricate the pan so that the other ingredients don't stick. So as it heats, especially as you make a chaunk, tilt the pan to swirl the oil or ghee around and coat its sides at least half way up. If you're using **mustard oil** you must remember to 'burn' it, as described on p. 11. Normally you turn down the heat after burning the oil, before you put in the other ingredients. **Dried red chillies,** however, go into the smoking oil and need to be fried on high heat for a minute or so till they turn plump and black and develop their wonderful earthy aroma.

Some whole spices like **mustard seeds** will pop and splutter almost immediately, so it's best to cover them for a few moments till they settle down, otherwise you'll get oil all over the stove. When the spluttering subsides it's a sign that they are ready and you can carry on to the next stage.

Cummin and **fennel seeds** take hardly a minute to turn golden brown. Finely diced **ginger** doesn't take long either. You need to be a bit careful with **whole spices** like **cinnamon, cloves** and **cardamom.** If they over-fry, their aroma is spoilt, so don't have the oil burning hot for these, and fry them on medium heat only as long as it takes them to release their fragrance.

If your chaunk or baghar involves **browning sliced onions,** be careful not to over-fry them (see p. 12).

If you're using chopped **tomatoes,** it's not a bad idea to turn the heat down as they go in, cover and cook on low heat for a couple of minutes till the juice runs. Then you can raise the heat and dry it up a bit.

Curry leaves lose flavour if over-cooked. Put them as the last ingredient into the baghar, and cover immediately, as they splutter like crazy. As soon as the spluttering subsides, turn the baghar out into the main dish.

South Indian cooking tends to be subtler than that of the north, and the baghar is often more discreet. A typical south Indian baghar is no more than half a teaspoon of mustard seeds in a couple of teaspoons of oil. They often exploit the nuttiness of **fried grains of dal,** especially husked **urad dal** and occasionally **chana dal.**

There is another special form of frying, often associated with the chaunk. This is the **bhuno.** To bhuno is to fry a mixture of spices and sometimes other ingredients, on high heat to just the point when they would burn if you didn't immediately add water or tomatoes or something to bring down the temperature—thus creating a new and rich flavour. There is a difference of opinion between the two authors of this book on the subject of bhuno. He bhunos rarely if ever, and reckons that it's not worth the trouble; you can produce excellent dishes without it. For busy young professionals, he argues, life is too short to get into the bhunoing business. She agrees up to a point, but suggests that surely generations of Indian cooks haven't been wasting their time and sweat stirring spice mixtures over high heat just for the heck of it; it does make a difference. It indubitably

Tamato per Eeda, recipe on page 209

Fried Eggs, recipe on page 206

does add to the effort of producing a dish but it's not such a big deal that it should be eliminated altogether. The compromise is that most of the dishes in this book don't involve bhuno, but a few, especially the meat dishes, do. It's a technique worth learning.

Actually, it's not that complicated, it just needs care. Obviously, if you are frying a masala and perhaps meat on high heat, there is a danger that it will burn and all your efforts so far will have gone for nothing. You take two precautions against this. One, you watch it with an eagle eye; and two, you keep stirring it without cease. The amount of time it takes to bhuno depends on the quantity in the pan. If it's just a mixture of spice powders made into a paste with a little water, it doesn't take more than a couple of minutes. However, if you're bhunoing, say, half a kilogram of meat, which has been marinated in a cup of spiced curd, it may take close to ten minutes for the moisture to be driven off. In that case, your stirring can be intermittent till it starts to look nearly dry, and the sound of the sizzle changes. The stirring can be intermittent, and even the eagle eye; but the vigilance must be constant. You can be doing something else in the kitchen—cutting vegetables for another dish, washing dal, cleaning the utensils—but you must remain constantly alert to what's going on in that pan. Once it starts to dry up, it needs your undivided attention. Another precaution is to keep a cup of water handy, so that if it does look like burning you can take emergency action by sprinkling a little water.

Often one of the first ingredients in a bhuno is sliced onions, which you have to brown. As the onions continue to cook after the other ingredients are added, they should be no more than pale gold before you start adding the other ingredients.

Many Indian recipe writers in their instructions for bhunoing tell you to 'fry till the oil separates' and it's quite true, as the temperature in the pan rises and the moisture is driven off, you can see the oil separating around the edges of the solid matter. If you carry on frying on high heat, in a few moments you'll find your masala beginning to stick to the surface of the pan. This is the point at which you must, without an instant's delay, add water or any other form of moisture, scraping frantically to loosen what's begun to stick, or it will burn on you. Sometimes you are required to add just a little water—a couple of tablespoons—and repeat the bhunoing process. But at the end, thankfully mopping your dripping forehead (because it's hot work no doubt), you slosh in as much water, or tomatoes, or curd as may be needed, scrape and stir well, and then your work is more or less done.

> *Take a tip from the authors' hard-won experience: never* never **never** **NEVER** *go out of the kitchen leaving a pan on high heat. Even if you have every intention to be back in an instant, you can't be certain that you won't be sidetracked by the telephone, or someone at the door. Making an invariable habit of checking that the gas is turned low as you leave the kitchen will save you a lot of grief as the years roll by. Naturally, if you're interrupted at a critical juncture—e.g. while bhunoing meat or spices or browning onions—you'll turn the gas off altogether till you can get back to it.*

If you want to make a masala with sliced onions that have been **softened but not browned,** you can put them in the pressure cooker along with oil, whatever spices are called for and a quarter cup of water, close the cooker, put the weight on the weight valve and cook on low heat for about ten minutes. The cooker won't come to full pressure, but it'll get the onions good and pulpy.

If you're of a frugal turn of mind and into fuel economy, you may like to experiment with 'alternative' cooking methods, like a solar cooker or the cook-in-the-blanket technique (see box on p. 39 for full instructions).

Of course, the pressure cooker is itself a fuel-saving device. There are no doubt people with super-sensitive palates who claim that pressure-cooking affects the taste of the food, and the best blend of flavours is achieved with long, slow cooking. If you subscribe to this, then it may be very well worthwhile experimenting with the above mentioned slow-cooking methods. Otherwise, we suggest that one way to achieve this is to cook today and eat tomorrow. It's an observed fact that dishes which rely on a blend of different flavours, are better after twenty-four hours in the fridge. Do your weekend entertaining on Sunday, but cook on Saturday. By such little gimmicks will your reputation as a cook be established.

Give a little thought to your systems of kitchen management. These for the most part you will evolve yourself as you gain experience. But let us just mention a few principles, mostly based on common sense.

In the kitchen as in the office, try to be as systematic as possible. A little forward planning will save you a lot of trouble in the long run. For instance, if you have someone who comes in to clean the house while you're in the office, see if you can't negotiate with her to cut vegetables, soak dal, and knead the dough for chapattis. Take five minutes every morning before you leave for work to think what there is for her to do, and lay it out for her. Remember things like the ginger and onions for the baghar/chaunk, as well as the main vegetable to be cleaned and cut.

If you plan your week's menus ahead, you can do your shopping accordingly in one major expedition. Of course, you have at the same time to be flexible. You may cook a meat or vegetable dish you expect to last for supper over two days, but it's so good it disappears on the first; or an unexpected guest turns up; or you're held up at the office on a day you'd planned to cook something special. So you have to be prepared for unforeseen eventualities. That means never running out of your basic items like rice, flour, oil, dal, spices, pasta, onions, potatoes and tomatoes. It also means having fall-backs available in the kitchen or the fridge at all times: eggs, UHT milk and cream, perhaps some boil-in-the-bag instant vegetable dishes. **This isn't very difficult if you cultivate the habit of religiously making a note, on a small pad kept handy to the cooking area, every time you notice you're running short of something.**

Don't plan anything remotely elaborate, or requiring a lot of time-consuming preparation, at a time when you're pushed with extra work in the office. If you're entertaining, work out your menu at least a couple of days in advance, check all the recipes, and ensure that you have everything you need, the store-cupboard items as well as the main ingredients. It's not sensible to experiment when cooking for guests. Always try out new recipes on the home team.

When you're on the job, try to avoid clutter as far as possible. Put each item away as you use it—spice-jars tightly closed and returned to their place, utensils stacked in the sink as soon as you're done with them, ready for washing. Clean up spills and any other mess immediately. Keep a sponge or a soft damp cloth handy for the purpose, or use kitchen paper. After cooking, clean your stove and work-surface with a damp cloth, which you must then rinse thoroughly and spread out to dry. If you leave it scrunched up and wet, it'll start stinking. Wash your kitchen cloths frequently, boiling them if necessary. There's nothing more unsavoury than filthy dusters in a kitchen.

If dishes and utensils are to be left for some time before washing, sluice them with water as you stack them in the sink. Make your life easier by getting rid of excess oil from frying pans and kadhais before washing them. It may not be a good idea to pour oil down the drain, as this could encourage the drain to clog up; rather let it cool, pour it into a used plastic bag, tie it up and put it into the garbage bucket. Wipe round the pan with old newspaper. This way you'll prevent the whole sink and its contents from getting oily, and save on both labour and detergent.

As an alternative to plastic garbage bags, line your garbage bucket with newspaper to avoid it getting messy.

And finally, a couple of safety tips. Always turn the handles of pans towards the wall, or over the counter, when you've finished attending to them, never protruding where a passer-by can knock into them. Don't leave spoons and spatulas in an unattended pan on the heat. And avoid, as far as possible, wearing loose clothes like shawls and saris when at the stove. If you wear a sari, tuck the pallu firmly in at the waist. Salwar-kameez wearers are advised to lay their dupattas aside altogether as long as they're in the kitchen.

4

Interpreting the Recipes

You'll save yourself a LOT of hassle if, from the outset of your culinary career, you make a habit of reading through every recipe before you embark on cooking it. Do I have all the ingredients? What do I need to put on my shopping list? What will the approximate working time be? How long will it take to cook? While it cooks does it need my undivided attention, or can I be getting on with something else at the same time?

As you gain experience, you may find yourself wanting to modify the given recipes. That's fine, but you should realise that in some processes there is plenty of room for individual interpretation, while in others the room for manoeuvre is much less. This can be illustrated by one of the very simplest recipes in the book: Spaghetti alla Marinara on p. 268. Not very helpfully for the anxious novice, it could well have been written out like this:

Spaghetti, as required
A little oil
A few cloves garlic
3-4 tomatoes, or more, or less
Mint, coriander, basil, *or* any other green herb available, *optional*
Salt
Black pepper powder

Chop or crush the garlic (or don't). Wash and chop the tomatoes, or quarter them. Wash the herbs, if used, and chop them, or leave them without chopping.

Heat the oil, add the garlic and cook till just taking colour—or if preferred till golden brown. Add the tomatoes, salt and pepper. Cook till the tomatoes are soft but still keeping their form; or cook to a mush if preferred. Add the herbs, if used, along with the tomatoes, or at the end after cooking is complete.

Bring plenty of water to the boil in a big pan with a handful of salt. Put in the spaghetti, bring back to the boil on high heat; adjust the heat so that it doesn't boil over, and cook uncovered till **al dente**—'to the tooth', i.e. with a little bite to it. Drain in a colander, tip into a warmed serving dish, sprinkle with salt and pepper and a tbsp or so of oil.

Mix the tomato sauce with the spaghetti, or serve separately.

This demonstrates quite neatly where you can use your own discretion, and where you can't.

There are really no two ways of cooking pasta. It has to be cooked as fast as possible in plenty of boiling salted water, and it has to be cooked al dente. Soggy, overcooked pasta is disgusting. It has to be well drained, and without being tossed in a little oil or butter, it is stodgy and uninteresting. It loses heat fast, so it has to be served immediately. Not a lot of scope for individual interpretation.

But look at the sauce recipe. You can vary the proportions, the way you prepare the ingredients, and how long you cook them. Each variation will alter the character of the dish, and if you prefer the garlic fried deep brown and the tomatoes cooked to a mush, rather than the lighter cooking of the classic recipe, there's really no law against it.

We have tried to write the recipes as clearly as possible; but in order to avoid undue repetition, like all cookery writers we've used certain conventions. It may help you to have a definition of terms and assumptions.

The quantities given in the lists of ingredients are fairly precise because we thought this would make things easier for beginners. However, for most of the recipes in this book, exact proportions are not an issue, and if you feel like putting in less of this or more of that, you should feel free to experiment. Where precision is needed, or the consequences of adding too much or too little are dire, we've said so.

Our measuring cup is of capacity 200 ml. A teaspoon (tsp) is 5 ml while a tablespoon (tbsp) is 15 ml. For solid ingredients assume level spoonfuls, not heaped.

The quantities of onions, potatoes and tomatoes are given in number, rather than by weight. These items are bought in bulk and are usually available in the kitchen, so there seems little point in weighing them out every time you want to cook a dish. In case you feel the need to avoid undue doubts and subjectivity in interpreting the terms 'small', 'medium' and 'large', refer to the following table. All the figures refer to weight in grams, and may be assumed plus/minus.

	Small	*Medium*	*Large*
Potatoes	50	100	200
Onions	40	80	120
Tomatoes	40	80	120
Eggs	45-50	55-60	65-70
Coriander or mint (bunch)	50-100	175	250

According to our measurements, different ingredients by the cup weigh in approximately as follows (weight in grams):

Rice	*Atta*	*Dal*	*Shelled peas*	*Kabuli chana*	*Sugar*
175	125	200	120	180	200

You'll get one cup of shelled **green peas** from 250-300 gms of unshelled ones.

Short of jeweller's scales, some items are almost impossible to quantify with precision, and for these we've adopted international norms, which are conceptual rather than strictly accurate. For a '3-cm piece' of **ginger,** for instance, imagine a knob about the size of a small walnut. **Cinnamon** is even trickier. Imagine the archetypal piece of cinnamon to be about one cm wide; your '3-cm' thus refers to the length of this conceptual one-cm wide stick.

Salt is a bit of a problem. We've suggested quantities but people's palates vary enormously. With experience, you'll get a feel for how much your taste buds require. For every recipe you can assume the phrase 'or to taste' after the quantity given. Similarly with **chilli powder**. For both these items, always add less rather than more. You can add but you can't take away.

By the same token, you can de-seed your **green chillies** (see p. 15) or not, according to your taste.

Bland oil means any of the lighter vegetable oils mentioned in the chapter on ingredients (see p.10), as opposed to mustard, sesame or coconut oil.

Onions and **garlic** are always peeled before chopping or slicing; this is taken for granted in the recipes.

Since **bay leaves** are included only for flavour and aren't eaten, it's a delicate touch to remove them before serving, though we haven't specified this every time.

Most meat, chicken, vegetable and dal dishes are the better with a garnish of chopped coriander leaves, so this is not usually specified. Even where it is, you can take it as optional. **Baghar** on the other hand is not garnish, but an essential element of the dish, which would be something else altogether without it.

Specified **cooking times** are estimates, and will vary according to the quality of the raw material, the size of the pieces, and how you like it, whether chewy, tender or mushy.

We haven't given even estimated **working times**, because everyone is different. You may manage to peel and slice three onions in three minutes; someone else may take ten. Each of our recipes does specify all the processes involved in preparing the ingredients as well as in the actual cooking, and this should help you to get an idea of the approximate time you'll take. As you gain experience, you'll realise that all the processes mentioned under the head **Preparation** don't need to be done right at the start. You can, e.g., cut the onions and tomatoes for a baghar while the dal is cooking.

To **reduce** a gravy etc., boil it on high heat to drive off some of the moisture. Keep stirring so that it doesn't stick and burn.

Simmer means to boil gently, and is always done on low heat.

The terms we have used to describe different ways of **cutting** are **dice**, to cut into more or less regular cubes, which may be anything from small (two to four mm) to bite-sized (two to three cm); and **chop**, to cut fine or coarsely without regard to shape.

The technique of mixing ingredients varies according to their nature. We use the term **stir** for predominantly liquid ingredients, and **toss** for solid ones. A substance with a delicate texture, like beaten egg white, is **folded** with a gentle, slightly rotary motion into another.

A lot of our recipes are followed by variations, and some others are in the form of master-recipes, which you can repeat, perhaps only changing the main ingredient. Thus we hope you'll feel that you've learnt several dishes for the price of a single recipe.

The large number of cross-references is in the interest of avoiding repetition while at the same time signposting the relevant processes.

We have on the whole avoided giving serving suggestions, especially for Indian dishes, because although you may be a novice cook you're not a novice eater, you must in twenty-odd years have developed some preferences as to what you like to eat with what. We have tried however to mention whenever an item is conventionally and deliciously served with another, like Sarson da Saag with Makki di Roti, or Choley with Pooris.

Our estimates for the number of people each dish may serve are based on the assumption that it is the main dish being served—together with rice or roti, in the case of Indian meat, chicken, dal and vegetable dishes. If you're going to stick to the more typical pattern of two or three dishes at one meal, you'll either reduce the quantities accordingly, or (as we've suggested earlier) reckon to cook for more than one meal at a time, and keep what's left in the fridge for another day. Salads, raitas and relishes are by definition side dishes.

That said, people are different, and a dish that might be more than adequate for four figure-conscious teenage girls, may be gobbled up entire by a sumo wrestler and leave him calling for more. We have tried to imagine 'average' young people with healthy appetites; but even so, numbers of servings can be no more than 'guesstimates', a rough guide, which we hope you'll find useful.

5

Ways with Rice

Whether your preference is for Indian or Western food, you have to know how to cook rice. And once you've mastered plain rice, Indian food offers a wonderful diversity of combinations of vegetables, spices and meat with the rice.

Hundreds of varieties of rice have been documented in India and people in different parts of the country swear by their own local varieties, which have their individual characteristics of shape, flavour and texture. If you have a strong local preference, fine; but it's possible in that case, that the quantity of water and cooking times given in the recipes may need some modification. Start with the quantities suggested and adjust according to the results.

The premium rice in north India, preferred for parties and festive occasions and particularly for making pulao, is **basmati**, but this is expensive; every region has its cheaper option for everyday use.

In south India they've developed a mind-boggling number of ways to deal with rice: they grind it, they ferment it, they aerate it, they fry it, they puff it, they do everything except throw it on the ground and jump on it. Many of these techniques are not, as we see it, for novice cooks in small kitchens. If you want to make dosas at home, buy a packet of dosa mix and follow the directions. Our recipes are confined to whole rice, soaked and boiled, and you'd be surprised the number of things you can do on that basis. The exception is rice ground to make phirni, one of the easiest and most delicious Indian-style desserts, and to thicken soup.

Rice keeps well, in fact connoisseurs prefer 'old' rice, i.e. not from the current harvest—as if you have the choice, with everything coming in plastic packets. Actually the cheaper varieties are often sold straight from the sack, and you may occasionally feel a bit put off to find insects in it, especially during the monsoon. If they are small and blackish, they are weevils, and as long as it's not a heavy infestation, they don't matter. As you wash the rice they float off, but you can remove them by picking through the rice first. If you find that you have kept some rice so long that it has become infested with whitish bugs, throw it out immediately. There's no way it can be salvaged.

Rice, dal, etc., that come in plastic packs are more or less guaranteed to be free of tiny stones and other impurities. But if for any reason you have bought it straight from the sack, it's wise to do a preliminary **pick-through**. Put your rice on a flat plate, or a pressure cooker separator, and spread it out. Tilt it slightly so that there is an empty space to one side, and with your fingers gently start pushing rice from the edge into the gap, scrutinising it as you do so, and picking out any foreign bodies.

The washing is best done in a pan or pressure cooker separator. Cover the rice with water, and work it with your hand. The water will turn milky-looking as the surface starch gets washed off. Pour off the water (if you're afraid of pouring out some of the rice, use a large strainer), and repeat the process till the water looks pretty clear. If you can then leave it to soak for thirty minutes or more, so much the better, you reduce the cooking time somewhat. But if you don't have the time, carry on regardless. You may need a little more water to cook it.

You can routinely cook double the quantity of rice you think you'll eat at one time, and reheat it the next day. The easiest way to reheat rice is in the microwave. Otherwise, put it in a pan on low heat with a tablespoon of water and half a tablespoon of bland oil, tossing it every now and then with a fork to prevent it sticking. You can also put it in a covered pan on the trivet in the pressure cooker, into which you've put a couple of cups of water. When the water boils, turn down the heat, put the weight on the cooker and leave it to heat through for five to ten minutes. This is perhaps a safer way, but it takes longer.

To grind rice for phirni, or to thicken a soup, wash the rice, soak it in water for thirty minutes, drain and dry in a clean cloth. Spread it out on the cloth and leave for fifteen minutes or so to dry further; then grind. If you are short of time and the rice looks clean, you can just grind it without washing, though this will result in a slightly less fine flour.

In pulaos and other rice recipes using oil, it's always a **bland oil** that's used, never mustard oil.

PLAIN RICE – 1

Ingredients for 4-6 servings:

2 cups rice Plenty of water

Preparation: Wash the rice well and soak it in water for 30 minutes or so.

Method: Bring the water to the boil, drain the rice through a large strainer, and put it in the water. Bring back to the boil and cook till ready. Test by crushing a few grains between finger and thumb. It should be soft but not mushy.

Drain, by pouring the entire contents of the pan out into a large strainer.

Put the rice back in the pan and return to very low heat for a minute or so to dry off. Fluff up with a fork and spoon out on to a serving platter.

PLAIN RICE – 2

Rice cooked in just enough water to be absorbed, without any waste of nutrients.

Ingredients for 4-6 servings:

2 cups rice 3-3½ cups water

Preparation: Wash the rice well and soak it in water for 30 minutes or so.

Method: Drain the rice. Bring the water to the boil in a heavy-bottomed pan with a tight-fitting lid, and add the rice.

Bring to the boil again, lower the heat, and cover the pan tightly. If the lid doesn't fit tightly, cover the pan with a sheet of foil and fold it down over the sides. Keep on the lowest heat possible, for 10 minutes or so, till all the water has been absorbed. If your stove doesn't give you really low heat, put the pan on a tava.

Fluff up with a fork and spoon out on to a serving platter.

As an alternative, after bringing the rice to the boil, cover and simmer for 1-2 minutes. When the rice begins to swell, cover the pan well so that no steam escapes, snatch it off the stove and wrap it in several layers of an old blanket, shawl or other insulating material, so that no heat escapes. The rice will cook in its own residual heat, which it will retain for at least a couple of hours. There's no way it can overcook, so you can prepare it well in advance and get on with the rest of your life till it's time to eat, when all you have to do is take it out, fluff it up and put it on the table. This method is particularly good for most pulaos.

BAGHAR FOR RICE

A splendid way of tarting up yesterday's leftover rice when you reheat it.

Ingredients:

2 tbsp bland oil
2 dried red chillies

Any combination of:
12 curry leaves
1 tsp cummin seeds
1 tsp mustard seeds
1 tsp sesame seeds

Preparation: Wash the curry leaves and strip them off the stem.

Method: Heat the oil in a small heavy-bottomed pan or kadhai, add the red chillies, and fry till they turn plump and black. Lower the heat and throw in the cummin seeds followed by the mustard seeds. Cover the pan till the spluttering subsides, then add the sesame seeds, and fry stirring over medium heat till the seeds are evenly golden brown. Add the curry leaves and fry for a few moments more till they start to shrivel.

Turn the contents of the pan into freshly cooked or warmed up leftover rice and toss together with a fork to mix.

Note: The given quantities will season 2-3 servings of rice.

CONJEE

A kind of rice soup, full of flavour but comforting and easy on the stomach.

Ingredients for 2 servings:

½ cup rice	1 tsp whole black pepper
½-1 lime	6-8 cloves
6-8 sprigs coriander leaves	½ tsp salt

Preparation: Wash the rice in minimum water till clean, but without removing all the starch, i.e. the water should still be cloudy. Drain. Wash the lime and squeeze out the juice, about 1½ tsp. Wash the coriander leaves and chop.

Method: Put all the ingredients except the lime juice and coriander leaves into a pan with 4 cups water. Bring to the boil, lower the heat and simmer till the rice is good and mushy. Remove from the heat, stir in the lime juice and coriander and serve.

GOLHAT

Golhat is rice cooked till very soft and mushy. It is ideal invalid food, especially for those with, or recovering from, stomach upsets. Cook rice to a mush, according to either of the recipes for Plain Rice, but add a little salt. Recommended is to use the recipe for Plain Rice–2, doubling the quantity of water. Serve it with curd.

THAYIR SHADAM
Curd Rice

A similar idea to Golhat, but demonstrating the sophistication of south Indian cuisine. Cooked rice mixed with milk and a 'starter' of curd, set as an amalgam of curd and rice—an inspired creation.

Ingredients for 3-4 servings:

1 cup rice
2 cups milk
½ tsp salt
2 tsp curd

Optional vegetables:
1-2 carrots
½ cucumber
A small piece of cabbage

Baghar:
2 tsp bland oil
1-2 dried red chillies, *optional*
1 tsp mustard seeds

Preparation: Wash the rice well and soak in water for 30 minutes. Boil the milk as for making curd (p. 21).

Wash and peel the carrots and cucumber, if used. Discard cucumber seeds. Cut both vegetables into fine dice. Shred the cabbage, if used.

Method: Cook the rice according to either of the recipes for plain rice, but make it slightly mushy, either by cooking it longer if going by Plain Rice–1, or by using about 1½ times the amount of water for Plain Rice–2. Add the carrots, if used, when the rice is half cooked.

Drain the rice, if necessary. Add the milk, and stir to mix till it becomes a thick batter. Stir in the salt and the rest of the optional vegetables. Check that the rice mixture is at the right temperature for setting curd (p. 21), and stir in the curd as the starter. Put the mixture into the dish in which it is to be served.

In a small pan heat the oil, add the red chillies, if used, and fry till plump and black. Add the mustard seeds and cover the pan till the spluttering subsides. Turn the baghar out on top of the rice, but do not stir in. Leave the dish in a warm place to set. It should take about 2 hours.

Serve it at room temperature with a chutney, pickle or salad.

Note: It can serve as invalid food, and is ideal for a packed lunch. Assemble it in the morning, and by mid-day the curd will be set but not sour.

Variation: **Short-cut Thayir Shadam**—Put about a cup of curd in the blender, with a cup of cooked rice and blend to a pasty consistency. Add salt, and give it a baghar as above.

PISH-PASH

As the patient begins to recover and gets tired of mushy rice, offer him or her the still bland but not utterly boring pish-pash.

Ingredients for 2 servings:

1 cup rice
3-4 chicken pieces
1 medium onion
2-3 black cardamoms
2-3 green cardamoms
6-8 cm cinnamon
2-3 cloves
1-2 bay leaves
½ tsp salt

Preparation: Wash the rice well and soak for about 30 minutes. Wash and drain the chicken, removing all fat. Coarsely slice the onion.

Method: Put the chicken in a pan or pressure cooker with the onion, whole spices and bay leaves, cover with water and bring to the boil. Skim off any scum that may rise, and cook till the chicken is tender, 0-1 minutes under pressure, 15-20 minutes without (see p. 191).

Using a slotted spoon, remove the chicken pieces to a plate. Take the meat off the bone and cut into bite-sized pieces. (You can omit this step if you think the patient is strong enough to cope with chicken bones.) Strain the stock and reserve, discarding the onion and spices. If the stock looks a bit too greasy—lots of fat floating in globules on the surface—degrease it (see p. 65).

Drain the rice. Put 2-2½ cups chicken stock into a pan and bring to the boil. Add the salt, rice and chicken, and cook according to the recipe for Plain Rice–2.

Note: Pish-pash is too good to be served only to convalescents. If you want to make it a one-dish meal for healthy people, add a little milk and a dollop of butter to the pan just before removing it from the heat, and serve it with slices of lime. You may also want to increase the number of chicken pieces.

CHILAU
Persian Rice

Ingredients for 4-6 servings:

3-4 cups basmati rice
4 tbsp bland oil
1 tbsp+1 tsp salt

Preparation: Wash the rice thoroughly in several changes of water to get rid of as much starch as possible. Soak for at least 1 hour in cold water with 1 tbsp salt. Just before cooking drain, wash again and drain once more.

Method: Bring plenty of water to boil in a large pan, with 1 tsp salt. Add the drained rice, bring back to the boil, and boil rapidly, till nearly ready. Test by crushing a few grains between finger and thumb—they should be just short of ready-to-eat, not hard but still firm. This may take about 5 minutes, but it depends on the quality of the rice.

Drain immediately, and wash again in several changes of cold water. Drain thoroughly once more.

Gently heat half the oil in a heavy-bottomed pan, with a tight-fitting lid. Put in the rice, and sprinkle the rest of the oil over it. Cover with the lid and tie a clean cloth around it, to absorb the steam and keep the rice dry and fluffy.

Cook over low to medium heat for 20-30 minutes. By this time, the rice at the bottom will be slightly burnt, to make a crisp golden crust. This is called tah deeg, is considered a delicacy, and is specially served to guests.

Pile the rice on a serving platter, and arrange the tah deeg, which you have dug out in pieces, around the edge.

This is not as complicated as it sounds, and the result is well worth the small extra trouble.

Note: We suggest rather larger quantities of rice than usual, because the tah deeg, being crisp, doesn't absorb the gravy of the other dishes, so people need more.

BUA'S PULAO

Ingredients for 4-6 servings:

2 cups basmati rice
1 small onion
1-2 tbsp bland oil
2 black cardamoms
3-4 green cardamoms
6-8 cm cinnamon
5-6 cloves
1-2 bay leaves
½ tsp turmeric powder, *optional*

Preparation: Wash the rice well and soak for about 30 minutes. Slice the onion fine. Measure 3½ cups water into a pan or kettle and bring to the boil.

Method: Heat the oil in a heavy-bottomed pan and fry the onion till golden. Using a slotted spoon, remove the onion from the pan and put aside on a small plate covered with kitchen paper to blot up the excess oil.

Throw the whole spices and bay leaves into the pan, and fry for 1-2 minutes on medium heat till fragrant.

Drain the rice well and add. Stir over medium heat for 1-2 minutes so that each grain is coated with oil.

Add the boiling water, and stir well to mix, ensuring that no dry grains are sticking to the sides of the pan above the water.

Stir in the turmeric if you want yellow rice. Cook according to the method described in Plain Rice–2.

Pile it on a serving platter and garnish with the fried onion.

Variation: Add the sliced onion after the whole spices, and stir-fry on medium heat till golden. Do not remove. Add the rice and continue as above. This approximates to the Parsi and Anglo-Indian **Brown Rice.**

GREEN PEA PULAO

Ingredients for 4-6 servings:

2 cups long-grain rice	1½ tbsp bland oil
1 small onion	1 tsp cummin seeds
1 cup shelled green peas	1 tsp salt

Preparation: Wash the rice well and soak in water for 30 minutes. Slice the onion fine.

Boil the green peas till nearly tender. If using frozen or dried green peas, prepare them according to the instructions on the packet. If you use less water for cooking the green peas, make up the amount to 3½ cups, and have it ready boiling.

Method: Heat the oil in a heavy-bottomed pan. Add the onion and fry on medium heat till golden. Remove from the pan using a slotted spoon, and put aside on a small plate covered with kitchen paper to blot up the excess oil.

Throw the cummin seeds into the pan and fry for a minute till golden. Drain the rice well and add. Stir over medium heat for 1-2 minutes so that each grain is coated with oil. Add the salt, and green peas with their water, and cook as for Plain Rice–2.

When it is ready, toss it gently with a fork to aerate and to mix the green peas evenly through the rice.

Pile it on a serving platter and garnish with the fried onion.

Variation: **Mushroom pulao**—Use the same method, substituting mushrooms (say a 200-gm packet) for the green peas. Wash the mushrooms, and cut fairly small. Add to the oil after the cummin seeds. As they start to cook, they give off a lot of moisture. Stir-fry on medium to high heat till dry, then add the rice and 3½ cups boiling water and continue as above.

MEAT PULAO

Ingredients for 6-7 servings:

½ kg meat, breast, chops or shoulder, for preference
2 cups basmati rice
1 medium onion
½ tsp whole black pepper
6+6 cloves

2+2 black cardamoms
12-16 cm cinnamon
2+2 bay leaves
2 tbsp bland oil
1 tsp cummin seeds
4 green cardamoms
1 tsp salt

Preparation: Wash and drain the meat, and remove any excess fat. Wash the rice well and soak in water for 30 minutes. Slice the onion as fine as possible.

Make a potli by tying the whole black pepper, 6 cloves, 2 black cardamoms and 6-8 cm cinnamon in a clean, thin, white cloth.

Method: Put the meat, potli and 2 bay leaves into a pan or pressure cooker with about 4 cups water, if cooking under pressure, otherwise 5-6 cups. Bring slowly to the boil. When it boils, skim off the scummy foam that rises to the surface.

Simmer or cook under pressure till the meat is just tender, 30-40 minutes without pressure, 10-12 minutes with, depending on the quality of the meat and the size of the pieces.

When the meat is cooked, lift it out with a slotted spoon, along with the potli, and reserve. Strain the stock, discarding the bay leaves. When the potli is cool enough to handle, squeeze out any remaining liquid into the stock and discard it. If the stock looks very greasy—lots of fat floating in globules on the surface—degrease it (see p. 65).

Measure the liquid, which should be about 3½ cups for your 2 cups of rice. If it has reduced too much, make up the quantity with water. Bring back to the boil.

Drain the rice. Heat the oil in a heavy-bottomed pan with a tight-fitting lid, and fry the onion till crisp and golden. Remove the onion from the pan with a slotted spoon, and keep aside on a plate lined with absorbent kitchen paper to blot up the excess oil.

Throw in the cummin seeds, and as soon as they turn light golden add the remaining spices. Fry for a few moments till the spices are fragrant, then add the rice. Stir over medium heat so that each grain is coated with oil, then add the meat and salt, and toss well.

Add the hot stock, and stir well to mix, ensuring that no dry grains are sticking to the sides of the pan above the level of the liquid. Cook according to the method described in Plain Rice–2.

Pile the pulao on a serving platter and garnish with the fried onion.

Variations: When you boil the meat, cook it for a shorter time till only ¾ done. Later, after browning and removing the onion, and before adding the rice to the oil, put in the meat and stir-fry on medium heat with 1 tsp ginger-garlic paste. When the meat is nicely browned, add the rice and continue as above.

- **Chicken Pulao**—Make it in exactly the same way, except that you need to cook the chicken for only about 0-1 minute under pressure (see p. 191).

KHICHDI

A filling dish, especially comforting in cold winter weather; it is cooked in innumerable versions all over India.

Ingredients for 3 servings:

1 cup rice
½ cup husked masoor *or* moong dal
1 small onion
4 green chillies
3 tbsp bland oil *or* ghee
1 tsp ginger-garlic paste
2 bay leaves
2 green cardamoms
2 black cardamoms
4 cloves
½ tsp red chilli powder
¼ tsp turmeric powder
1 tsp salt

Preparation: Wash the rice and dal together, and soak for 30 minutes. Slice the onion fine. Wash the green chillies but leave them whole.

Method: Heat the oil in the pressure cooker or a heavy-bottomed pan. Add the onion and stir-fry till golden. Remove from the pan into a small metal bowl along with about ½ the oil.

Add the ginger-garlic paste to the oil in the cooker, and stir-fry over medium heat till golden. Add the bay leaves and whole spices and fry for a minute till fragrant. Add the rice, dal, green chillies, spice powders and salt, and stir all together for another couple of minutes. Add water to cover by 3 cm, bring to the boil and either simmer for 10-15 minutes till well done and the water is absorbed, or cook under pressure for 3-4 minutes. Adjust consistency if necessary, adding water if it seems too thick.

Serve with plain curd or raita, and Aloo ka Bharta, and hand round the fried onions and oil to sprinkle over individual servings.

Note: You can actually make the Aloo ka Bharta in tandem with the Khichdi. Double the amount of oil and fried onions, and reserve half. Put 3-4 medium, peeled potatoes into the pan when you add the water. When the khichdi is cooked, remove the potatoes, rinse them, and proceed as given for Aloo ka Bharta on p. 228, using the reserved onions and oil.

Variation: You can make khichdi with chana dal, whole masoor or arhar/toover; but in that case wash and soak the rice and dal separately, and half cook the dal before adding the rice.

6

Rotis

Chapattis have been described as 'a vulgar feudal luxury', and it's true that you get the best value from chapattis if there's someone standing in the kitchen making them and bringing them one by one, hot and golden and puffed out with scalding steam, to the table. Many busy young professionals may feel this is too much for them to do on a regular basis. But a few chapattis, roasted on the tava as the food is being heated, are a treat that may not be too much trouble to organise for yourself every now and then; and the oftener you make them, the less the effort will seem.

The basic dough for making **chapattis** and **parathas** is **atta (whole wheat flour)** and water, seasoned with a little salt. But it can be varied in any number of ways. You can substitute **refined flour (maida)** for half, or even all of the atta, and half-half is what is usually recommended for making **pooris**. You can mix the dough with milk, or half milk and half water. For parathas and pooris, some cooks recommend kneading a little oil or ghee into the dough.

For a change of flavour, you can knead a teaspoonful of **ajwain** or **powdered fennel** into the dough.

In the metropolitan cities you can get various ready-made kinds of bread that you can substitute for roti—pizza bread, for example, which only needs to be put into the toaster. These may be worth looking out for if you like to eat rotis but find it too much of an effort to make them at home every day.

CHAPATTIS

Ingredients for 10-12 chapattis:

2 cups atta
½ tsp salt
1 cup water

Method: To prepare the dough, you need a thali or a large platter with a raised rim. Sieve the atta with the salt into this.

Start adding the water, say ¼ cup at a time, mixing it in with your fingers till it is absorbed and the atta starts to cohere into a stiffish dough. As the dough starts to form and only a little of the atta remains dry, add the water with circumspection. The idea is to use only as much as is needed to form the dough, which should not be wet and sticky, but also not so stiff as to make it difficult to work with.

Once you have a nice firm ball of dough, the trick of making soft chapattis is to knead it well. It's quite hard work, but satisfying, once you get the knack. Punch the ball of dough with the heel of your hand, and as it flattens out go all over it with your knuckles. When it gets thin, pull the far edge of the dough towards you with your fingers, and fold it over. Punch, knuckle and pull; punch, knuckle and pull, turning the platter with your other hand as you do so. And that's it. Keep at it for about 5 minutes, till the dough loses its stickiness, and you have the makings of lovely soft supple chapattis.

> *Kneading atta is perhaps the only kitchen job for which the working surface should be lower rather than higher, so that you can bear down on the dough with your weight behind your knuckles. It's actually quite tiring trying to do it on the surface high enough to be comfortable for cutting, etc. If possible, take the dough elsewhere (e.g. the dining table) to knead it.*

This process is best done 1-2 hours in advance, both because you don't want the hassle of kneading dough as you're getting the meal on the table, and because the kneaded dough improves further if it's allowed to 'rest' for a bit. If you're really sold on the whole chapatti bit, you can even make double quantities, and keep half in the fridge for the next day. But remember that the surface of resting dough has to be protected from drying out, so you must either cover it with a clean damp cloth, or keep it in a food-grade plastic bag or other airtight container.

When the time comes to make the chapattis, put the tava on medium heat. Put a couple of tbsp dry atta on a small plate beside your work surface. Give the rested dough a couple of kneadings, then divide it into 10-12 portions, each about the size of a large lime. Take each portion and roll it into a ball between your palms, then squeeze it between the heels of your hands to flatten it a bit. In summer, cover the flattened balls with a clean barely damp cloth so that the surfaces don't dry out.

Sprinkle some dry atta on your chapatti board or clean smooth working surface. Take one flattened ball and dip it in dry atta to coat it on both sides. Put it on the atta-sprinkled surface, and press it down again with the heel of your hand to flatten it further.

Now you have to roll it out, turning it as you do so, with the aim of achieving as near as you can to a perfect circle. Never mind if your first efforts look like the map of Australia; you'll learn by doing (and in any case there's no reason why a map-of-Australia-shaped chapatti shouldn't taste perfectly fine).

As you roll the rolling pin down towards yourself, give it a little extra pressure with the right hand. This makes the chapatti turn automatically. Till you develop the knack, you'll need to turn it manually. If it offers to stick to the surface, or to the rolling pin, dip it into the dry atta.

When the dough is rolled out as thin as you can reasonably get it, to a diameter of 12-14 cm, test the heat of the tava. A drop of water flicked onto it should jump and evaporate instantly. Now pick up the chapatti carefully, peeling it off the working surface, and toss it gently from palm to palm to get rid of any dry atta that may still be sticking to it. Lay it flat on the tava, and start rolling out the next chapatti, all the time keeping an eye on the tava.

When you see the upper surface beginning to look dry and slightly blistered, about 30 seconds, turn it over with flat-bladed tongs. The underside should also have a blistered appearance, and some golden patches. Give it another 30 seconds, then take the tava off the heat, and using the tongs, put the chapatti, first side down, directly on the flame. It should puff up immediately. Turn it over (leaving it for a few seconds on the flame if you like a slightly burnt taste to your chapattis); then take it off the fire.

Another technique for the final cooking—instead of toasting it directly on the flame, turn it over once more on the tava, and with a clean kitchen cloth folded into a pad, press down the sides with a gentle rotating movement. This should make it puff.

If you like your chapattis spread with ghee or butter, it's easier to do this at the table than in the kitchen, where it becomes just one more process to cope with. Make sure that the fat is softened, or even melted, for easy spreading.

Either way, put the chapatti straight into a dish, or better, a basket, lined with a clean napkin. Fold the napkin over it. Repeat the process, till all the chapattis are made.

Theoretically, the rolling out of each chapatti takes almost the same time as the previous chapatti is on the tava. It's not that easy in the beginning to get it all perfectly co-ordinated, but as you get practice, you may find that you get into a rhythm and have an assembly line going.

To reheat chapattis: There is really no satisfactory method of reheating chapattis. Some writers recommend wrapping them in foil and reheating in the oven, but then they lose their crispness. In the toaster they get hard. The least unsatisfactory method, we find, is to toast them a second time briefly on the flame. It won't be as good as freshly made chapattis, but one option is to make them in advance omitting the toasting process, which you can then do at the time of serving the meal.

POORIS

Ingredients for 10-12 pooris:

1 cup atta
1 cup maida
1 tsp salt
1 cup water *or* ½ cup water and ½ cup milk
1 cup bland oil for deep frying

Method: Using all the ingredients except the oil, make a dough in exactly the same way as for chapattis. Knead well and allow to rest for at least an hour.

Knead the dough briefly and divide into portions about the same size as for chapattis, and roll out.

Since pooris cook faster than other rotis, it's often suggested that you roll them all out before you start cooking them. But they have to be kept separate, which means that on top of each one as you roll it out you must put a piece of clean paper, foil or plastic film. If you do this ahead of time (e.g. before the arrival of guests), cover the whole arrangement with a barely damp cloth to prevent them drying out.

> *When making any of the fried rotis—paratha, poori or doodhi roti—try to minimise the amount of dry atta you use in rolling them out. You can brush loose atta off a dry tava; but not from an oily surface, where it burns and forms an unattractive black grime in the oil, some of which may stick to the rotis. The counsel of perfection is to use a few drops of oil instead of dustings of atta to prevent them sticking. If you find this too messy, use atta anyhow, but try to dust off as much as possible before the rotis go onto the tava or into the cooking oil.*

Pour the oil into a medium-sized kadhai, to fill it to a depth of 3-5 cm. Set the pan on medium heat, and let the oil get really hot—it should be just short of smoking. Lower a poori gently into the hot oil with the help of a spatula or slotted spoon. It will sink at first, then, as it rises, keep pushing it down into the oil with small quick strokes. Within a few seconds it will puff out, and the underside will have turned golden brown. Turn it over and cook for a few seconds more till the other side turns gold.

Lift out and place on a plate lined with absorbent paper to blot up excess oil. When the next poori is ready to be blotted, put the first one into a serving basket lined with napkin over which you have placed a sheet of foil.

Note: Don't try to reheat pooris; just make as many as you think will be eaten at one time.

Variations: Add 2 tbsp semolina to the flour when kneading the dough. The pooris won't be so soft, but they'll stay puffed longer. The choice is yours.

- For **Khasti Poori,** when kneading the dough use ¾ cup beaten curd thinned down with about ¼ cup water, and add 2 tbsp oil or ghee.

DOODHI ROTI

Ingredients for 6-8 rotis:

1 cup atta
1 cup maida
1 tsp salt
1 cup milk
½ cup bland oil

Method: Using all the ingredients except the oil, make a dough in exactly the same way as for chapattis. Knead well and allow to rest for at least an hour.

Pour the oil into a medium-sized frying pan, to fill it to a depth of about 1 cm. Set the pan over medium heat.

Knead the dough briefly and divide into portions almost twice the size as for chapattis. Roll each portion into a roti about ½ cm thick and 8-10 cm in diameter. Brush off as much of the dry atta as possible, and use a spatula to lower the roti into the oil, which should be medium hot.

Start rolling out the next roti, keeping an eye on the one in the pan. After a minute, check it by lifting with the spatula. If the underside is beginning to brown, turn it carefully and cook the other side. It will rise and puff out slightly. When the second side is nice and brown, remove the roti and put it in a basket, which you have lined with foil on top of a napkin.

Note: It's never easy to judge the heat of oil for frying, but you can break the first roti open to check whether you've got it right. The roti should be golden brown and barely crisp on the outside, and soft but cooked through on the inside. If it's crisp and hard most of the way through, the heat was too low and you had to cook it too long to get the right colour on the outside. If it's soggy and undercooked inside, it was too hot and turned brown before it was cooked through. Adjust the heat accordingly.

PARATHAS

Ingredients for 6-8 parathas:

2 cups atta	1 cup water
½ tsp salt	½ cup bland oil *or* ghee

Method: Using the atta, salt and water, make and knead the dough, and put the tava on to heat, exactly as for chapattis.

Half fill a small bowl with the oil or ghee, and keep it handy next to the plate of dry atta. Knead the dough briefly and divide it into portions about 1½ times larger than for chapattis.

In exactly the same way as for chapattis, roll one portion into a roti as thin as you can. Smear ½ tsp oil all over the surface. Fold it in half, smear oil over the surface again and fold again. Roll it out, doing your best to maintain the triangular shape.

For parathas, the tava should be a little less hot than for chapattis. Test by sprinkling a pinch of dry atta on it; it should take 5 seconds to turn brown. When it is at the right temperature, place the paratha gently on it and start rolling out the next one. As soon as the upper surface of the paratha begins to rise in blisters, turn it. Smear the surface with ½ tsp oil, and when the underside begins to show flecks of brown turn it again and smear oil on that surface. Press down around the edges with the tongs or the back of the teaspoon, and cook a minute or so more on each side till both are a rich brown.

Remove the paratha and put it in a basket, which you have lined with foil on top of a napkin. Repeat till all the parathas are made.

Note: You can reheat parathas quite successfully by toasting them on the direct flame, as in the last step of making chapattis. They come up *almost* as good as new.

STUFFED PARATHAS

Ingredients for 5-6 parathas:

2 cups atta
½ tsp salt
1 cup water
½ cup bland oil *or* ghee
About 1½ cups stuffing *(see below)*

Method: Using the atta, salt and water, make and knead the dough, and heat the tava, exactly as for plain parathas, and divide into slightly larger portions.

Take one portion and roll it into a ball between your palms. Flatten it slightly, and rotating it between your fingers and thumbs mould it into the shape of a small cup, using your thumbs to hollow it out. Fill the cup almost to the brim with stuffing, and draw the sides together to seal well. You now have a stuffed ball of dough. With the seal on top, flatten it slightly, dip both sides in dry atta, and lay it on the rolling surface, sealed side down. Roll it out gently, so that the stuffing doesn't break through. (If it does, pinch it together as best you can.)

Cook as for plain parathas.

Stuffings for Parathas:

- For **Aloo ka Paratha,** make Aloo ka Bharta (p. 228).

- For **Ande ka Paratha,** make Scrambled Egg (p. 216) or Egg Bhujia (p. 219).

- For **Mooli ka Paratha** or **Gobhi ka Paratha,** grate one large white radish or one small cauliflower. To make the stuffing, sprinkle the grated vegetable with salt and put it aside for 10-15 minutes. The salt will draw out the moisture. Squeeze out the excess water from the vegetable and season to taste with ½ tsp red chilli powder or 1-2 green chillies chopped fine, 1 tsp cummin powder or black pepper powder or ½ tsp fennel seed powder, and optionally, chopped coriander leaves and/or grated ginger (better for this purpose than commercial ginger paste). These stuffings don't need to be cooked before they go into the parathas.
  The grated cauliflower is rather crumbly in texture, so rolling out a Gobhi ka Paratha isn't that easy—the stuffing keeps trying to break through the dough. Better to start with Aloo ka Paratha, and proceed to Mooli ka Paratha, and only when you've mastered these go on to try Gobhi ka Paratha.

MAKKI DI ROTI

This is considered the essential accompaniment to Sarson da Saag. Not easy to make; best learn the knack by watching someone who's skilled in working the fragile dough.

Ingredients for 6-8 rotis:

2 cups makki ka atta *or*
1½ cups makki ka atta and ½ cup atta
¼ tsp salt

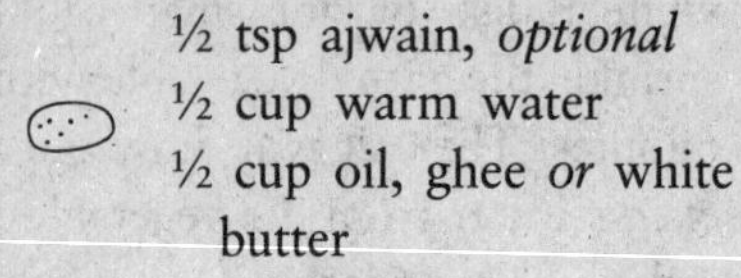

½ tsp ajwain, *optional*
½ cup warm water
½ cup oil, ghee *or* white butter

Method: Sieve both the flours together, if used, into a platter, and sprinkle in the salt and ajwain, if used. Using your hands, mix it into a dough with the warm water. The dough will not cohere in the same way as dough made with atta, and the optional ½ cup atta is a cheat to give it a little more stability. Knead for a couple of minutes till it is about as integrated as it seems to be getting.

Put the tava on low to medium heat. These rotis will cook on a slightly less hot tava than chapattis.

This dough is much more fragile than wheat flour dough, so you have to shape the rotis between your palms. Keep a small bowl of water beside your work surface, and keep wetting your hands with it. Divide the dough into portions each about twice the size of a chapatti. Take one portion and roll it into a ball between your wetted palms. Flatten it, and press it repeatedly, rotating it as you do so till you have a circle the size of a chapatti, but twice as thick. As it offers to break at the edges, pinch the sides of the break together as best you can.

Place one roti on the hot tava and roast it for about 2 minutes. The underside should have brown spots. Turn it over and smear a little oil, ghee or butter over the cooked side. Remove the roti from the tava after another 2 minutes, smear butter on the other side and keep warm in a basket lined with foil over a clean napkin.

7

Soups

While soup is not likely to be on the daily menu of most busy young working people, it can be a useful standby for several culinary occasions. Hot or cold, thin or thick—it comes in an extraordinary variety of tastes and textures and lends itself to creative and imaginative combinations of ingredients.

A **hot thick soup** is one of the most comforting of foods in cold weather, and can serve as a light meal in itself, needing only some toast and butter to complete it. **Cold soup,** on the other hand, is refreshing, ideal for tempting appetites jaded by the heat of the Indian summer; it makes an elegant starter for a lunch or dinner party.

There are several short-cut soups in tins and packets available in the market, but many of them are heavy on monosodium glutamate and not very nice. In any case, tinned or packet soups, are expensive. It's certainly cheaper, as well as more satisfying, to make your own.

> *You can always cheat by using concentrated meat, chicken or vegetable cubes for the stock if you can find ones that aren't overdosed with monosodium glutamate; they are a perfectly acceptable substitute for the real thing. Reconstitute according to the instructions on the packet or sprinkle directly into the soup. But remember, they're already salted, so you have to allow for this when you're making the soup.*

Non-vegetarians tend to look down on vegetarian soups, and to think that the only soup worth talking about is made on the basis of **chicken** or **meat stock.** But it's possible to make a very tasty **vegetable stock.** There are also many combinations of vegetables, essentially purées, that are delicious and nourishing. Many of the supposedly non-vegetarian soups are perfectly acceptable when made using vegetable stock, milk, or even water—though water is obviously the least preferred option.

The preliminary softening of onions in oil or butter, which is the first step of many of the following recipes, adds richness and body to the soup. But it's possible to omit this step and just boil the onions up in stock or water with the rest of the ingredients. Figure-and-health-conscious cooks may prefer this way.

For many soups, you need to **blend** the ingredients after cooking, to get a purée. For this you really need an **electric blender**. Sure you can strain it through a coarse sieve or vegetable mill, or at a pinch mash it with a fork or a potato masher, but that's hard work.

> *SIPPETS*
>
> *Also called croutons. Fried bread cubes to add crunch, especially to a thick puréed soup.*
>
> *Use white bread, preferably not very fresh. Use 1 slice per serving, remove the crust and cut into 1-1½ cm cubes. Fry in hot oil in a kadhai, over medium heat till dark brown and crisp. Remove from the oil with a slotted spoon, and put them on a couple of layers of kitchen paper to absorb the excess oil. Hand around with the soup.*

Soups can be **thickened** with **refined flour, cornflour, ground rice** or **semolina**. Refined flour is either incorporated as a roux (see p. 258) or mixed with water in a jam jar etc. (see p. 259); cornflour and ground rice need to be blended with a little water to a runny paste; semolina can be sprinkled in dry. Keep stirring as you add the thickening agent to the hot soup.

The technique of thickening a soup with eggs is described in the recipe for Soupa Avgolemone. You can also incorporate eggs into almost any hot soup by the Chinese **egg-drop** method. Beat 1-2 eggs till well blended. Have the soup boiling fast. Stir it vigorously, and dribble the beaten egg into it. The eggs set on contact with the hot liquid as ribbons through the soup.

There doesn't seem to be a lot of point in making small quantities of soup. The recipes given below are for four to five servings, if it is to be eaten as a starter. Double the quantities if you are going to serve it as a meal in itself.

CHICKEN STOCK

Ingredients for 5 cups stock:

½ kg chicken pieces, the bonier the better
1 onion
2 black cardamoms
2 bay leaves
6 cloves
6 cm cinnamon
½ tsp whole black pepper

Preparation: Wash and drain the chicken. Chop the onion coarsely.

Method: Put all the ingredients into the pressure cooker with about 6 cups water and bring slowly to the boil. When it boils, skim off any foamy scum that rises. Close the cooker and cook under pressure for 20 minutes. Let the pressure come down and strain the stock.

If the recipe calls for bits of chicken, it's easy to pick off the meat from the bones. Discard the bones and the spices. Cool and degrease the stock, and use as required.

To degrease stock: Cool the stock, refrigerate it till the fat congeals and skim it off. In case there isn't time for this, after straining it, give it 5 minutes to settle and for the fat to rise. Gently lay on the surface torn bits of brown paper, rough side down, which will blot up nearly all the fat. You could also use kitchen paper, but it's rather flimsy and difficult to pick up when saturated with fat.

Note: You can serve chicken stock as a soup by itself, with a seasoning of salt and pepper, a squeeze of lime juice and a sprinkling of coriander leaves.

It's advisable not to salt stock; add salt when preparing the soup.

Variation: **Hamud**—Dice 1-2 stalks of celery, and chop the leaves. Chop 1 medium onion or a leek. Cut 3-4 cloves garlic into tiny dice. Add the vegetables to 5 cups stock with 1 tsp salt, ½ tsp black pepper powder and 1½-2 tbsp lime juice. Simmer till the celery is al dente, about 15-20 minutes. Garnish with 8-10 sprigs of chopped fresh coriander leaves. This is a favourite soup with the Egyptians, who stir in a cup or so of boiled rice just before serving.

MEAT STOCK

Same method as for chicken stock, and same ingredients; only substitute meat bones and any odd pieces of meat you can spare, in place of the chicken, removing as much of the fat as possible.

Stock, whether of chicken, meat or vegetables, doesn't keep awfully well; goes off in about 3 days even in the fridge. You can prolong its life by bringing it up to the boil and then cooling and refrigerating it again. But better to use it sooner rather than later; or freeze it for up to a week.

When you order pasandas you may have to pay for the bones as well and the butcher will give them to you in a separate packet. Similarly, when he prepares chops he'll often take out half the bones. You can ask him for bony cuts like ribs; some butchers may even sell bones for soup.

VEGETABLE STOCK

Ingredients for 8 cups stock:

1 kg vegetables—any combination of:
celery, spinach, green peas, onions, carrots, leeks *or* spring onions, turnips, capsicums, french beans, tomatoes and mushrooms

Seasoning—any combination of:
2 cloves garlic
2 bay leaves
6 cloves
6 cm cinnamon
½ tsp whole black pepper
2 tsp malt vinegar

Preparation: Cut the root off the celery, separate the stalks and wash. Pick through the spinach as given on p. 109, and wash. Shell, defreeze or rehydrate the green peas. Peel the onions. Wash the rest of the vegetables. Scrape the carrots. Cut the roots off the leeks or spring onions. Discard any yellowed leaves and the coarse green part at the very top. Peel the turnips and rinse again. Halve the capsicums, scrape out the seeds and discard. Top and tail the french beans. Roughly chop all vegetables except the green peas.

Method: Put all the ingredients into the pressure cooker along with about 10 cups water. Bring slowly to the boil and cook under pressure for about 10 minutes. Let the pressure come down, and simmer for a further 10 minutes.

Cool and strain the stock. Leave the vegetables in the strainer to drip for a few minutes, shaking occasionally to get out all the stock, but don't press or squeeze them, or the stock may not be as clear as it is supposed to be.

Note: Go easy on strong-flavoured vegetables like turnip and capsicum, even tomatoes, which tend to dominate.

SOUPA AVGOLEMONE
Greek Lemon Soup

A light, nourishing and delicious soup which is a staple of Greek cuisine.

Ingredients for 4-5 servings:

¼ cup long-grain rice
1 small onion
1 lemon *or* 2 limes
5 cups chicken stock
1 tsp salt
½ tsp black pepper powder

2-3 eggs, depending on their size

Garnish:
8-10 sprigs fresh parsley *or* coriander leaves

Preparation: Wash and drain the rice. Chop the onion as fine as possible. Wash the lemon or limes and squeeze out the juice, 1½-2 tbsp. Wash the herb and chop fine.

Method: Put the rice and onion into the stock with the salt and pepper, and simmer for 15 minutes till the rice is tender.

When ready to serve, reheat the stock till just about to boil and remove from the heat. Break the eggs into a bowl, and beat till well blended. Beat in the lemon or lime juice. Pour a ladleful of hot stock slowly onto the egg mixture, beating all the time. Repeat with one more ladleful. Pour the egg mixture into the stock, stirring all the time.

> *Never reheat a soup after thickening it with eggs, as the eggs will scramble. If you need to reheat it, place the pan containing the soup into a larger pan containing simmering water, until heated through.*

Garnish with the parsley or coriander, and serve immediately.

Variations: You could grind the rice as given on p. 38, work it into a thin paste with 1 cup water before adding it to the stock. This thickens the soup so you have to stir it every now and then as it simmers, to prevent it sticking.

- Instead of rice, use pasta, either regular egg noodles broken into small pieces, or vermicelli, adjusting the cooking time accordingly. The pasta should, as always, remain al dente, and remember that vermicelli cooks almost instantaneously.

CREAM OF CHICKEN SOUP

Ingredients for 4-5 servings:

5 cups chicken stock	1 tsp salt
1½ tbsp bland oil	½ tsp black pepper powder
1-1½ tbsp flour	1 cup cream

Method: Heat the stock and if there are any scraps of chicken meat from making it, cut them up and throw them in.

Make a roux of the oil and flour by heating the oil on medium heat for 1-2 minutes. Lower the heat, stir the flour into the oil and work it in well to blend. It should have the consistency of a rather dry paste. Cook, stirring all the time, for a couple of minutes to get rid of the raw flour taste, taking care that it does not turn brown.

Take the pan off the heat and let it cool till it stops sizzling. Then add the hot stock all at once. Immediately start stirring the soup. It will begin to thicken. Stir till well amalgamated, return the pan to the heat and bring slowly to the boil stirring all the time.

Add the salt and pepper, and simmer for a few minutes, stirring often to ensure it doesn't stick.

Stir in the cream and pour into individual bowls.

MIXED VEGETABLE SOUP

Ingredients for 5-6 servings:

2 medium onions
2 cloves garlic, *optional*
2 large potatoes
½ kg mixed vegetables as given for vegetable stock (see p. 67)
1 tbsp bland oil *or* 25 gms butter
2 bay leaves
½ tsp black pepper powder
1 tsp salt
5 cups any stock *or* water
A small bunch fresh coriander leaves *or* dill, *or* 8-10 sprigs mint *or* basil, *optional, but adds flavour and freshness*

Preparation: Slice the onions. Chop or crush the garlic, if used. Peel, wash and cut the potatoes into medium dice. Wash and prepare the other vegetables as given in the recipe for vegetable stock, and chop roughly. Wash and chop the green herb.

Method: Heat the oil over medium heat in a heavy-bottomed pan or pressure cooker, lower the heat, add the onions, cover and cook till soft and translucent.

Add the rest of the ingredients except the stock or water and herb. Toss over medium heat for a few minutes.

Pour in the stock or water, bring up to the boil and cook till the vegetables are well softened. If using the pressure cooker, cook under pressure for 5 minutes, release the pressure and simmer for a further 15 minutes.

Stir in the green herb, if used, and mash or blend the soup to a purée.

Reheat till piping hot and serve immediately.

Variations: Reduce the amount of stock by about 1½ cups, and after blending the soup add the same quantity of milk.

- You can use any one vegetable along with the onions and potatoes, and the same basic recipe to make for example, **Celery Soup, Green Pea Soup, Carrot Soup,** or **Spinach Soup**. Spinach Soup is improved by the addition of a grated nutmeg.

- You can hardly have a better **Tomato Soup** than one made as above using only 1-2 onions, 3-4 medium potatoes and 6-8 medium tomatoes. Tomatoes being so full of water, you may like to reduce the amount of water or stock. The inclusion of mint, dill or basil, coarsely chopped and added just before puréeing, lifts it into the gourmet class.

- The classic cold soup **Vichyssoise** is exactly this recipe, using only 3-4 potatoes and ½ kg leeks, if available, otherwise use spring onions or regular onions. Chill and stir in ½ cup cream just before serving. If served hot it is called **Potage Bonne Femme** and can be enriched with cream or 25 gms butter.

- You can invent your own variations: **Mushroom and Green Peas; Celery and Turnip; Capsicum and Leeks; Spinach and Carrot**—endless possibilities.

MUSHROOM SOUP

Ingredients for 4-5 servings:

- 400 gms/2 packets mushrooms
- 2 medium onions
- 2 cloves garlic, *optional*
- 5 cups any stock *or* water
- 1 tbsp bland oil *or* 25 gms butter
- 2 bay leaves
- 1 tbsp refined flour
- ½ tsp salt
- ½ tsp black pepper powder
- 3-4 tsp Worcestershire sauce, *optional*

Preparation: Wash the mushrooms and chop coarsely. Slice the onions. Chop or crush the garlic, if used. Heat the stock to nearly boiling point.

Method: Heat the oil or butter over medium heat in a heavy-bottomed pan, lower the heat, add the onions, and garlic, if used, cover and cook till the onions are soft and translucent.

Add the mushrooms and the bay leaves. When the mushrooms begin to sweat, raise the heat and cook stirring till nearly dry.

Lower the heat, sprinkle in the flour and work it in well to blend. Cook, stirring all the time, for a couple of minutes, taking care not to let it turn brown.

Remove the pan from the heat and leave for 1-2 minutes till it stops sizzling. Add the hot stock all at once. Immediately start stirring the soup. It will begin to thicken. Return it to medium heat and keep stirring till it comes to the boil. Lower the heat and simmer for 10-15 minutes stirring occasionally.

Remove the bay leaves and blend the soup. Add the salt, pepper and Worcestershire sauce, reheat and serve.

Variations: Use milk instead of stock.

- Add a squeeze of lime juice before serving.

- For a more substantial soup, add 50 gms pasta (ordinary egg noodles, broken into manageable lengths would be fine) after the soup is blended, and simmer till the pasta is al dente. This is called **Postnaya Lapsha,** a Russian soup.

ALMOND AND CELERY SOUP

Ingredients for 4-5 servings:

½ cup almonds	1½ tbsp bland oil
½ cup milk	1 tbsp refined flour
1 medium onion	1 tsp sugar
4 sticks celery	1 tsp salt
5 cups stock, preferably chicken stock	½ tsp black pepper powder

Preparation: Blanch and peel the almonds. Grind them in the electric grinder. Boil the milk and pour it over the ground almonds. Leave for about 30 minutes.

Chop the onion fine. Wash the celery and dice small. Bring the stock to the boil.

Method: Heat the oil over medium heat in a heavy-bottomed pan. Lower the heat, add the onion, cover, and cook till the onion is soft and translucent. Sprinkle the flour and stir it in till well blended. Cook stirring for 1-2 minutes more, taking care it does not turn brown.

Remove the pan from the heat and leave for 1-2 minutes till it stops sizzling. Add the hot stock to the pan all at once and immediately start stirring the soup. It will begin to thicken. Return it to medium heat and keep stirring till it comes to the boil.

Stir in the sugar, salt, pepper and almond-milk, mix well and add the diced celery. Simmer for a few minutes more till the celery is barely cooked and still crunchy.

COLD CUCUMBER SOUP

There are any number of variations on the theme of cold cucumber soup, some with, some without curd. Here are two of them.

Ingredients for 4-5 servings:

2 medium cucumbers
1 medium onion
1 small potato
3-4 sprigs mint, dill *or* basil *or* failing any of these a small bunch fresh coriander leaves
1 tbsp bland oil
5 cups stock, preferably chicken stock
1 tsp salt
½ tsp black pepper powder
¾-1 cup cream

Preparation: Wash the cucumbers, cut a 5-cm piece from one of them and slice into thin rounds without peeling. Cover and set aside in the fridge. Peel the remaining cucumbers, cut into quarters lengthwise, cut out the seeds and discard. Chop the flesh coarsely.

Slice the onion. Peel, wash and dice the potato. Wash the herb of choice, and chop the leaves fine.

Method: Heat the oil over medium heat in a heavy-bottomed pan, lower the heat, add the onion, cover the pan and cook till the onion is soft and translucent.

Add the cucumber, potato, stock, salt and pepper, and bring up to the boil. Cover and simmer for 20 minutes or so, till the vegetables are soft.

Blend the soup. Cool, stir in the cream and chill thoroughly.

Stir in the chopped green herb and garnish with the reserved slices of cucumber.

COLD CUCUMBER AND CURD SOUP

Ingredients for 4-5 servings:

2 medium cucumbers
2 sprigs mint
3 cups curd
½ tsp salt
¼ tsp black pepper powder
1 tsp sugar

Optional ingredients:
2 spring onions *or*
½ small onion
1 clove garlic
1 cup chicken *or* vegetable stock in place of 1 cup curd

Preparation: Wash and peel the cucumbers and cut into quarters lengthwise. Cut out the seeds and discard. Chop the flesh coarsely. Wash the mint and strip the leaves off the stem. Beat the curd till smooth and blended.

Of the optional ingredients, wash the spring onions and chop coarsely. Chop the onion. Crush the garlic.

Method: Put the cucumber into the blender jar with the onion and garlic, if used, and give it all a whirl. Add the rest of the ingredients, reserving a few mint leaves, and whirl again. Taste and adjust the seasoning. Chill thoroughly.

Stir well, garnish with the reserved mint leaves and serve.

GAZPACHO
Cold Spanish Soup

An inspired creation of Spanish cuisine. Lends itself to any number of variations.

Ingredients for 4-5 servings:

1 medium cucumber
2 large capsicums
6 medium, red, juicy tomatoes
.100 gms spring onions *or* 1 medium onion
1-2 cloves garlic
2-3 limes *or* 2-3 tbsp malt vinegear
1 tsp salt
½ tsp black pepper powder
4 tbsp olive oil *or* other good-quality salad oil

Optional ingredients:
2 slices white bread
12 black olives
1½-2 cups chicken stock
1½-2 cups tomato juice
½ cup cream

Preparation: Wash all the vegetables thoroughly. Peel the cucumber and cut into quarters lengthwise. Cut out the seeds and discard. Deseed the capsicums.

Reserve about ¼ cucumber, ½ capsicum, 1-2 nice firm tomatoes and 1-2 spring onions or ¼ regular onion. Roughly chop the rest of the vegetables. Dice the reserved vegetables fine and set aside. Crush the garlic. Wash the limes, if used, and squeeze out the juice, 2-3 tbsp.

Of the optional ingredients, remove the crusts from the bread slices, soak in cold water, squeeze out the moisture and set aside. Stone the olives and cut them into quarters.

Method: Put the roughly chopped vegetables with the garlic, salt, pepper, and bread, if used, into the blender, and reduce to a purée.

Add half the lime juice or vinegar, and oil, and whirl some more. Taste, and judge how much more of these ingredients to add.

If the soup seems too thick, thin it down with the chicken stock and/or tomato juice. Stir in the cream, if used, and chill.

Toss the diced vegetables together in a small serving bowl with the quartered olives, if used.

Serve the soup in individual bowls, garnished with a spoonful of the diced vegetables.

INSTANT COLD TOMATO SOUP

An elegant starter for a summer lunch or dinner. Takes all of five minutes to assemble.

Ingredients for 4-5 servings:

4-5 sprigs fresh dill, mint *or* basil *or* failing these, a small bunch coriander leaves
3 cups curd, not too sour
½ lime, *optional*
3 cups tomato juice
½ cup unsweetened orange juice
½ tsp salt
¼ tsp black pepper powder

Preparation: Wash the green herb and reserve a few whole leaves for garnish. Wash the lime and squeeze out the juice, about 1 tsp.

Method: Put all the ingredients except the reserved garnish into the blender and give it a whirl. Taste, and adjust seasoning.

Thin down with a little cold water or milk if it seems too thick. Chill.

Pour out into individual bowls and garnish with the reserved leaves.

8

Dals

Several varieties of **dal (lentils** or **pulses), gram (chana)** and **beans** are used in Indian cookery. Most dals come in different forms—whole, including the outer husk; split, but not husked; and husked and split. To add to the confusion, there is little agreement on their English names, some of them being quite unfamiliar. You don't have to learn about all of them at one time. It may help to have the information regarding the ones in common use, in tabular form.

Hindi name	English name	Forms available
Arhar/toover (also called toor)	Pigeon peas	Husked (arhar/toover)
Kabuli chana	Chickpeas	Whole (kabuli chana)—the cooked dish is known as **Choley**
Kala chana	Bengal gram	Whole (kala chana); husked (chana dal)
Lobia	Black-eyed beans	Whole (lobia)
Masoor	Egyptian lentils, red lentils	Whole (sabut masoor); husked (masoor dal/dhuli masoor/malka masoor)
Moong	Green beans, green gram	Whole (sabut moong); split (chilke ki moong dal); husked (dhuli moong/ moong dal)

Hindi name	English name	Forms available
Rajma/rajmash	Red beans, kidney beans	Whole (rajma or rajmash)
Urad (also called maan)	Black beans, black gram	Whole (sabut urad); split (chilke ki urad dal); husked (dhuli urad/urad dal)

Arhar/toover and **chana dal** are easy to confuse, but the grains of arhar are smaller and glossier. Arhar is much used in Gujarati cooking, and is the basis of the south Indian sambar.

You won't want to keep all of this lot in your store cupboard at any one time. You might want to start by laying in a kilogram of two or three different varieties, that you like and find easy to cook. Don't buy too much at a time, as they don't keep indefinitely, especially during the monsoon.

As protection against insects, put a couple of dried red chillies in each dal container.

The basic dal technique is simplicity itself. By way of preliminary preparation pick through the dal using the method described for cleaning rice (see p. 37), discarding any dicey-looking grains, and especially looking out for tiny stones. Even though dals now come well cleaned and hygienically packed in plastic bags, it makes sense to check them over for small stones, unless and until you develop confidence in a particular brand. Wash the dal in several changes of water till most of the cloudiness disappears, and if you have the time, soak it for an hour or so.

Whole dals and beans **must** be soaked, and then washed well in several changes of water before cooking. They release harmful toxins while soaking, which need to be washed away. What is toxic for humans, however, is said to be highly nutritious for plants. So if you're into keeping pot-plants, save the soaking water for them.

To cook the dal, put it in a pan or pressure cooker with water, salt and spice powders—often the basic combination of red chilli, turmeric and coriander. Boil till the dal is soft and the water is more or less absorbed. If you're in a tremendous hurry, or have taken a vow of austerity, you can eat it just like that. But to transform an edible and nourishing but not frightfully interesting gruel into a really tasty dish, you need to give it a baghar.

In a small frying pan or kadhai, heat a tablespoon or two of oil, burning it if using mustard oil. Into this throw any combination of the following ingredients: cummin seeds, mustard seeds, panch-poran, finely diced ginger, slit green chillies (de-seeded if liked), whole dried red chillies, chopped or finely sliced onions, chopped garlic, chopped tomato, pieces of unripe mango, curry leaves, bay leaves, asafoetida. Some recipe writers suggest a baghar incorporating spice powders like red chilli, garam masala or sambar powder, or even ginger-garlic paste; others add half a teaspoon of sugar or a little jaggery. Fry, usually on high heat, and turn the lot into the dal, covering it immediately to trap the aroma. You can stir it in before serving, so that the oil is absorbed, or serve the dal with the baghar floating on top.

All the dal recipes in this book are for liquid dals. Some dals can be cooked dry, but this needs a very precise judgment of the amount of water needed in relation to the amount of dal, the length of time it has been soaked and the time it takes to cook; it is not for beginners.

The process for cooking kabuli chana and the different kinds of beans is rather different from that for dal.

Since the different dals can be cooked by one basic method, we give below a master recipe, explaining the method in detail, followed by others in an abbreviated form, with special instructions when necessary. Though all of the combinations are tried and tested, that doesn't make them sacrosanct. The possibilities are endless; once you get the hang of it, you can ring the changes to your heart's content.

Many people like a couple of teaspoons of lime juice stirred into the dal before the baghar is added, and any dal is improved by being given a garnish of chopped coriander leaves.

The one cup (about 200 gms) of dal that is specified for each recipe may last two to three people for two meals, assuming that the meal also includes rice and/or roti and a vegetable or meat dish.

Don't forget that most kinds of whole lentils, pulses and beans can be sprouted and lightly cooked, or used in salads.

CHANA DAL
(Master Recipe)

Ingredients for 4-6 servings:

1 cup chana dal
½ tsp red chilli powder
½ tsp turmeric powder
1 tsp coriander powder
1 tsp salt

Baghar:
2 tbsp oil
1 tsp cummin seeds
1 small onion
1-2 green chillies
1 medium tomato

Preparation: Wash the dal and soak in water for 1 hour. Slice the onion fine. Wash and slit the green chillies. Wash and chop the tomato.

Method: Drain the dal and rinse. Put it in the pressure cooker with the spice powders, salt and fresh water to cover by 1-2 cm. Stir and bring to the boil. Cook under pressure till soft, 6-8 minutes.

Heat the oil in a small frying pan or medium-sized kadhai, burning it if using mustard oil. Lower the heat, add the cummin seeds and cook for a few seconds, till golden and fragrant. Add the onion and green chillies and fry on high heat till the onion starts turning golden. Lower the heat and add the tomato, cover and cook for 1-2 minutes, till the tomato softens and disintegrates. Raise the heat, stir-fry for another 1-2 minutes till it dries and becomes slightly gooey, then turn the contents of the pan into the dal. Cover immediately to trap the aroma.

> *Best not to use one of those very small kadhais for a baghar with a watery ingredient like tomato, as the tomato can froth up on contact with the hot oil, boil over on to the heat-source, and your whole baghar goes up in flames. Believe us, we speak from experience. A smallish frying pan is OK.*

Stir in the baghar before serving or not, as you like it.

MASOOR AUR URAD DAL

Use ¾ cup husked masoor dal and ¼ cup husked urad dal. Wash and soak the dals together, drain and combine with salt, water and the same spice powders as in the recipe for Chana Dal. Cook for 3-4 minutes under pressure.

To make the baghar, fry 1 tsp cummin seeds till golden and fragrant. Add 1 small chopped onion and 1-2 slit green chillies. Fry on high heat till the onion turns golden. Add 10-12 curry leaves, fry for a few seconds more and pour the baghar into the dal.

MASOOR AUR MOONG DAL

Use ½ cup husked masoor dal and ½ cup husked moong dal. Wash and soak the dals together, drain and combine with salt, water and the same spice powders as in the recipe for Chana Dal. Cook for 3-4 minutes under pressure.

To make the baghar, fry 2-3 dried red chillies on high heat till they turn plump and black. Lower the heat, add 1 tsp cummin seeds and ¼-½ tsp asafoetida powder. Fry till the cummin is golden and fragrant, and add 1 small chopped onion. Fry on high heat till the onion is golden, and pour the baghar into the dal.

MASOOR DAL

Wash and soak 1 cup masoor dal, drain and combine with salt, water and the same spice powders as in the recipe for Chana Dal. Cook for 15 minutes without pressure.

> *Masoor dal is the only dal we recommend should be cooked without pressure, as it is tender enough to cook in a reasonable time, and becomes mushy under pressure.*

To make the baghar, fry 1 tsp of cummin seeds till they are golden and fragrant. Pour the baghar into the dal.

Variations: When the dal is cooked, mix in about 2 tsp tamarind paste thinned down with a little water. To make the baghar, put 2 dried red chillies into the hot oil and fry on high heat till plump and black. Lower the heat, add 1 small finely sliced onion and a couple of cloves of finely chopped garlic, and fry till golden.

- To make the baghar, throw in a couple of dried red chillies into the hot oil, and cook for a few seconds till plump and black. Lower the heat, add 1 tsp mustard seeds, cover till the spluttering subsides, then add the flesh of an unripe mango cut in medium slices. Cover and cook till the mango softens. Pour the baghar into the dal, and simmer for another 10 minutes till the mango is cooked through. Stir in 2 tsp sugar before serving. This makes a really delicious dal.

CHILKE KI MOONG DAL

Wash and soak 1 cup split moong dal, drain and combine with salt, water and the same spice powders as in the recipe for Chana Dal. Cook for 5-6 minutes under pressure.

To make the baghar, fry 1 tsp each of cummin and fennel seeds till they are golden and fragrant. Add 1 small chopped onion, 1-2 slit green chillies and a 3-cm piece of ginger, finely diced. Fry on high heat till the onion turns golden and pour the baghar into the dal.

MOONG DAL

Cook 1 cup husked moong dal according to the recipes for Masoor Dal, Masoor aur Moong Dal, or Chilke ki Moong Dal. It will cook in 3-4 minutes under pressure.

Note: Some people think that husked moong dal has a peculiar 'raw' flavour when cooked by the standard method. To avoid this, you might like to start by **dry-roasting** the dal in a heavy frying pan over low heat till the colour turns a shade or two darker (but beware of over-roasting it). Wash it after roasting. Alternatively, cook it with a chaunk instead of a baghar, using the ingredients suggested for the baghar and frying the dal in the chaunk for a couple of minutes before adding the spice powders, salt and water.

ARHAR/TOOVER

Ingredients for 4-6 servings:

1 cup arhar/toover
½ tsp turmeric powder
½ tsp red chilli powder
1 tsp fennel powder
1½ tsp sugar
1 tsp salt

Baghar:
2 tbsp oil *or* 1 tbsp ghee
1 tsp cummin seeds
¼-½ tsp asafoetida powder

Preparation: Wash the dal and soak in water for 1 hour.

Method: Drain the dal and rinse. Combine with the spice powders, sugar, salt and water as in the recipe for Chana Dal. Cook for 5-6 minutes under pressure.

When the pressure has gone down, open the cooker and whisk the dal. Adjust the consistency by adding more water, or reducing it on high heat, stirring constantly to prevent it sticking and burning. It is supposed to have the consistency of a thick puréed soup.

To make the baghar, fry the cummin seeds in the oil or ghee till golden and fragrant. Add the asafoetida, and fry for only a few seconds more. Pour the baghar into the dal.

URAD SABUT

Ingredients for 4-6 servings:

1 cup whole urad
1 cup creamy curd *or* cream
½ tsp turmeric powder
½ tsp red chilli powder
1 tsp coriander powder
1 tsp salt

Baghar:
1 small onion
3-cm piece ginger
2 tbsp oil
1 tsp cummin seeds

Preparation: Wash the dal and soak in water for 1 hour. Beat the curd till smooth and blended. Chop the onion. Peel and wash the ginger, and dice fine.

Method: Drain the dal and rinse. Combine with the spice powders, salt and water as in the recipe for Chana Dal. Cook under pressure for 15-20 minutes.

When the pressure has gone down, open the cooker, stir in the curd or cream, and bring back gently to the boil.

To make the baghar, fry the cummin seeds in the oil till golden and fragrant. Add the onion and ginger and stir-fry on high heat till the onion is golden. Pour the baghar into the dal.

Variation: You can cook split urad or whole moong by the same recipe. Cook the split urad dal for 10 minutes and the whole moong for 12-15 minutes under pressure.

MASOOR SABUT

Ingredients for 4-6 servings:

1 cup whole masoor
7-8 cloves garlic
½ tsp turmeric powder
½ tsp red chilli powder
1 tsp coriander powder
1 tsp salt

Baghar:
1 small onion
3-cm piece ginger
2-3 green chillies
2 tbsp oil

Preparation: Wash the dal and soak in water for 1 hour. Chop the garlic and the onion fine. Peel and wash the ginger, and dice fine. Wash and slit the chillies.

Method: Drain the dal and rinse. Combine with the garlic, spice powders, salt and water as in the recipe for Chana Dal. Cook for 6-8 minutes under pressure.

To make the baghar, stir-fry the onion, ginger and green chillies in the oil on high heat till the onion is golden. Pour the baghar into the dal.

DAL PANCHRATAN

Ingredients for 4-6 servings:

1 tbsp arhar/toover
1 tbsp chana dal
1 tbsp husked moong dal
1 tbsp whole urad
1 tbsp husked masoor dal
1 lime
1 tsp salt
1 tsp coriander powder

½ tsp red chilli powder
½ tsp turmeric powder
½ tsp garam masala powder

Baghar:
1 large onion
2 tbsp oil
1 tsp ginger-garlic paste

Preparation: Wash the dals and soak in water together for 1 hour. Wash the lime and squeeze out the juice, about 1 tbsp. Chop the onion fine.

Method: Drain the dals and rinse. Combine with the salt, water and all the spice powders except the garam masala, as in the recipe for Chana Dal. Cook for 10-15 minutes under pressure.

To make the baghar, stir-fry the onion and ginger-garlic paste in the oil on high heat till the onion is golden. Pour the baghar into the dal.

Before serving stir in the lime juice and sprinkle the garam masala.

DAL WITH VEGETABLES

For the sake of getting, as it were, two dishes for the price of one, you can combine a vegetable with dal. The usual combinations are **chana dal** with **vegetable marrow** or **spinach**; and **husked masoor dal,** or **husked** or **split moong dal** with **spinach.** In Kashmir, they cook **split moong dal** with **turnips.**

Cook the dal for a little less time than indicated in the foregoing recipes, let the pressure come down, and add the vegetable. Use 300 gms washed and peeled vegetable marrow, cut into medium dice, or 300 gms spinach prepared as given on p. 109, or 200 gms turnips, washed, peeled, rinsed again and cut in medium chunks, for 1 cup of dal. Cook for 2-3 minutes under pressure, or cook without pressure till the dal and the vegetable are tender.

Give a baghar according to the recipe for the relevant dal, perhaps omitting the tomato in the case of chana dal. You may like to step up the quantities of salt and spices by say 1½ times the quantities given in the recipes above. For husked moong dal with spinach, dry-roast the dal as suggested on p. 84.

You could experiment by adding **cauliflower,** cut into small florets, to the dal (don't overcook the cauliflower); or **karela, toori, pumpkin, french beans, green peas, mushrooms.**

Here's a recipe to show how it works.

CHILKE KI MOONG DAL AUR SHALGAM

Ingredients for 4-6 servings:

1 cup split moong dal
200 gms turnips
3-cm piece ginger
1½ tsp sugar
1 tsp coriander powder
½ tsp turmeric powder
½ tsp red chilli powder
½ tsp salt

Baghar:
1 tbsp oil
1 tsp cummin seeds
¼-½ tsp asafoetida powder

Preparation: Wash the dal and soak in water for 1 hour. Wash and peel the turnips, rinse again and cut into medium chunks. Peel and wash the ginger, and dice fine.

Method: Cook the dal with all the ingredients except the turnips and baghar under pressure for 2 minutes. Let the pressure go down, add the turnips, and cook for another 2 minutes under pressure, or 15 minutes without, till the turnips are tender but not mushy.

To make the baghar, fry the cummin seeds in the oil or ghee till golden and fragrant. Add the asafoetida, and fry for only a few seconds more. Pour the baghar into the dal.

RAJMA/LOBIA AUR TAMATAR

Ingredients for 4-6 servings:

1½ cups rajma *or* lobia

Tomato gravy:
4-6 medium tomatoes
3 medium onions
2 tsp ginger-garlic paste
½ tsp red chilli powder
½ tsp turmeric powder
2 tsp coriander powder
2 tbsp oil
2 tsp cummin seeds
½ tsp salt

Garnish:
8-10 sprigs coriander leaves

Preparation: Wash the beans and soak in water for several hours or overnight. Wash and chop the tomatoes fine. Slice the onions fine. Mix the ginger-garlic paste with the spice powders. Stir to combine into a paste with a tbsp or so of water. Wash the coriander leaves and chop coarsely.

Method: Drain the beans, wash again and put in the pressure cooker with fresh water to cover by 1-2 cm. Cook till tender, 10-15 minutes for rajma and 5-6 minutes for lobia, depending on the quality of the beans. When the pressure goes down, check the amount of water. There should be only a little left. Boil it down over high heat for another few minutes if there seems to be too much.

Make the Tomato Gravy according to the directions on p. 102, and stir into the beans. Garnish with the coriander leaves.

Variation: Instead of Tomato Gravy, you can use the Tomato and Aubergine Sauce on p. 276.

CHOLEY

The standard recipe for Choley uses tamarind paste for sourness. This one has lime juice instead, which is used to marinate a seasoning of onion, chilli and ginger.

Ingredients for 4-6 servings:

1½ cups kabuli chana
3-cm piece ginger
1-2 green chillies
4 medium onions
4 medium tomatoes
2-3 limes
1½ tsp salt
½ tsp bicarbonate of soda, *optional*
2 tbsp oil

2 tsp cummin powder
2 tsp coriander powder
½ tsp turmeric powder
½ tsp red chilli powder
2 tsp garam masala powder

Garnish:
A small bunch fresh coriander leaves

Preparation: Wash the chana and soak in water for several hours, preferably overnight. Peel and wash the ginger, and dice fine. Wash the green chillies and chop fine. Chop the onions fine. Wash and chop the tomatoes. Wash the limes and squeeze out the juice, 2-3 tbsp. Wash and chop the coriander leaves.

> *In case you forgot to soak the chana beforehand, pour the washed chana into a thermos, half-filling it, and fill up with boiling water. Screw the lid on tight and leave for an hour. Empty out into a strainer, and wash in 2-3 changes of clean water. The chana are now as good as if soaked overnight. Use this method for rajma and lobia also.*

Method: Put the ginger, green chillies, lime juice, 1½ tbsp of chopped onion and ½ tsp of salt in a small bowl, mix well and reserve.

Drain the chana, wash again and put into the pressure cooker with bicarbonate of soda, if used, and fresh water to cover by 1-2 cm. Cook till the chana is tender. The time taken will depend on the variety of chana, but chana can hardly be overcooked. Try 20 minutes for a start. When it's cooked, take out a cupful of chana, and mash it with a fork or potato masher. Return to the pan and stir into the gravy to thicken it.

Heat the oil in a large heavy-bottomed pan or kadhai, burning it if using mustard oil. Add the remaining onions, and fry on medium to high heat till beginning to turn golden.

Add the spice powders except the garam masala and stir well to mix. Stir in the tomatoes, lower the heat, cover and cook for a couple of minutes till they give up their juice. Raise the heat and stir-fry for another few minutes till nearly dry.

Add the tomato masala to the chana, together with the garam masala and the remaining salt. Bring back to the boil, cover, reduce the heat to low, and simmer for 10-15 minutes, stirring occasionally. Check that it is of the right consistency, neither too dry nor very watery. If too dry, stir in a cup of water; if watery, cook uncovered during this final simmer.

Stir in the reserved onion mixture and serve hot or lukewarm, garnished with the coriander leaves.

Note: Kabuli chana used to be the very devil to tenderise, even after prolonged soaking, and the standard method was to add a little bicarbonate of soda in the cooking, which did the trick but changed the taste slightly. Nowadays improved varieties are being cultivated, which tend to be less recalcitrant.

KADHI

One of many versions of a standard enjoyed all over India.

Ingredients for 4-6 servings:

2 cups sour curd
1 sprig curry leaves
1 cup gram flour
½ tsp turmeric powder
1 tsp salt
2 tbsp oil
2-3 dried red chillies

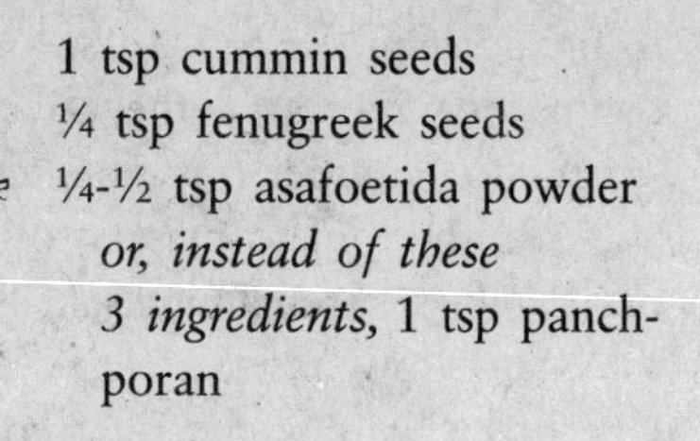

1 tsp cummin seeds
¼ tsp fenugreek seeds
¼-½ tsp asafoetida powder *or, instead of these 3 ingredients,* 1 tsp panch-poran

Preparation: Beat the curd till smooth and blended. Wash the curry leaves and strip them off the stem.

Method: Sieve the gram flour into a large mixing bowl. Gradually add the curd, beating and stirring all the time till you have a smooth paste. Slowly stir in 6 cups water, beating continuously till you have a thin batter without lumps. Sprinkle in the turmeric and salt, and beat and stir well.

Heat the oil in a large heavy-bottomed pan or kadhai, burning it if using mustard oil. Add the red chillies, and fry till black and plump. Reduce the heat and add the cummin and fenugreek seeds, and as soon as they turn golden and fragrant add the asafoetida. Alternatively add the panch-poran, covering the pan till the spluttering subsides.

Add the curry leaves and immediately pour in the curd-gram flour mixture. Bring to the boil on medium heat stirring constantly. Lower heat and let it simmer uncovered, stirring occasionally, till it is thick, creamy and reduced to about half its original bulk, 30-40 minutes.

Serve with plain rice.

Note: Kadhi does not reheat all that well, so it's one dish that it's best to make only as much as will be eaten at one meal.

Variations: The given quantities make a medium-consistency Kadhi. Reduce the quantity of water if you like it thicker, as the Punjabis do, or increase it if you prefer it much thinner, as they make it in Gujarat and south India.

- Slice one medium onion and add to the chaunk before the curry leaves, stir-frying over high heat till golden.
- Cut the flesh of one unripe mango into medium dice and add to the chaunk instead of the curry leaves. Cover the pan and cook on low heat till the mango is soft, then add the curd-gram flour mixture and proceed as above. Add 1-2 tsp sugar if it seems too sour.
- Incorporate some spinach, say 300-500 gms, cleaned, washed and chopped fine as described on p. 109. Add it to the chaunk before the curd-gram flour mixture goes in. Lower the heat, cover and cook till the spinach has wilted and lost its bulk, then add the curd-gram flour mixture and proceed as above.
- Add 1 tsp ginger powder and the liquidised pulp of 3-4 ripe mangoes to the curd-gram-flour mixture for a gourmet Kadhi.

PAKODAS FOR KADHI

Plain kadhi is a perfectly satisfactory dish on its own, but it is traditionally made more substantial by the addition of pakodas, which you can make while the kadhi is cooking. The procedure is as follows:

Ingredients for 20-25 pakodas:

½ cup curd
1 small onion, *optional*
2 green chillies, *optional*
1 cup gram flour

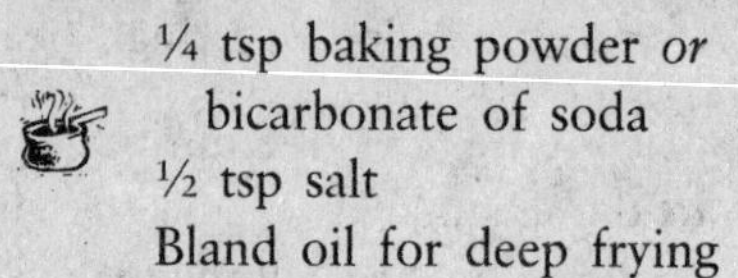

¼ tsp baking powder *or* bicarbonate of soda
½ tsp salt
Bland oil for deep frying

Preparation: Beat the curd till smooth and blended. Chop the onion very fine. Wash the green chillies, if used, and chop very fine.

Method: Sieve the gram flour into a mixing bowl with the baking powder or bicarbonate of soda and salt. Add the beaten curd gradually, beating and stirring all the time to make a smooth thickish batter. Beat in the onion and green chillies if used. Beat well for a few minutes to aerate the batter.

Put the oil in a deep frying pan or kadhai to a depth of about 2-3 cm, and place on medium heat for 3-4 minutes.

Drop in the batter by teaspoonfuls, filling the pan but leaving yourself room for manoeuvre. Keeping the heat low, cook till they are golden brown on the underside. Turn them with a slotted spoon and continue to cook till the second side is golden, 1½-2 minutes each side. Cook in several batches and put aside on a plate lined with kitchen paper to blot up the excess oil.

Ten minutes before serving, reheat the kadhi, adding ½-1 cup water if it has thickened too much. Drop in the pakodas, simmer for 10 minutes and serve immediately.

SPROUTS

Fresh sprouts are supposed to be the ultimate health food—a combination of roughage with some carbohydrate and all sorts of minerals and vitamins that do you no end of good. You can sprout any kind of whole, unhusked dal—masoor, moong, urad, kabuli chana, kala chana; or bean—lobia, rajma. Moong is probably the lightest and kala chana is supposed to have the most nutritious properties.

Start by soaking the grains in water as you would before cooking. In fact, whenever you cook any of these, you could soak some extra and put it aside to sprout. Leave them in the water for about 24 hours, till they soften and swell.

Drain and wash them, and wrap in a clean cloth, thick rather than thin, soaked in water. It shouldn't be wringing wet, but more than just damp. Keep it in a warmish place, and be sure not to let it dry out. Different varieties take different amounts of time to sprout, but within a day or two, you'll see white or pale greenish sprouts breaking out. Let them grow for another 12-24 hours, till the sprouts are about 1 cm in length, then decant them into a bowl, cover and put in the fridge.

Special sprout-making containers which claim to maintain the ideal humidity for sprouting, are available in kitchenware shops; but our experience is that they don't work, and you're better off with the clean-rag method.

You can eat sprouts as a salad, seasoned with some finely chopped onion, a couple of teaspoons each of lime juice and salad oil, salt and pepper, with or without some chopped tomato and coriander leaves, mint, or any other herb. You can also serve them as a kind of raita, folded into beaten curd which you've seasoned with salt, a little chopped onion, perhaps some cummin powder or black pepper powder, and the same optional herb. Chopped tomato too, why not? Whichever combination you plump for, sprouts are not a bad option for a packed lunch.

Sprouts can also be cooked using the recipe for Matar Piaz (see p. 134) or the one that follows. To retain their health-giving properties they should be undercooked and eaten while still slightly crunchy.

COOKED SPROUTS

Ingredients for 2-3 servings:

1 small onion
1 green chilli, *optional*
8-10 sprigs fresh coriander *or* mint leaves
1 lime
1 tbsp oil
1 tsp cummin seeds
1½ cups sprouts (moong, masoor, urad, kala chana *or* beans)
½ tsp red chilli powder
½ tsp salt

Preparation: Chop the onion fine. Wash the green chilli and chop fine. Pick through the coriander or mint leaves, wash well and chop fine. Wash the lime and cut it into quarters.

Method: Heat the oil, burning it if using mustard oil. Add the cummin seeds and fry till they are golden and fragrant. Add the onion and fry till just taking colour. Stir in the sprouts, chilli powder and salt, and stir-fry for 2-3 minutes. Pour in ½ cup water, bring to the boil, lower the heat, cover and simmer for 10-15 minutes till the water has dried and the sprouts are al dente.

Stir in the green chilli, if used, and coriander or mint and mix well.

Serve hot or cold with lime quarters. Curd is a good accompaniment.

Variation: If served cold, stir in 1-2 kakdi, cut in thin rounds, or a small cucumber, peeled, de-seeded and diced, or 1-2 tomatoes, chopped fine.

9

Vegetables

Vegetables are an important element in most Indians' diets, even among non-vegetarians. Western as well as Indian nutritionists recognise the importance of vegetables and fruit in a healthy diet. To maximise the benefit, vegetables should not be overcooked. Many varieties are at their best if cooked only till they are al dente, the way the Italians like their spaghetti—with just a little bite in them.

The first thing you have to know about vegetables is how to buy them, and how long they will keep. Experience will teach you all, but even as a novice you can probably make out whether the vegetables you have your eye on are fresh. That usually means a good bright colour, smooth skin, and firm to the touch. You don't want to go shopping for vegetables every day. What's a fridge for? So it's best to have an idea of what will keep for several days, and what you ought really to cook today or tomorrow. We've tried to indicate this in talking about individual vegetables.

For all your best efforts, you'll find every now and then that something has been kept a bit longer than is good for it. It may be OK if you are going to cook it—bits beginning to go bad can be cut out—but *not* if it's to go into a salad, or to be eaten raw in any manner. You have to use your judgment, remembering the overriding rule: 'If in doubt, chuck it out'.

Naturally, vegetables have to be washed before you do anything else to them. Then often peeled, and/or cut into pieces conveniently sized for cooking and eating. For the most part, it hardly matters if the pieces are big or small. Roughly speaking, the smaller you cut, the faster it will cook; but then the actual cutting takes longer, so what you gain on the swings you lose on the roundabouts. What is obviously desirable is that the pieces should be roughly even in size, so that they cook evenly.

Nutritionists recommend that to maximise food value, you wash vegetables before peeling and cutting them, and this seems to make sense. The exception is perhaps root vegetables. You want to be very sure that they are washed clean of every particle of earth, which means also washing them carefully after peeling, but before cutting. You need to take extra care with washing any vegetable or herb that grows close to the earth.

There is a pattern to the basic vegetable recipe in north Indian cooking. Heat the oil or ghee, make a chaunk with whole spices, add the prepared vegetable, sprinkle on a few selected spice powders for seasoning and some salt, and either stir-fry on medium heat or cover and cook on low heat with or without a little water depending on the vegetable. You can, in fact, if you're hassled and don't want the bother of checking recipes every time, cook almost any vegetable, or combination of vegetables, to the recipe for Bund Gobhi ki Subzi, given below, the only difference being whether or not to add water in the final cooking, and how long to cook it.

Another technique is to create a **masaledar gravy,** or a standard **dry masala,** with, for example, ginger, garlic, tomato and spice powders, (see p. 102-103) and cook the vegetable in that.

It might become boring to cook vegetable dishes only according to these two basic methods. Fortunately, there is plenty of variation. For some of the best potato dishes, you boil the potatoes first, dice them and reheat them in a chaunk. There's a lovely dish of turnips, in a masala of onions cooked to a mush and mixed with curd; and one of small aubergines with dry masala smeared onto their inside surfaces, then fried. Occasionally, instead of a chaunk you do a baghar. But master the basic procedure, which is not difficult, and the rest follows naturally.

BUND GOBHI KI SUBZI
(Master Recipe)

Ingredients for 2-3 servings:

½ cabbage, 300-400 gms
1 tbsp oil
1 tsp cummin seeds
½ tsp red chilli powder

½ tsp turmeric powder
1 tsp coriander powder
½ tsp salt

Preparation: Discard the coarse outer leaves of the cabbage and chop as described on p. 118.

Method: Heat the oil in a kadhai, burning it if using mustard oil. Lower the heat and throw in the cummin seeds. When they turn golden and fragrant, add the cabbage, spice powders and salt. Toss together till the cabbage begins to sweat. Cover and cook on low heat for not more than 5 minutes.

Note: Once you get the hang of it, you can start thinking of possible variations. Substitute panch-poran for the cummin seeds, for instance, or add ¼-½ tsp asafoetida powder to the other spice powders.

This recipe comes out particularly well with **toori, matar aloo, parval, okra, and beans.** If you want to try spinach, cauliflower, pumpkin or any other, it'll probably be fine too.

TOMATO GRAVY

From this basic recipe you can make either a gravy or a dry masala with which you can cook a variety of dishes The given quantities are enough to make a dish with ½ kg paneer, fish or any vegetable, or 250 gms (1½ cups) of uncooked beans or chickpeas.

Ingredients:

4-6 medium tomatoes
3 medium onions
2 tsp ginger-garlic paste
½ tsp red chilli powder
½ tsp turmeric powder
2 tsp coriander powder
2 tbsp oil
2 tsp cummin seeds
½ tsp salt

Preparation: Wash and chop the tomatoes fine. Slice the onions fine. Mix the ginger-garlic paste with the spice powders and a tbsp or so of water, to make a paste.

Method: In a kadhai, heat the oil, burning it if using mustard oil. Lower the heat, and put in the cummin seeds. As soon as they turn golden and fragrant, add the onions, and stir-fry on medium to high heat till beginning to turn golden. Add the spice paste, and bhuno till the oil separates.

Stir in about ¼ cup of the chopped tomatoes, cover and lower the heat till they release their juice, raise the heat and bhuno again till the oil separates once more. (This step is optional but sharpens the tomato flavour.)

Add the rest of the tomatoes along with the salt. Stir well, cover and lower the heat. Simmer for 30-40 minutes, stirring occasionally, till the tomatoes disintegrate and all the ingredients are well blended.

Note: If you are pushed for time complete the cooking in a pressure cooker for 8-10 minutes. But long, slow cooking gives a richer flavour. This gravy makes a good **Aloo Tamatar** (see p. 104).

To make **Tamatar Paneer** fry ½ kg paneer as given on p. 23 and fold into the gravy. If you'd like to cook some green peas in the gravy before adding the paneer, who's stopping you?

Variation: For **Dry Tomato Masala**, omit the onions and halve the number of tomatoes. Bhuno once with all the chopped tomatoes as described above, then add your prepared vegetables, with salt and as much water as will be needed to cook the vegetable.

Use this masala to make **Tamatar Beans** (see p. 136) or **Bhindi Tamatar** (see p. 120).

Potatoes (aloo)

They are an amazingly versatile vegetable, and can be cooked in all sorts of ways. Buy them good and hard; if they're already a bit soft, they won't keep. They can be stored for several days outside the fridge, but keep them in a vegetable rack, not in a plastic bag. If they turn slightly soft and wrinkled with keeping, you can still cook them; likewise if they start sprouting—cut or dig out the sprouts—but obviously there are limits.

When potatoes are to be boiled, you can either peel and then boil, or peel after boiling. Some people find it easier to boil them with the skin and then peel. You also save marginally on the nutritional aspect. When they're fully cooked, the skin detaches itself from the flesh and slips off easily.

When you boil potatoes without peeling, take extra care when washing them. In fact, it's a good idea to keep a small brush beside the sink to scrub them with. Nice well-scrubbed new potatoes can be cooked and eaten skin and all.

Even peeling raw potatoes isn't such a big deal. It's best to use a vegetable peeler, which ensures that only a thin layer of peel is removed. After peeling, if they are not to be cooked immediately, put them in a pan and cover with cold water, otherwise they will get discoloured. Cut them to size or dice them just before cooking.

For boiling, have them even-sized, cutting the larger potatoes into chunks approximately the size of the smaller ones. Cut larger ones in 2-3 pieces anyway, they'll cook faster.

For **Aloo Tamatar**, peel, wash and dice 4-5 medium potatoes, and make a tomato gravy as given on p. 102. Add the potatoes to the gravy, stir well, bring back to the boil, cover, lower the heat and simmer for 15-20 minutes till the potatoes are tender.

ALOO DUM

Ingredients for 3-4 servings:

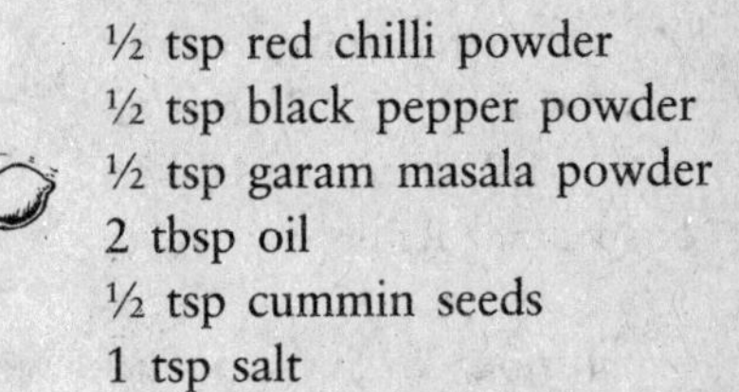

10 small new potatoes, about ½ kg
1½ tbsp curd
1 tsp ginger-garlic paste
½ tsp turmeric powder
1 tsp coriander powder
½ tsp red chilli powder
½ tsp black pepper powder
½ tsp garam masala powder
2 tbsp oil
½ tsp cummin seeds
1 tsp salt

Preparation: Peel and wash the potatoes. If only large ones are available, cut them into roughly equal-sized pieces.

Beat the curd in a large bowl till smooth and blended, add the ginger-garlic paste and spice powders. Stir well to blend. Prick the potatoes all over with a fork, and add them to the curd-spice mixture, spooning the mixture over them so that the potatoes are well coated.

Method: Heat the oil in a pan with a tight-fitting lid, burning it if using mustard oil. Throw in the cummin seeds and fry for a moment till golden and fragrant.

Add the potatoes, and any extra curd mixture remaining in the bowl, and cook on high heat, stirring all the time, till the masala dries and the oil separates.

Add ½ cup water, and the salt, turn the heat to low, cover tightly and cook till the potatoes are tender.

SOOKHE ALOO

Ingredients for 3-4 servings:

5 medium potatoes
1-2 tbsp oil
1-2 dried red chillies
2 tsp dried fenugreek leaves

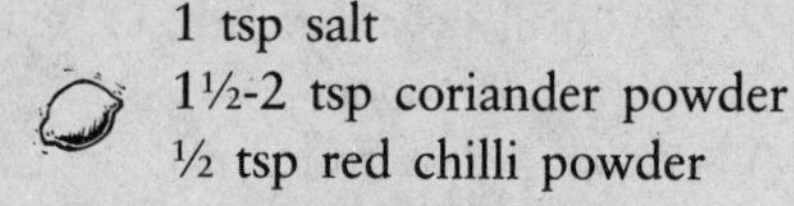

1 tsp salt
1½-2 tsp coriander powder
½ tsp red chilli powder

Preparation: Wash the potatoes well and peel, or don't if you prefer to peel boiled potatoes. If they are large, cut them into medium chunks, for faster cooking.

Boil just enough water in a pan to cover the potatoes. Put in the potatoes and bring back to the boil. Boil for 15-20 minutes. If using the pressure cooker, boil 2 cups water, put in the potatoes and cook under pressure for 2-3 minutes. Let the pressure fall naturally before opening the cooker.

Drain off the water, place the pan on low heat, and shake it a couple of times, to dry out the potatoes. Let them cool, peel if you haven't done it already, and cut into medium dice.

Method: Heat the oil in a kadhai, burning it if using mustard oil, and put in the red chillies. Let them turn plump and black, then take the kadhai off the heat. A few moments later, when the oil has cooled a bit, add the dried fenugreek leaves.

Mix in the potatoes, salt and spice powders. Return to low heat and stir gently till the potatoes are thoroughly impregnated with the seasonings and heated through.

Variations: Substitute the following for the dried chillies and fenugreek leaves:

- 1 tsp each of sesame, cummin and mustard seeds; and if you like, sprinkle in 1 tsp of lime juice just before taking the pan off the heat.
- 1 tsp mustard seeds, 2 green chillies sliced and de-seeded, 2 cloves garlic chopped fine and 10-12 curry leaves.
- 1 tsp fennel seeds fried in the oil. Omit the red chilli powder and season with ½ tsp each of aamchur, garam masala, and coriander powders.
- Or use your imagination.

SOOKHE ALOO CHILKEWALE

Ingredients for 3-4 servings:

½ kg small new potatoes, the size of limes
1 medium onion
2 tbsp oil
½ tsp red chilli powder
½ tsp turmeric powder
½ tsp cummin powder
1 tsp salt
1 tsp garam masala powder

Preparation: Wash and scrub the potatoes thoroughly. Chop the onion fine.

Method: Heat the oil, burning it if using mustard oil. Add the onion and stir-fry till light brown.

Add all the other ingredients except the garam masala, and stir-fry on medium heat for 5 minutes.

Pour in 1 cup water, bring to the boil, cover, turn down the heat and cook till the potatoes are nearly tender, 10-12 minutes.

Add the garam masala, turn up the heat and cook stirring often till the water has dried.

ALOO IMLIWALE

Ingredients for 3-4 servings:

5 medium potatoes
2 green chillies
1½ tsp tamarind paste
2 tsp sugar
2 tbsp oil
1 tsp mustard seeds
½ tsp red chilli powder

½ tsp turmeric powder
1 tsp coriander powder
1 tsp salt

Garnish:
A small bunch fresh coriander leaves

Preparation: Peel, wash and cut the potatoes into more or less even dice. Wash and slit the green chillies. Put the tamarind paste into a small bowl with the sugar, and thin down with a little water. Wash and coarsely chop the coriander leaves.

Method: Heat the oil, burning it if using mustard oil. Lower the heat, throw in the mustard seeds and cover till the spluttering subsides.

Add the potatoes, spice powders and salt, and toss together till well mixed. Add ½ cup water, bring up to the boil, cover and simmer till the potatoes are all but done.

Add the green chillies and the tamarind-sugar mixture and cook for a few minutes more on high heat, stirring all the time, till the water has dried.

Garnish with the coriander leaves.

Green leafy vegetables (saag)

There are a variety of green leafy vegetables—**spinach** or **sorrel (palak), mustard greens (sarson ka saag), fenugreek (methi), amaranth (cholai), bhatua ka saag** (a type of cress, available during the winter and spring months), and many others.

Of these, the most commonly used is spinach, a quite delicious vegetable. Fenugreek has a strong flavour that not everyone likes. So strong, in fact, that its dried leaves are used as a masala **(kasoori methi).** Whichever you go for, buy leaves which are fresh-looking and not wilted or damaged, and store in a plastic bag in the fridge for up to three days.

The problem with most greens is that they are full of water and disappear to practically nothing in the cooking, so you have to cook at least twice as much in raw weight as of other vegetables. They are also low in bulk, so your one kilogram looks like an awful lot of greens. As if this weren't enough, consisting as it does of bunches of loose leaves, it's the very devil to clean. You have to open out the bunches of leaves and pick through them for any nasty ones, or strands of grass, etc, that may have found their way into them; and you have to cut off the coarse stem of each and every leaf. This is done by bunching them into bundles again and cutting across them. The entire process, it must be said, is laborious and time-consuming, best entrusted to an obliging servant or part-timer if you have one.

In any case, you have to be very particular about washing it. After the preliminary sorting and de-stalking, plunge the leaves into a large basin of water. Work it about with your hands, then lift it out into a large colander. You may be surprised how much earth is left in the water—that's why we suggest you lift it out rather than tilting the basin to let the water drain off, which will leave a deposit of earth on the leaves. Repeat the process a couple more times till the water seems to be absolutely clean. *Then* you have to cut it, though not necessarily very fine. Take it in handfuls onto the chopping board, and chop with a large knife. Return to the colander to drain as much as possible. That's all there is to it.

Once you have this great mass of chopped leaves, it's hard to believe you're going to be able to cook it in one lot. But just wait.

Most of its bulk is water, which starts to come out as you cook it. Sure enough, you probably won't get it all into the pan in one go. Put into the pan as much as will fit, with or without oil but no added water, just as much water as is clinging to the washed leaves, and even that's too much, and set it on low heat. It will almost immediately start to wilt and give up its moisture, and its bulk will collapse in on itself. Stir it around a bit, and after a few minutes you'll find there is room to add more, and finally the whole lot will fit in quite easily.

> *Spinach is deceptive to the eye, looking such a lot in its raw state; accordingly, it's best not to add salt until a late stage in the cooking, when you can see how much you've got, and can judge accordingly. Otherwise, there's a definite tendency to over-salt.*

The laborious process of preparing it is probably why people usually cook less and stretch it with potato, to make **Palak Aloo** (see p. 113), a perfectly legitimate dodge.

One more warning, in case you haven't been totally put off already. If your concentration wavers and you succeed in burning your spinach dish, write it off. There are things you burn a bit, and they can be salvaged, most dishes with tomatoes, for example. A slightly burnt tomato taste by no means ruins a dish. Even dal, if it's not too badly burnt—you can often decant the top layer into a fresh pan and carry on. But burnt spinach—not only is the taste disgusting, it permeates the whole dish, so that even the top layer which may look all right, tastes awful. Believe us, we speak from experience.

PANCH-PORAN KA PALAK

Ingredients for 3-4 servings:

1 kg spinach
1-2 green chillies
2 tbsp mustard oil
1 tsp panch-poran
½ tsp sugar
½ tsp salt

Preparation: Pick through, wash, drain and chop the spinach. Wash and slit the green chillies.

Method: Burn the mustard oil in a heavy-bottomed pan or kadhai. Lower the heat, throw in the green chillies and the panch-poran, and cover till the spluttering subsides.

Add the spinach by handfuls, till it all fits in. Stir occasionally as the leaves begin to wilt and give up their moisture. Cover and cook till ready.

Stir in the sugar and salt. If it seems too wet, turn up the heat and boil away the excess water. It should be moist, but without extra liquid sloshing about.

Variation: Cook cholai to the same recipe.

PALAK AUR SUA SAAG

Ingredients for 3-4 servings:

1 kg spinach	*Baghar:*
250 gms dill	2 tbsp oil
½ cup cream *or* creamy curd	2-3 dried red chillies
½ tsp coriander powder	1 tsp cummin seeds
½ tsp salt	1 tsp mustard seeds

Preparation: Pick through, wash, drain and chop the spinach and dill. Beat the curd till smooth and blended.

Method: Put the spinach and dill together by handfuls into a large pan or kadhai, without any oil, and set on low heat. They will gradually start to wilt and release their moisture. Stir occasionally, and cook till the leaves are tender. Mix in the coriander powder and salt, and stir over high heat till nearly dry. Stir in the cream or curd.

In another small heavy-bottomed pan, heat the oil, burning it if using mustard oil. Throw in the red chillies and cook on high heat till they are plump and black. Lower the heat, add the cummin and mustard seeds and cover till the spluttering subsides. Turn the contents of the pan into the spinach, and stir well to mix.

Note: If dill is not available, coriander leaves are an acceptable substitute.

PALAK MUGHLAI

Ingredients for 3-4 servings:

1 kg spinach
3-cm piece ginger
3 medium onions
2 tbsp oil
½ tsp fennel seeds
3 green cardamoms
½ tsp red chilli powder
½ tsp cummin powder
½ tsp salt
½ tsp garam masala powder

Preparation: Pick through, wash, drain and chop the spinach. Peel and wash the ginger, and dice fine. Slice the onions.

Method: Heat the oil, burning it if using mustard oil. Throw in the fennel and the cardamoms, stir for a few moments, add the ginger and onions and fry till the onions are well browned.

Lower the heat, and add the spinach by handfuls. Once it is all in, stir well to mix, cover and cook gently till wilted and moist, stirring occasionally.

Sprinkle in the chilli powder, cummin powder and salt, and continue cooking till the spinach is tender.

Uncover, add the garam masala and stir over high heat till dry.

Variations: **Palak Aloo**—Use any of these 3 recipes, but add, or substitute for some of the spinach, 3-5 potatoes (depending on their size), peeled, washed and cut into medium-small dice, added with the last of the greens. Cook till the potatoes and spinach are tender and continue as given.

- **Palak Paneer**—Cut about 300 gms paneer into medium cubes, fry till they are evenly browned, as described on p. 23, and set aside. Prepare any of the 3 dishes described above, and purée the greens. Now fold the paneer gently into the purée and simmer for a few minutes.

SARSON DA SAAG

A favourite Punjabi dish.

Ingredients for 3-4 servings:

½ kg mustard greens
150 gms spinach *or* bhatua
½ tsp salt
½ tbsp atta
½ tsp red chilli powder

Baghar:
2 tbsp ghee *or* oil
3-cm piece ginger
1-2 green chillies

Preparation: Pick through, wash, drain and chop the greens. Peel and wash the ginger, and dice fine. Wash and slit the green chillies.

Method: Put the greens by handfuls into a large pan or kadhai without oil, and set on low heat. They will gradually start to wilt and release their moisture. Stir occasionally, and cook till tender.

Stir in the salt and blend to a purée in a blender or food processor.

Return to the heat, and mix in the atta and chilli powder. Stir, and adjust consistency, drying it up if too moist or adding a little water, probably not more than 1-2 tbsp, if too dry.

In a small pan, heat the oil or ghee, burning it if using mustard oil. Throw in the ginger and green chillies, and fry till brown. Pour the contents of the pan into the greens, and stir to mix.

Sarson da Saag is traditionally served with makki di roti, but if you find them difficult to make it's delicious with chapatti too.

Variation: Mustard greens are available for only a few months in winter. If you have a craving to eat them at other seasons, you can cook spinach to the same recipe, adding a couple of tsp of mustard powder along with the chilli powder, and making the baghar in unburnt mustard oil. It's not quite the genuine article, but somewhat reminiscent.

Cauliflower (phool gobhi)

It is a favourite winter vegetable, cooked either on its own, or with potatoes for **Gobhi Aloo** (see p. 117). When buying, choose a flower that is compact and creamy white, with no brown marks, or only a few. It should feel firm to the touch, and the leaves should not be wilted. Cut off the stalk and outer leaves (which the subziwala will insist on including in the weight), and store in the fridge, wrapped in plastic. It will keep for three or four days. If by the end of that time it has developed some brown patches on the flower, cut them off and carry on.

To prepare, cut off the remaining stalk and leaves till you are left with the whitish flower. This, you will observe, is made up of similar but smaller florets, each on its own stem, which you can cut and separate into convenient-sized pieces. You can also chop the inner part of the stalk and use. Another method is to treat the flower as an undifferentiated mass, and chop it into pieces regardless of the growth of the florets. This, according to some, enables the masala to penetrate better. Either way, because of its structure, which can trap particles of earth, and in which slugs and other undesirables may find a convenient resting-place, cauliflower is about the only vegetable other than root vegetables that it is advisable to wash *after* you have cut it. (Before you let this put you off, you should understand that the presence of a slug, etc, is a compliment to the vegetable, and a guarantee of its freshness.)

Overcooked cauliflower really isn't nice, it develops a peculiar flavour; so you have to be a bit careful. Better to have it al dente, or even slightly crunchy, especially if you're cooking more than you need for one meal and planning to reheat it. Another thing to watch, is not to overfill the kadhai in which you cook it, or the pieces will cook unevenly, and some will become mushy before others are even tender.

MIRCHWALI GOBHI

Ingredients for 3-4 servings:

1 medium cauliflower, about 650 gms
5-6 dried red chillies
2 tbsp oil

1 tsp mustard seeds
1 tsp urad dal
¼-½ tsp asafoetida powder
½ tsp salt

Preparation: Trim the coarse stalk and leaves from the cauliflower, and cut the flower into convenient pieces. Wash well. If you like your food good and fiery, break the chillies to let the seeds escape through the dish, otherwise keep them whole.

Method: Heat the oil in a kadhai, burning it if using mustard oil. When it is hot, throw in the dried chillies, and fry on high heat till black. Turn the heat down, add the mustard seeds and cover till the spluttering subsides. Add the dal and fry for 1-2 minutes, stirring gently till the grains turn reddish. Stir in the asafoetida, and add the cauliflower.

Raise the heat to medium and toss gently to mix well for a minute or so. Sprinkle in the salt, and add ¼-½ cup water. Toss once more, bring to the boil, cover, lower the heat, and cook till ready, 6-8 minutes if you like it al dente. Toss a couple of times to ensure even cooking.

This is meant to be a dry dish. If there is a little water left by the time the vegetable is cooked, raise the heat and stir till it evaporates.

SOOKHI GOBHI

Ingredients for 3-4 servings:

1 medium cauliflower, about 650 gms
3-cm piece ginger
2 tbsp oil
1 tsp cummin seeds
¼-½ tsp asafoetida powder

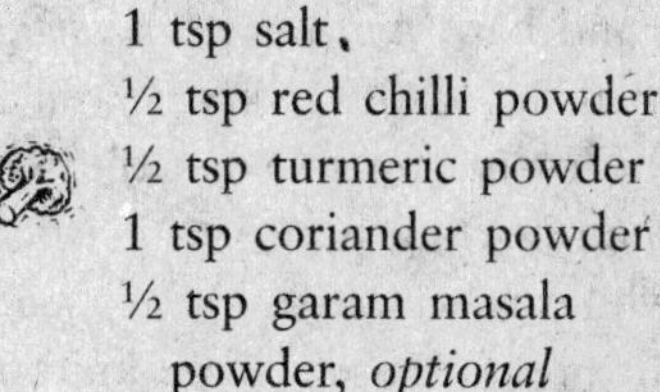

1 tsp salt
½ tsp red chilli powder
½ tsp turmeric powder
1 tsp coriander powder
½ tsp garam masala powder, *optional*

Preparation: Trim the coarse stalk and leaves from the cauliflower, and cut the flower into convenient pieces. Wash well. Peel and wash the ginger, and dice fine.

Method: Heat the oil in a kadhai, burning it if using mustard oil. When it smokes, turn down the heat and throw in the cummin seeds. As soon as they turn golden and fragrant, stir in the ginger. When this in its turn becomes golden, add the asafoetida.

Almost immediately add the cauliflower, stir briefly then sprinkle in the salt and spice powders except garam masala.

Stir in ¼-½ cup water, and bring up to the boil on high heat. Cover, lower the heat and cook till tender, 6-8 minutes if you like it al dente, tossing a couple of times to ensure even cooking.

This is meant to be a dry dish. If there is a little water left by the time the cauliflower is cooked, raise the heat and stir till it evaporates.

Sprinkle with the garam masala, if used, before serving.

Variation: **Gobhi Aloo**—Peel, wash and cut 3 medium potatoes into smallish dice. Add to the dish after the chaunk, i.e. before you put in the cauliflower. Stir, cover and let the potato cook in its own moisture on low heat for about 5 minutes. When it is about half cooked, add the cauliflower and complete the cooking as above.

Cabbage (bund gobhi)

This is a less interesting vegetable than cauliflower, but nice for a change. When buying, the essential thing is to see that the piece is good and hard, with the leaves tightly packed. Store in the fridge wrapped in plastic. It keeps well for up to a week or even more. If you don't want to cook the whole cabbage at one time, a half wrapped in cling film or a plastic bag will keep almost as long as the whole vegetable.

To prepare, use a large knife to cut off the stalk end together with the base of the outer leaves. Peel off two to three layers of the outer leaves, and discard. These leaves have completely insulated the inside of the vegetable from the outside world, so there is no need to wash, even if you happen to be preparing a raw cabbage salad.

Stand the cabbage on its flat cut end, cut through it down the middle into halves and then quarters. Cut out the coarse inner stalk from each quarter. Lay it down on one of the cut sides, cut it lengthwise into strips and then across the strips into pieces.

Cabbage cooks fast and even more than cauliflower is truly unpleasant when it is overcooked. Since it can also be eaten raw, it hardly matters how undercooked it is. So try cooking it a little less than you think is right, especially if it is to be reheated.

Cabbage is quite versatile, and you could cook it according to either of the cauliflower recipes above, omitting the water, or either of the first two of the spinach recipes, reducing the cooking time to about five minutes. Or of course simply follow the master-recipe given on p. 101. It doesn't lend itself to a wet masala.

BUND GOBHI AUR KAJU

Ingredients for 2-3 servings:

½ cabbage, about 300-400 gms	½ tsp mustard seeds
1 medium onion	1 tsp urad dal
2 green chillies	¼ cup broken cashew nuts
1 sprig curry leaves	2 tsp coconut powder, *optional*
1 tbsp oil	1 tsp salt

Preparation: Discard the coarse outer leaves and chop the cabbage. Slice the onion. Wash the green chillies and chop fine. Wash the curry leaves and strip them off the stem.

Method: Heat the oil in a kadhai, burning it if using mustard oil. Lower the heat, throw in the mustard seeds and cover till the spluttering subsides. Mix in the urad dal and fry for a minute or so till reddish.

Add the onion, cashew nuts and green chillies. Cover and cook for 5 minutes till the onion is soft and translucent. Add the curry leaves and fry for a few seconds more.

Mix in the cabbage, coconut powder, if used, and salt, and toss together till the cabbage begins to sweat. Cover, and cook on low heat for not more than 5 minutes.

Okra or lady's fingers (bhindi)

A native of tropical Africa, it is a favourite summer vegetable, with a distinctive taste, but some people with delicate stomachs find it a bit tough on the digestion.

Make sure to buy tender young pods, a nice fresh green, and slightly soft; if very large and hard, with the seeds palpable through the walls of the pod, they are bound to be indigestible. Also discard at the time of purchase any pods that are not quite straight. A pronounced curve means that a worm or caterpillar has infiltrated, and the pod is probably inedible.

They will keep in the fridge in a plastic bag for three or four days.

Okra exude a slimy substance when cut. This is not terribly noticeable till you make the mistake of trying to boil them without preliminary frying, when the whole thing becomes a slimy mess. So it's essential to fry or bhuno at the start of cooking. It also helps to wash them well ahead of cooking, so that they have time to dry; or alternatively, pat them dry with a clean cloth before cutting.

You can cook **Bhindi ki Subzi** according to the master-recipe for cabbage given on p. 101. Wash, top and tail ½ kg okra, and cut into medium rounds, 1-2 cm thick. After adding the spice powders, stir-fry over medium heat for 3-4 minutes, lower the heat and cook covered till the okra is tender but not mushy, about 8-10 minutes. Add ¼ cup water, only if it seems to be getting too dry.

For **Bhindi Kurkur,** same ingredients, except halve the amount of cummin seeds and double the amount of oil. Cut the okra into thin rounds, and after adding the spice powders, stir-fry over medium heat till crisp, taking care not to burn the vegetable, 12-15 minutes. Add salt a couple of minutes before the end of cooking time.

For **Bhindi Tamatar,** prepare ½ kg okra, as for Bhindi ki Subzi, and make a dry tomato masala as given on p. 103. Add the okra along with salt to the masala; and stir-fry over medium heat for 3-4 minutes. Lower the heat, cover and cook till the okra is tender but not mushy, 8-10 minutes.

Capsicum, green pepper or bell pepper (simla mirch)

Despite its name, it is not 'hot' at all, though it has a strong and distinctive flavour. It can be eaten raw in salads, or cooked. Either way it has a great affinity with tomato.

When buying, choose pieces that look fresh and smooth, and have a sheen. Softish and slightly wrinkled, means they're not very fresh. They weigh relatively light, so a little goes a long way.

Store in a plastic bag in the fridge; they will keep for two to three days, but once they develop soft spots they go off very fast.

To prepare, wash the capsicum, and cut it into quarters lengthwise. Carefully cut and scrape out the pith and seeds together with the stalk. Cut lengthwise into strips, and then cut the strips into convenient, bite-sized pieces.

SIMLA MIRCH ALOO

Ingredients for 2-3 servings:

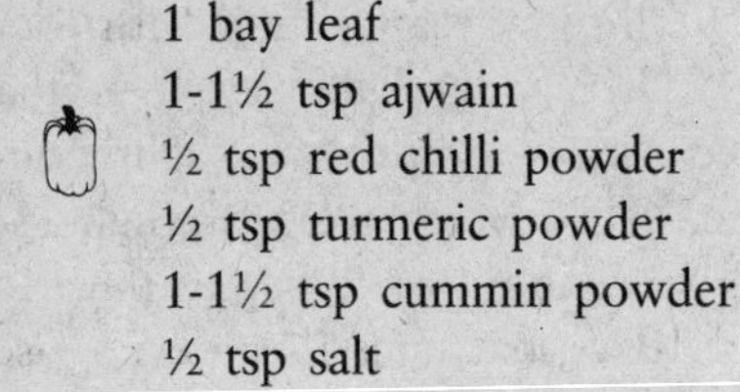

3 medium potatoes
2-3 medium capsicums, about 200 gms
2 medium tomatoes
2 tbsp oil
2 tsp coriander seeds
1 bay leaf
1-1½ tsp ajwain
½ tsp red chilli powder
½ tsp turmeric powder
1-1½ tsp cummin powder
½ tsp salt

Preparation: Peel, wash and cut the potatoes into smallish dice. Wash the capsicum, de-seed and dice. Wash and chop the tomatoes.

Method: Heat the oil, burning it if using mustard oil. Lower the heat, throw in the coriander seeds, bay leaf and ajwain, and cook for a few seconds till golden and fragrant.

Add the potatoes, toss with the spices and cook covered for a few minutes. Add the capsicum, sprinkle in the spice powders and salt and toss well.

After a couple of minutes, add the tomatoes. Stir well, cover and cook till ready.

It should not need any added water, but if it offers to dry up and stick to the pan, you can add ¼ cup water.

Variation: **Baingan Aloo**—The same dish can be made using aubergine instead of capsicum. Cut the aubergine into chunks, and add it a couple of minutes after the potatoes. Raise the heat and stir-fry till the aubergine starts turning limp, then add the spice powders and tomatoes and proceed as above. Don't worry if it all looks rather dry till the tomatoes go in, only don't let it burn.

Bhindi ki sabzi, recipe on page 120

Cucumber and Moong dal salad, recipe on page 226

Aubergine, brinjal, eggplant (baingan)

Baingan may be a dirty word to some who spent part of their youth in hostels and were forced to survive on a diet of badly cooked vegetables, but it can be quite delicious and is also amazingly versatile. Depending on how it's cooked, its flavour changes completely. You roast it for Baingan ka Bharta, and you'd hardly know it was the same vegetable as the fried slices in the raita labelled as Baingan aur Dahi. Boiled or cooked without enough oil, it can admittedly be quite nasty.

The other unusual thing about aubergine is the widely varying shapes and forms it comes in. There are little egg-shaped ones that presumably are responsible for the appellation 'eggplant', which can be either whitish or purple; then long thin ones, also purple; and the large round ones, the size of a cabbage. For some recipes, it doesn't matter which you use. Others are quite specific. For bharta, where the aubergine is roasted in its skin, you have to use the large round ones, while for Baingan Masaledar–1, you need the small egg-shaped ones.

When buying aubergines, go for a deep or bright purple colour and a glossy sheen on the skin. They should be firm to the touch. Look out for a little hole, which has been made by a worm or caterpillar. If one such has infiltrated, part or whole of the vegetable will need to be discarded. Aubergines keep for up to four days in the fridge, preferably wrapped in plastic.

Not much preparation is needed before cooking; most recipes don't even call for peeling them. In frying they soak up an amazing amount of oil, so be prepared to add more if necessary; and lay the fried slices on absorbent paper to blot up excess oil.

For more distinctive and delicious aubergine dishes, see p. 229-230.

BAINGAN MASALEDAR – 1

A particularly delicious dish; and surprisingly as good cold as hot.

Ingredients for 3-4 servings:

½ kg small aubergines
1 tsp fennel powder
½ tsp cummin powder
1 tsp coriander powder
½ tsp turmeric powder
½ tsp garam masala powder
½ tsp aamchur
1 tsp salt
3 tbsp oil

Preparation: Wash the aubergines, leaving on the stems. Make 2 slits from the base almost up to the stem, in the shape of a cross, being careful to keep the segments connected.

Method: Mix the spice powders and salt in a small bowl. Rub a little of this masala inside each aubergine. To do this, hold the aubergine so as to separate the segments slightly. Using the handle of a teaspoon, insinuate the masala into the cracks between the segments so that all the inner surfaces are smeared with it.

Heat the oil in a large enough kadhai, burning it if using mustard oil. Add the aubergines and stir-fry on high heat for a couple of minutes. Lower the heat, cover and cook for 15-20 minutes, turning occasionally, till the aubergines are tender.

You may find that they don't cook evenly, and you have to remove them 2-3 at a time from the kadhai, as they get ready.

Variation: Make a raita by beating up about 2 cups slightly sour creamy curd, till smooth and blended. Stir in ¼ tsp salt, ½ tsp cummin powder, a small bunch of fresh coriander leaves and a couple of green chillies, washed and chopped fine, and dunk the fried aubergines in this while still warm.

BAINGAN MASALEDAR –2

Ingredients for 3-4 servings:

½ kg aubergines, any shape or size
3 tbsp oil
1 tsp panch-poran
¼-½ tsp asafoetida powder

1 tsp coriander powder
½ tsp cummin powder
½ tsp turmeric powder
½ tsp red chilli powder
1 tsp salt

Preparation: Wash the aubergines and cut into medium pieces without peeling.

Method: Heat the oil in a kadhai, burning it if using mustard oil. Lower the heat, throw in the panch-poran and cover till the spluttering subsides. Stir in the asafoetida and immediately add the aubergines.

Raise the heat to medium-high and stir-fry for a couple of minutes. Sprinkle in the spice powders and salt, and toss together till well mixed. Lower the heat and continue to cook, tossing every now and then so that it doesn't stick, till the aubergines are tender and slightly browned.

If it seems to be offering to dry up and burn, add 1-2 tbsp water.

Gourds

The gourd family is reckoned by some to be on the boring side, but that is not entirely true, and even the more bland members like the **indian squash (tinda)**, and **vegetable marrow (lauki** or **ghia)** can be tarted up into very tasty dishes. **Pumpkin (kaddu** or **sitaphal)** has a distinctive, sweetish taste. **Ridged gourd (toori),** something like the western **courgette** or **zucchini** but not identical, also has lots of flavour; and **bitter gourd (karela)** is, well, bitter. Some people are fond of **wax gourd (parval).**

Many of the gourds are full of water, and cook without added water.

Pumpkin: It is a massive vegetable and the subziwala will cut a piece as large as you want. The cut surface should look fresh and light orange or golden, and the rind should be glossy. It doesn't keep very well, so plan to cook it the day you buy it, or at most within the next couple of days. In the meantime, wrap it in plastic and into the fridge with it.

To prepare, take the cut segment, and scrape out and discard the pith and seeds from the centre. Wash it well. The rind is thick, tough and hard, so to peel it, first cut the segment into manageable pieces, and then cut the rind off each piece. You have to take away a relatively thick layer. Once it is peeled, cut into convenient, bite-sized chunks.

SITAPHAL KHATTA

Ingredients for 2-3 servings:

- ½ kg pumpkin
- A small bunch fresh mint leaves *or* 1 tsp dried mint, *optional, but adds zing*
- 2 tbsp oil
- 1 whole dried red chilli
- ½ tsp panch-poran
- ½ tsp turmeric powder
- ½ tsp red chilli powder
- ½ tsp salt
- 1 tsp aamchur
- ½ tsp sugar

Preparation: Peel the pumpkin, and cut it into largish cubes. Wash the fresh mint, if used, strip the leaves from the stalks, and chop fine.

Method: Heat the oil, burning it if using mustard oil. Add the red chilli and fry for a minute till black and plump.

Lower the heat and throw in the panch-poran. Cover till the spluttering subsides, then add the pumpkin. Sprinkle in the turmeric, chilli powder and salt. Toss well together, cover, and cook over low heat. It should not need any added water, but if it seems to be offering to stick and burn, you can add ¼ cup.

When the pumpkin is tender but not mushy, stir in the aamchur, sugar and mint, if used.

Ridged gourd (toori): It looks like a slender cucumber, with a darker skin. Choose pieces that are firm and dark green without black patches. It keeps in the fridge for two to three days.

To prepare, wash carefully, and peel, or don't, according to the recipe. Cut into rounds of as uniform thickness as possible.

You can cook **Toori ki Subzi** according to the master-recipe for cabbage given on p. 101. Cut ½ kg toori into rounds about 2 cm thick, without peeling. After adding the spice powders, stir-fry on medium to high heat till the toori pieces begin to show signs of softening, about 5-7 minutes. Add the salt and toss for just 1-2 minutes more till tender but not mushy. That's why the salt isn't added earlier; it draws the water out of the vegetable and the dish becomes mushy.

TOORI PIAZ

For this dish, the toori *is* cooked to a mush, which completely changes its character.

Ingredients for 2-3 servings:

½ kg toori
1 large onion
2 tbsp bland oil
½ tsp red chilli powder
½ tsp turmeric powder
2 tsp coriander powder
½ tsp black pepper powder
½ tsp salt

Preparation: Wash the toori, peel and cut into thin rounds. Slice the onion fine.

Method: Heat the oil in a kadhai and stir-fry the onion till brown. Add the remaining ingredients. Stir well, cover and cook over low heat for 10-15 minutes, stirring occasionally, till the toori is tender and mushy. If it seems too dry, stir in 1-2 tbsp water.

Vegetable marrow (lauki or ghia): It really does seem to be a vegetable quite lacking in taste or character. But for that very reason it lends itself to being cooked in interesting combinations of spices. There are two recipes given below, both of which are equally applicable to **indian squash (tinda).**

Because of its thick rind, lauki keeps well; no need to wrap it in the fridge. To prepare, wash, peel and cut into convenient chunks. No need to discard the seeds.

Tinda should be kept in a plastic bag in the fridge and doesn't need to be peeled.

LAUKI DAHIWALI

Ingredients for 2-3 servings:

1 medium vegetable marrow, about ½ kg	1 tsp fennel seeds
3-cm piece ginger	¼-½ tsp asafoetida powder
½-1 cup curd	½ tsp red chilli powder
2 tbsp oil	½ tsp ginger powder
	½ tsp salt

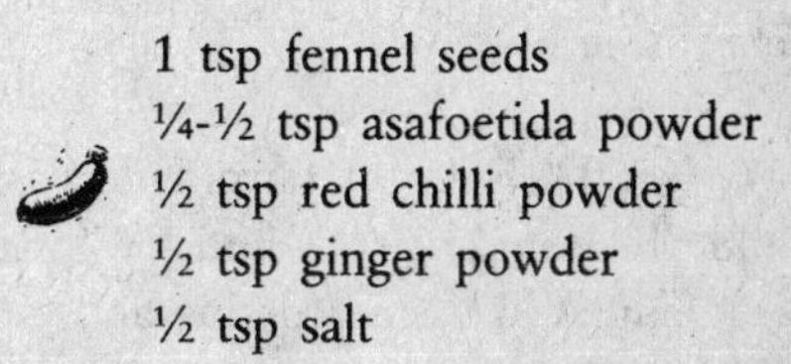

Preparation: Wash and peel the marrow and cut into medium dice. Peel and wash the ginger, and dice fine. Beat the curd till smooth and blended.

Method: Heat the oil, burning it if using mustard oil. Lower the heat, throw in the fennel, and when it turns golden, in just a few seconds, add the ginger and asafoetida. Stir for a few seconds more till the ginger turns golden.

Add the marrow, stir in the spice powders and salt, and toss gently together till well mixed. Cover and simmer till marrow is tender, adding ½ cup water if necessary.

Remove from the heat and stir in the curd before serving.

LAUKI TAMATARWALI

Ingredients for 2-3 servings:

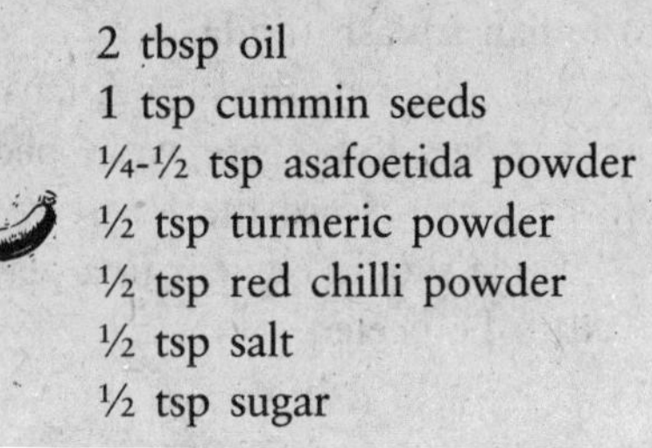

1 medium vegetable marrow, about ½ kg
3-cm piece ginger
2 medium tomatoes
A small bunch fresh mint leaves *or* 1 tsp dried mint, *optional, but adds zing*

2 tbsp oil
1 tsp cummin seeds
¼-½ tsp asafoetida powder
½ tsp turmeric powder
½ tsp red chilli powder
½ tsp salt
½ tsp sugar

Preparation: Wash and peel the marrow, and cut into medium dice. Peel and wash the ginger, and dice fine. Wash and chop the tomatoes. Wash the fresh mint, if used, strip the leaves from the stalks and chop fine.

Method: Heat the oil, burning it if using mustard oil. Lower the heat, add the cummin seeds and fry for a few moments till golden and fragrant. Add the asafoetida and ginger and stir for a few seconds till the ginger turns golden.

Mix in the marrow. Sprinkle the spice powders and salt over the marrow, and toss gently together till well mixed. Cover and cook for about 5 minutes, then stir in the tomatoes. Continue simmering till the tomatoes are done and the marrow is tender but not mushy. Stir in the sugar and mint, if used.

Wax gourd (parval): Another unremarkable member of the gourd family. Its USP seems to be its crunchy seeds. Buy parval fresh, green, and firm to the touch. They will keep for four or five days in the fridge. To prepare, wash and scrape the vegetable and cut in half lengthwise.

You can cook **Parval ki Subzi** according to the master-recipe for cabbage given on p. 101. Wash and cut ½ kg parval. After adding the spice powders and salt, stir in ½ cup water and bring to the boil. Cover, lower the heat and cook till tender, about 10 minutes. The water should have just about dried. If it's still too wet by the time the vegetable is ready, turn up the heat and dry it off, taking care not to burn it.

Bitter gourd (karela): Many people dislike it for its bitterness, and even those who like the vegetable may want to cook it in such a way as to counteract the bitterness to some extent. The usual way of doing this is to stuff the karela with a strongly flavoured masala. A simpler method is to cut them into rounds and brine them, i.e. toss them with about half a tablespoon of salt and leave them for an hour or so for the bitter juices to be drawn out. Then you wash the slices thoroughly, drain them and cook in a chaunk of onions—the sweetness of which also works against the bitterness—panch-poran or whatever. A souring agent like aamchur may also be used.

Choose pieces that are a good fresh lightish green, and not too big. They'll keep in the fridge for three to four days.

To prepare, wash and cut according to the recipe. No need to remove the seeds, or to peel, if they are fresh and tender; otherwise the rough skin can be scraped.

KARELA KI SUBZI – 1

Ingredients for 2-3 servings:

½ kg karela
½ tbsp+¼ tsp salt
1 large onion
1 medium tomato, *optional*

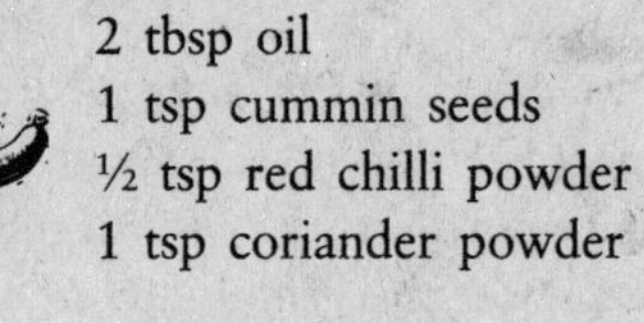

2 tbsp oil
1 tsp cummin seeds
½ tsp red chilli powder
1 tsp coriander powder

Preparation: Wash the karela, cut into rounds and brine them with ½ tbsp salt. Rinse well and drain. Chop the onion. Wash and chop the tomato, if used.

Method: Heat the oil, burning it if using mustard oil. Lower the heat, throw in the cummin seeds, and as soon as they turn golden and fragrant add the onion. Stir-fry over high heat till the onion is golden.

Lower the heat, add the karela and stir to mix. Sprinkle in the spice powders and mix well. Add the tomato, if used, or else ½ cup water, stir again, cover and cook till the karela is tender. Check for salt and add if needed.

KARELA KI SUBZI – 2

Ingredients for 2-3 servings:

½ kg karela
½ tbsp+¼ tsp salt
2 tbsp mustard oil
1½ tsp panch-poran

½ tsp red chilli powder
½ tsp turmeric powder
¾ tsp aamchur

Preparation: Wash the karela, cut into thick rounds and brine them with ½ tbsp salt. Rinse well and drain.

Method: Heat the oil, burn it, turn down the heat, throw in the panch-poran and cover till the spluttering subsides. Immediately add the karela, chilli powder and turmeric, and toss together till well mixed.

Cover tightly and cook on the lowest possible heat, stirring occasionally. The karela shouldn't turn brown, but remain greenish-yellow. If it offers to stick and burn, sprinkle in 1 tbsp water. When tender add the aamchur, and salt if required.

Serve with rice.

Green peas (matar)

They are an old faithful. Buy pods with a good fresh green colour, that seem well filled, but not too large and hard. You can save yourself the trouble of shelling the peas by spending a little more on frozen or dried green peas. The flavour is virtually indistinguishable. Defrost or rehydrate according to the instructions on the packet. Frozen green peas need less cooking—barely five minutes without pressure. Fresh or dried and rehydrated peas may take two to three minutes under pressure, depending on their size and age, or ten to twelve minutes without pressure.

MATAR PIAZ

Ingredients for 3-4 servings:

4 cups shelled green peas
2 medium onions
4 green chillies
2 tbsp bland oil
3 tsp coriander powder
½ tsp black pepper powder
½ tsp sugar
½ tsp salt

Preparation: Defrost or rehydrate green peas if using frozen or dried peas. Slice the onions fine. Wash the green chillies but leave them whole.

Method: Heat the oil in the pressure cooker. Add the onions and ¼ cup water. Close the cooker, and put the pressure weight on the weight valve. Leave on low heat for 10-15 minutes (this way it won't come to full pressure). Remove from the heat, and let the pressure go down naturally. The onions should be soft and pulpy, but not brown.

Add the spice powders and sugar, and cook stirring over medium heat for a couple of minutes, till well integrated. Add the green peas, chillies, salt, and ½ cup water, and cook till ready. If it seems too wet, stir for 1-2 minutes over high heat till it is the consistency you like.

Variations: **Matar Paneer**—Use the same basic recipe, but with a little more water. Fry the paneer as given on p. 23, and fold gently into the cooked peas.

- **Matar Aloo**—Using the same basic recipe, reduce the amount of peas to about 2½ cups and add 2-3 medium potatoes, diced. If using frozen peas, cook the potatoes for 1½ minutes under pressure, then add the peas and cook without pressure for another 4-5 minutes. Otherwise, cook the potatoes and peas together for about 2 minutes under pressure.

- You can make a different **Matar Aloo** according to the master-recipe for cabbage given on p. 101. If using fresh or rehydrated peas, add along with the potatoes; if frozen, cook the diced potatoes with the spice powders and salt, covered on low heat, for 5 minutes, and then add the peas. Stir in ½ cup water and bring to the boil. Cover, lower the heat and cook till the potatoes and peas are tender. The water should have just about dried. If it's still too wet by the time the vegetables are ready, turn up the heat and dry it off, taking care not to burn it.

French beans (farash beans) and sheet beans (saem phalli):

Both are useful standbys. To test the freshness of french beans, take one and bend it till it breaks. It should snap cleanly. Sheet beans should be bright green and slightly glossy, without blemishes. French beans keep reasonably well in the fridge—four or five days in a plastic bag. Sheet beans perhaps not quite so long.

Both often have a string down each side, at the seams between the two halves of the pod, which has to be removed. To do this, wash and cut off the tops and the tails, pulling the knife down the side as you do so and removing the string. Rather a pain, as each pod has to be dealt with individually. The younger and tenderer the pods, the more likely they are to be without this feature. Either way, since they have to be topped and tailed, it's best to check while doing so. After topping and tailing them, cut into convenient, bite-sized dice.

You can cook **Farash Beans ki Subzi** or **Saem ki Subzi** according to the master-recipe for cabbage given on p. 101. After adding the spice powders, stir in ½ cup water and bring to the boil. Cover, lower the heat and cook till the beans are tender, about eight to ten minutes for sheet beans, twenty minutes for french beans. (For french beans you may need to add more water.) The water should have just about dried. If it's still too wet by the time the vegetable is ready, turn up the heat and dry it off, taking care not to burn it.

For **Tamatar Beans:** Prepare ½ kg french beans or sheet beans as above, and make a dry tomato masala as given on p. 103. Add the beans with salt and 1 cup water for french beans and ½ cup water for sheet beans. Stir well, bring back to the boil and simmer till tender (15-20 minutes for french beans, 8-10 minutes for sheet beans).

SAEM PIAZ

Ingredients for 3-4 servings:

½ kg sheet beans
1 medium onion
1-2 green chillies
1 cup milk *or* curd
2 tbsp oil

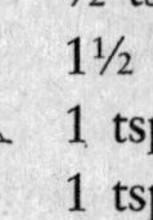

½ tsp mustard seeds
1½ tsp ginger-garlic paste
1 tsp turmeric powder
1 tsp coriander powder
1 tsp salt

Preparation: Wash beans, top and tail, and cut into convenient pieces. Chop the onion fine. Wash the green chillies and chop fine. Beat the curd, if used, till smooth and blended.

Method: Heat the oil in a heavy-bottomed pan or kadhai, burning it if using mustard oil. Lower the heat, throw in the mustard seeds and cover till the spluttering subsides.

Add the onion, green chillies and ginger-garlic paste, and stir-fry till the onion begins to turn golden. Sprinkle in the spice powders, and fry for 1-2 minutes.

Add the beans, milk or curd and salt, bring to the boil, lower the heat and cook covered, stirring now and then, till the beans are just tender.

Mushrooms (dhingri)

Mushrooms are a quite delicious vegetable, expensive to match, and readily available in the big cities at most seasons. They usually come ready-packed in plastic bags of 200 gms. Go for fresh-looking ones, good and white without too many brown marks. They keep well in the fridge, but the bags should be pierced, if not already furnished with holes, to preclude the formation of toxic anaerobic bacteria. Once they develop brown patches, they go off very quickly.

Wash well before cooking, and cut out any brown soggy patches. Cut into convenient and more or less even-sized pieces. Large ones can be quartered, medium ones halved, and small ones left whole. No need to discard the stalks.

Mushrooms can be cooked with green peas, french beans or potatoes. For **Dhingri Matar,** make an onion masala according to the recipe for Matar Piaz (see p. 134), add the mushrooms and stir-fry till dry (they give off a lot of water). Add the shelled green peas and 1 cup water, and cook till the green peas are tender.

You could also make a dry tomato masala according to the recipe on p. 103. Add the mushrooms and stir-fry till dry. Add shelled green peas, sliced french beans or diced potatoes and ½ cup water, bring to the boil, lower the heat and cook till the vegetables are ready.

Or, if you're feeling extravagant, cook it as a separate vegetable.

DHINGRI MASALEDAR

A bit expensive, but as easy as it is delicious.

Ingredients for 2-3 servings:

400 gms/2 packets mushrooms
1 medium tomato
1-2 tbsp oil
¼-½ tsp fennel seeds
½ tsp ginger powder
¼ tsp turmeric powder
½ tsp red chilli powder
½ tsp salt

Preparation: Wash and drain the mushrooms, and cut into convenient-sized chunks. Wash and chop the tomato fine.

Method: Heat the oil, burning it if using mustard oil. Lower the heat, put in the fennel and fry for a few seconds till golden.

Add the mushrooms, and stir-fry on medium heat. They will give out a lot of water, so keep on stirring till they are nearly dry.

Sprinkle in the spice powders and stir-fry for 1-2 minutes more. Stir in the tomato and salt, lower the heat, cover and cook till the tomato disintegrates, about 5 minutes.

Turnips (shalgam)

Turnips are an unfairly neglected vegetable, which can be the basis for at least one quite delicious dish. They keep well, and would really have to be weeks in the fridge before they started to go off. If they begin to sprout, no matter, carry on.

For preference buy small to medium-sized turnips, and store them in the fridge in a plastic bag for as long as you like (within reason).

Wash well, peel and rinse again before cutting them.

SHALGAM KI SUBZI

Ingredients for 2-3 servings:

½ kg turnips
2 large onions
1½-2 cups curd
2 tbsp oil
6 cloves
6 green cardamoms
2 black cardamoms
3 cm cinnamon
½ tsp turmeric powder
½ tsp red chilli powder
½ tsp cummin powder
1 tsp coriander powder
½ tsp salt
15-20 sultanas, *optional*

Preparation: Wash and peel the turnips, rinse again and cut into chunks or quarters. If you like them cut small rather than chunky, no hassle, only you'll have to adjust the cooking time accordingly. Slice the onions fine. Beat the curd till smooth and blended.

Method: Heat the oil in the pressure cooker, burning it if using mustard oil. Lower the heat, put in the whole spices and fry for a minute till fragrant.

Add the onions and ¼ cup water. Close the pressure cooker, and put the pressure weight on the weight valve. Leave on low heat for 10-15 minutes. Remove from the heat, and let the pressure go down naturally. The onions should be soft and pulpy.

Sprinkle in the spice powders, turn up the heat and stir-fry for a minute or so till well integrated.

Stir in the turnips along with the curd, salt and sultanas, if used, and cook under pressure for about 2 minutes. If cut small, cook without pressure till tender, about 5 minutes.

UPAMA
Semolina with Vegetables

A one-dish meal from south India, capable of many variations.

Ingredients for 2-3 servings:

1 cup semolina
1½ tbsp bland oil
1 tsp mustard seeds
1 tsp urad dal
1 tsp chana dal
2 small tomatoes
1-2 small green chillies
1 tsp salt

Optional ingredients for the chaunk:
3-cm piece ginger
1 sprig curry leaves
3-4 cashew nuts

¼-½ tsp asafoetida powder

Optional ingredients added to the dish:
1 small or medium onion
1-2 small carrots
1 small potato
50 gms french beans
½ cup shelled green peas

Garnish:
A small bunch fresh coriander leaves

Preparation: Dry-roast the semolina in a heavy frying pan over low to medium heat, stirring every now and then, till the colour darkens a shade or two, and it gives off a toasted earthy fragrance. This may take 10-15 minutes, and meanwhile you can be getting on with other preparations.

> *If you like upama and cook it often, you can roast the semolina in bulk and keep it in an airtight container.*

Wash the tomatoes and green chillies, and chop fine. Of the optional ingredients, peel and wash the ginger, and dice fine. Wash the curry leaves and strip them off the stem. Chop the cashew nuts and onion. Wash, peel and dice the carrots and potato. Wash, top and tail the french beans, and dice.

Blanch the vegetables in a little boiling water, till barely tender. Allow to cool in the water, and then drain. Wash and chop the coriander leaves. Bring 2 cups water to the boil.

Method: When the semolina is ready, heat the oil on medium heat in a kadhai, and add the mustard seeds. Cover till the spluttering subsides, then add the urad and chana dals, and when they turn red, add the cashew nuts and ginger, if used. When these turn golden, put in the curry leaves, if used, and immediately the tomato and green chillies. Give it a stir, cover and cook on low heat till the tomato softens, just a couple of minutes.

Open, and stir for 1-2 minutes more, till more or less dry. Add the optional vegetables, salt, and asafoetida, if used.

Pour the boiling water into the kadhai, stir and bring back to the boil. Now pour the semolina in slowly, stirring all the time. On contact with the hot water, the semolina immediately swells and the whole thing becomes thick and pasty. Cook stirring till the thickening process is obviously complete, about 3 minutes.

Serve with chopped coriander leaves sprinkled over the top, and accompanied by curd, raita, pickle, sauce or chutney.

Variation: Instead of boiling vegetables, dice any leftover cooked vegetables and add them just before you pour in the roasted semolina.

10

Meat

If you're going to cook and eat meat, the first thing you must find within reasonable reach of your flat is a good butcher's shop. This means an establishment where the wares are fresh and the premises clean, with adequate refrigeration facilities and staff who are skilled at their job and pleasant to deal with. Fortunately, most of the upmarket shopping centres of India's major cities have at least one such shop.

It's possible to get buffalo meat and pork in the metropolitan cities. If you eat pork, you have to be particularly careful about your source of supply, as pork that's been raised in anything but the most hygienic conditions can carry various horrible and life-threatening infections. (No kidding.)

The standard meat over most of India is the great Indian goat, and that's what we assume in all the recipes that follow.

When you shop for meat, check out the colour. The darker red it is, the older the goat it came from, and the more cooking it may need to become tender. Lightish pink means a young animal whose meat will cook faster.

Obviously, there are as many different cuts of meat as there are parts of a goat's carcase. As a novice cook you may prefer to confine yourself to **the hind leg haunch (raan), shoulder, chops (chaamps), ribs**—for the delectable Kashmiri dish Tabaq Maaz—**liver (kaleji)** and of course **mince (keema)**.

Meat is normally sold on the bone, and the best value in terms of meat to bone ratio is the hind leg haunch. Many people, however, reckon that even for a curry or korma, **breast (seena)**, comprising chops and ribs, has a better flavour. If the butcher asks you how you want your chosen meat cut, you're probably better having the pieces larger rather than smaller, till you get the experience to know what's better for which dish. In a good shop, they'll clean the meat of extra fat and bits and bobs while cutting it, without being asked; but there's no harm in keeping an eye on what they're doing. You'll get respect and better service if you seem to know what you want and how you want it.

A few dishes call for **pasandas,** strips of meat without any bone, which have been tenderised—the fibres broken down by being beaten with the blunt side of the chopper. Pasandas are best ordered in advance, because they take time to prepare, and the assistants in the shop may not be able or willing to produce them at short notice (especially if you wander in during the evening, on your way home from work, when the shop is likely to be at its most crowded). The same goes for chops for frying, which also need to be tenderised.

If you want to do a **roast**, or more likely a **pot roast**, your choice will be a whole **raan**. Before buying it, check the diameter of the pressure cooker in which you're going to cook it; it's no fun buying a luscious juicy haunch and finding it won't fit into your cooker. If necessary, have the butcher break the bone to bring it to the required dimensions.

Well wrapped in plastic, meat cut into pieces will keep in the chiller compartment of the fridge for up to five days; mince for three days.

Wash your meat well, piece by piece, before cooking; take the opportunity to check the butcher's cleaning, and let it drain for a few minutes in a colander. If you find you're spending too much time cutting off gobs of fat and pieces of membrane, change your butcher.

It's impossible to wash **mince**. Carry on as we all do, and hope for the best.

The traditional method for cooking most meat curries is to simmer them for up to an hour on the lowest possible heat, covering the pan with a tight-fitting lid, sealed if necessary with a flour and water dough. Today, most of us are ready to settle for the convenience of the pressure cooker. Your average pieces for curry will cook in ten to twelve minutes under pressure, or thirty to forty minutes without, depending on their size, the age of the goat and how long a preliminary cooking—bhuno—it has had. Mince is usually cooked for about the same amount of time.

A whole haunch may take twenty to twenty-five minutes depending on its size, a bit less if it's been treated with a tenderiser like unripe papaya. You're better not to try cooking it without pressure.

Liver doesn't need pressure and cooks, depending on the thickness of the slices, in five to ten minutes. It tends to get tough if overcooked.

> *You may often find that the curd-based gravy of a meat or chicken dish, especially if cooked in the pressure cooker, looks watery and not well integrated when you open the cooker. Never fear, once you've stirred it over high heat for a few minutes, it will homogenise. If in this process the gravy reduces too much stir in a little milk till it is as you want it.*

There are some meat dishes, the cooking of which involves nothing more than marinating the meat in a curd-based marinade, and then putting it on to cook. It's a simple can't-go-wrong technique, and the result is often as delicious as that of more elaborate dishes. We start with three such recipes, spelling the method out only once.

KALIA RIZALA
Mild Meat Curry

Subtly flavoured, and couldn't be simpler.

Ingredients for 3-4 servings:

½ kg meat, cut into pieces
2 large onions
3-4 green chillies
A small bunch fresh coriander leaves
1 cup curd
2 tsp cummin powder
1 tsp ginger-garlic paste
2 tbsp oil *or* ghee
½ tsp salt

Preparation: Wash and drain the meat. Slice the onions as fine as possible. Wash the green chillies and leave whole. Wash the coriander leaves and chop as fine as possible. Beat the curd in a large bowl till smooth and blended.

Add all the ingredients except the oil and the salt to the curd and mix well. Leave to marinate for 1-2 hours, or all day or overnight in the fridge.

Method: Heat the oil or ghee, burning it if using mustard oil. Add the meat and its marinade with the salt, and bring to the boil over low to medium heat stirring occasionally. Cover, and cook till the meat is tender, 10-12 minutes under pressure.

When the pressure has gone down, open the cooker, and stir for a few minutes over high heat to homogenise the gravy.

HINGWALA GOSHT

Another simple recipe, depending on the distinctive flavour of asafoetida.

Ingredients for 3-4 servings:

½ kg meat, cut into pieces
2 cups curd
2 bay leaves
1 tsp cloves
1½ tsp garam masala powder
½ tsp asafoetida powder
1 tsp black pepper powder
½-1 tsp red chilli powder
2 tbsp oil
½ tsp salt

Method: Marinate the meat with curd and spices, and cook as for Kalia Rizala (see p. 147).

BANJARA MAAS

Supposedly a recipe of the nomadic Banjara tribe of Rajasthan.

Ingredients for 3-4 servings:

- ½ kg meat, cut into pieces
- 1 cup curd
- ½ tsp whole black pepper
- ½ tsp cloves
- 4-6 cm cinnamon, broken into small pieces
- 5 dried red chillies
- 2 large onions
- 5-6 cloves garlic
- 2 tbsp oil
- ½ tsp salt

Preparation: Marinate the meat in the curd and all the spices, as for Kalia Rizala, but don't add the onions and garlic. Slice the onions fine. Crush the garlic.

Method: Heat the oil, burning it if using mustard oil. Add the onion and garlic, and cook over high heat, stirring often, till golden. Add the meat and its marinade, with the salt and ½ cup water.

Cook according to the method described for Kalia Rizala (see p.147).

SOOKHE PASANDE

Using a marinade similar to the previous recipes, you can get a completely different effect by cooking pasandas or chops in plenty of oil over low heat till dry. Equally easy and foolproof.

Ingredients for 3-4 servings:

½ kg pasandas (boneless slices of meat)
1 cup sour curd
½ tbsp bland oil
1½ tsp ginger-garlic paste
½ tsp turmeric powder
½ tsp red chilli powder
½ tsp garam masala powder
½ tsp salt
3 tbsp oil, preferably mustard oil

Preparation: Have the butcher cut and tenderise the pasandas for you. Wash the meat and drain thoroughly. Beat the curd in a large bowl till smooth and blended. Add the bland oil, ginger-garlic paste, spice powders and salt to the curd, and beat and stir till well mixed. Add the meat and toss it in the curd mixture till well coated. Allow to marinate for 2 hours, or overnight or the whole day in the fridge.

Method: Heat 3 tbsp oil in a kadhai, burning it if using mustard oil. Add the meat with its marinade, and cook over low heat for 30-40 minutes, turning the meat occasionally and basting with the marinade till it has dried and the meat is tender and golden brown.

It goes better with chapatti than with rice.

Variation: **Chaamps**—You can cook chops in exactly the same way.

MEAT CURRY WITH HERBS

Ingredients for 3-4 servings:

½ kg meat, cut into pieces
2 large onions
A medium bunch fresh coriander leaves
A medium bunch fresh mint leaves
3 green chillies
1-2 limes
½ tsp salt
1 tsp cummin powder
½ tsp red chilli powder
½ tsp turmeric powder
1 tsp ginger-garlic paste
2 tbsp bland oil

Preparation: Wash and drain the meat. Slice the onions fine.

Pick through and wash the coriander leaves. Wash the mint and strip the leaves off the stems. You should have about ½ cup (well-packed) of each herb. Wash the green chillies and chop coarsely. Wash the limes and squeeze out the juice, about 1½ tbsp.

Put the coriander leaves, mint, green chillies and lime juice into a blender with 1-2 tbsp water and blend to a purée.

Method: Put all the ingredients except the blended herb mixture into the pressure cooker with about ¾ cup water. Cook under pressure for 10 minutes, till the meat is nearly done.

Open the cooker after the pressure has gone down and boil down the gravy on high heat to a thick consistency.

Pour in the blended herb mixture, bring back to the boil, stir and simmer gently for 3-4 minutes.

MUTTON ISHTOO

A version of a classic, popular in the Muslim restaurants of Old Delhi. Delicious and easy, but very rich.

Ingredients for 3-4 servings:

½ kg meat, cut into pieces
3 large onions
3-cm piece ginger
10 cloves garlic
1 cup curd
6 dried red chillies
5 tbsp bland oil *or* ghee
½ tsp whole black pepper
10-12 cloves
6 green cardamoms
1 bay leaf
½ tsp red chilli powder
½ tsp salt

Preparation: Wash and drain the meat. Slice the onions fine. Peel and wash the ginger, and dice fine. Chop the garlic roughly. Beat the curd till smooth and blended. Break the red chillies and shake out the seeds.

Method: Heat the oil or ghee in the pressure cooker and fry the onions over low heat for about 5 minutes till soft and translucent, but not at all brown. Add all the other ingredients and stir to mix thoroughly. Cook under pressure for 10-12 minutes. When the pressure has gone down, stir over medium heat for a couple of minutes to integrate the gravy.

KHATTA KORMA

One of the few recipes in which the mustard oil is NOT to be burnt before cooking. The raw mustard oil taste is part of the character of the dish, which otherwise relies completely on whole spices.

Ingredients for 3-4 servings:

½ kg meat, cut into pieces
2 large onions
3-cm piece ginger
1 cup slightly sour curd
12-15 cloves garlic
2 tsp coriander seeds
2 bay leaves
2 dried red chillies
1 tsp whole black pepper
4-6 green cardamoms
2 black cardamoms
4-6 cloves
1 tsp cummin seeds
½ tsp caraway seeds
½ tsp salt
½ cup mustard oil

Preparation: Wash and drain the meat. Chop the onion. Peel and wash the ginger, and dice fine. Beat the curd till smooth and blended.

Method: Put all the ingredients except the curd in the pressure cooker. Mix well, put on high heat and bring to the boil. Cook under pressure for about 10 minutes.

Stir in the curd, and simmer till the meat is well cooked and the gravy is the consistency you like.

CHAMBA GOSHT

No onions, garlic or ginger. Whole spices, asafoetida and curd are the name of the game. The classic dish of the district of Chamba in Himachal Pradesh, where it is called Cha.

Ingredients for 3-4 servings:

½ kg meat, cut into pieces
1½ cups curd
2 tsp gram flour
2 tbsp oil
3 dried red chillies
4 cloves
½ tsp whole black pepper
4 black cardamoms
½ tsp powdered cinnamon
1 tbsp cummin seeds
12-15 fenugreek seeds

2 bay leaves
½ tsp turmeric powder
¼-½ tsp asafoetida powder
½ tsp red chilli powder, *optional*
½ tsp salt

Garnish:
8-10 sprigs fresh coriander leaves

Preparation: Wash and drain the meat. Beat the curd till smooth and blended. Mix the gram flour with ½ cup water to a runny paste, and blend with the curd. Wash and chop the coriander leaves.

Method: Heat the oil in the pressure cooker, burning it if using mustard oil. Add the red chillies and fry for 1-2 minutes, till they turn plump and black.

Take the cooker off the heat and let it cool for 1-2 minutes. Add the whole spices and bay leaves, return the cooker to medium heat and fry for a minute or so till the spices give off their fragrance.

Add the meat, stir well, and cook over medium heat stirring often, till the meat has dried and is beginning to turn brown, about 15-20 minutes.

Take the cooker off the heat again, and allow it to cool a little. Add the curd and gram flour mixture, stir well to blend all the ingredients, return to the heat and bring to the boil slowly, stirring often. Sprinkle in the spice powders and salt. Stir well and cook under pressure for 8-10 minutes, according to the quality of your meat, till it is nearly tender.

When the pressure goes down, open the cooker and continue cooking for another 10-15 minutes, stirring occasionally, till the meat is well done.

Garnish with the chopped coriander leaves.

TABAQ MAAZ
Kashmiri Ribs

An easy recipe from the delectable cuisine of Kashmir.

Ingredients for 3-4 servings:

1 kg tabaq maaz (ribs)
1½ tsp fennel seeds
2 bay leaves
15 green cardamoms
8 cloves
6 cm cinnamon, broken into small pieces
1 tsp whole black pepper
1 tsp ginger powder
2½ tsp cummin powder
1 tsp salt
1 tsp+½ tsp garam masala powder
2 tbsp bland oil

Preparation: Ask the butcher for tabaq maaz (ribs), and have him cut it into large pieces with 2-3 bones each. Wash and drain the meat. Make a potli by tying all the whole spices in a piece of clean thin white cloth.

Method: Bring 2½ cups water to the boil in the pressure cooker. Add the potli and all the other ingredients except the oil and ½ tsp garam masala. Cook under pressure for 8-10 minutes till the meat is tender.

Using a slotted spoon, remove the meat from the cooker and drain in a colander or pat dry on kitchen paper. Heat the oil in a frying pan, add the meat and fry on high heat till crisp on the outside.

Before serving, sprinkle with the remaining ½ tsp garam masala, and a little more salt if necessary.

Note: The meat stock can be strained, degreased (see p. 65) and used to make a soup. The meat can be pressure-cooked several hours or even a day ahead, and kept covered in the fridge till you're ready to complete the cooking.

AABGOSHT
Kashmiri Meat with Milk

A modified version of the famous Kashmiri dish; dead easy.

Ingredients for 3-4 servings:

½ kg meat, cut into pieces
6-8 strands saffron
4 cups full-cream milk
2 tbsp bland oil
6 cm cinnamon
6 green cardamoms
6-8 cloves
2 bay leaves
1½ tsp fennel powder
1 tsp ginger powder
4 dried red chillies
1 tsp salt

Preparation: Wash and drain the meat. Soak the saffron in 1 tbsp warm milk. Bring the rest of the milk carefully to the boil, and simmer till reduced to about 2½ cups.

Method: Heat the oil in a heavy-bottomed pan. It shouldn't be very hot. Add the whole spices and bay leaves and fry for a minute till fragrant. Add the meat, milk, fennel and ginger. Mix well, bring carefully to the boil and simmer without covering till the meat is tender and the milk and oil have more or less amalgamated to form a thinnish gravy, about 25-40 minutes depending on the quality of the meat and how it's cut. Give it a stir every now and then to ensure that the milk doesn't stick and burn.

This unfortunately can't be done in the pressure cooker, as the milk will froth up and boil over.

Add the saffron, red chillies and salt, and simmer for another 10 minutes.

Serve with plain rice.

Note: On no account add the salt at the start of cooking, or the milk may curdle.

YAKHNI
Kashmiri Meat with Curd

Another classic Kashmiri dish, first cousin to the previous one.

Ingredients for 3-4 servings:

- ½ kg meat, preferably shoulder or ribs
- 3 cups slightly sour curd
- 5-6 cloves
- 4-5 black cardamoms
- 5 cm cinnamon, broken into small pieces
- ¾ tsp fennel seeds
- 2 bay leaves
- 1 tsp ginger powder
- 1½ tbsp bland oil
- 3-4 green cardamoms
- 1 tsp salt

Preparation: Wash and drain the meat. Beat the curd till smooth and blended. Tie the cloves, black cardamoms, cinnamon and fennel in a piece of clean thin white cloth to make a potli.

Method: Put the meat, potli, bay leaves, ginger powder and 1 cup water in the pressure cooker. Cook under pressure till the meat is nearly tender, about 10 minutes.

When curd is used in such a large quantity there's a danger that it may split when heated. It's to avoid this that you raise its temperature gradually by whisking in the hot stock, and don't add the salt till the end of the cooking time. If by chance it does split, there's no help in it; just carry on. It won't look so good, but it'll still taste OK. If after trying the recipe a couple of times you find you really have a problem and the curd keeps splitting on you, you can cheat by stirring 1-2 tsp of cornflour or gram flour, thinned down to a runny paste with a little water, into the curd when you beat it up.

When the pressure goes down, open the cooker, and slowly ladle the hot stock into the curd, whisking it as you do so.

Put the oil in a heavy-bottomed pan or large kadhai with the green cardamoms, and heat till the cardamoms are fragrant. It shouldn't be very hot. Pour in the curd-stock mixture, and bring to the boil on medium heat, stirring often.

Remove the meat from the pressure cooker, and add it to

the curd-stock mixture. When the potli is cool enough to handle, squeeze out the juice into the dish and discard it, along with the bay leaves.

Simmer without covering for 10-15 minutes till the gravy is well integrated and has the consistency of thin custard. Add the salt a couple of minutes before the end of the cooking time.

Serve with plain rice.

Variation: If you slice a couple of onions fine and fry them in the oil till just golden, before you add the curd-stock mixture, and then along with the salt stir in a medium bunch of coriander leaves, washed and chopped fine, you get a very fair approximation to another classic Kashmiri dish, **Dhaniwal Korma.**

SHORT-CUT MEAT CURRY

A fairly basic recipe, illustrating the use of the bhuno.

Ingredients for 3-4 servings:

½ kg meat, cut into pieces
2 large onions
1 cup curd
2 tbsp oil
1 tsp ginger-garlic paste
½ tsp red chilli powder
½ tsp turmeric powder
1 tsp coriander powder
½ tsp whole black pepper
3-4 cloves
3-4 black cardamoms
1 bay leaf
3 cm cinnamon
½ tsp salt

Preparation: Wash and drain the meat. Chop the onions fine. Beat the curd till smooth and blended.

Method: Heat the oil, burning it if using mustard oil. Put in all the rest of the ingredients and cook without covering on high heat stirring every now and then till it dries.

Bhuno till the oil separates, adding ¼ cup water once or twice as it starts offering to stick.

Add 1½-2 cups water, and cook for about 8-10 minutes under pressure till nearly tender. Let the pressure go down, then simmer, uncovered, for 5-10 minutes, reducing the gravy or adding a few tbsp water till it is the consistency you like.

Variation: For the curd substitute 3-4 medium tomatoes, washed and chopped fine, and there's your Tamatar Gosht.

KORMA

A basic version of a classic north Indian dish.

Ingredients for 3-4 servings:

½ kg meat, cut into pieces
1 cup curd
1 tsp ginger-garlic paste
½ tsp salt
2 large onions
1 tsp cummin powder
1½ tsp coriander powder
½ tsp red chilli powder
½ tsp turmeric powder

2 tbsp oil
3 cm cinnamon
4-5 cloves
1-2 black cardamoms
4-5 green cardamoms
1-2 bay leaves
1 tsp garam masala powder *or* 1 tsp kewra-water, *optional*

Preparation: Wash the meat and drain. Beat the curd till smooth and blended, add the ginger-garlic paste and salt, and beat and stir well to blend. Add the meat and mix to cover completely. Leave to marinate for 2 hours, or overnight or all day in the fridge.

Slice the onions fine. Mix all the spice powders except the garam masala with a little water to a thin paste.

Method: Heat the oil, burning it if using mustard oil. Lower the heat, throw in the whole spices and bay leaves, and fry till fragrant. Raise the heat, add the onions, and fry, stirring constantly, till beginning to turn golden. Add the meat and curd mixture, and cook on high heat stirring constantly till it dries up. Bhuno till the oil separates, adding ¼ cup water 2-3 times as it dries.

Stir in the mixed masala paste and bhuno once or twice more. Pour in 1-1½ cups water, and cook under pressure for about 10 minutes till the meat is nearly done.

When the pressure goes down, open the cooker and simmer for another 10-15 minutes, reducing the gravy or adding a few tbsp water till it is the consistency you like.

Sprinkle with garam masala or kewra-water, if used, and serve.

ROGAN JOSH

Another Kashmiri classic.

Ingredients for 3-4 servings:

½ kg meat, cut into pieces
4-5 cloves garlic
3-cm piece ginger
2 large onions
½ cup curd
1 tsp fennel powder
1 tsp ginger powder
½ tsp red chilli powder
1 tsp turmeric powder
2 tbsp oil
4-5 cloves
1-2 black cardamoms
4-5 green cardamoms
2-3 bay leaves
½ tsp salt

Preparation: Wash and drain the meat. Chop the garlic coarsely. Peel and wash the ginger and chop coarsely. Slice the onions fine. Beat the curd till smooth and blended. Place all the spice powders into a small bowl, add a little water and blend into a thin paste.

Method: Put the meat, garlic and ginger into a pan with 2 cups water. Cover pan, bring up to the boil on high heat, lower the heat, skim off any scummy foam and simmer for 15-20 minutes. Remove the meat with a slotted spoon and set aside. Strain the stock, discarding the ginger and garlic, and reserve.

Heat the oil, burning it if using mustard oil. Lower the heat, add the whole spices and bay leaves and fry for a minute till fragrant. Put in the onions and fry over high heat, stirring continuously, till beginning to turn golden. Add the mixed masala paste and bhuno, adding ¼ cup water a couple of times as it dries. Add the curd, and bhuno yet once more till the oil separates.

Add the meat, salt, and reserved stock. Stir well, and cook under pressure for 6-8 minutes till the meat is nearly done.

Open the cooker after the pressure goes down, and simmer for another 10-15 minutes, reducing the gravy or adding a few tbsp water till it is the consistency you like.

KORMA SHIRAZI

Ingredients for 3-4 servings:

½ kg meat, cut into pieces
2 large onions
20 almonds
12-15 dried apricots
6-8 strands saffron, *optional*
1 lime, *optional*
2 tbsp oil
4 cloves
4 green cardamoms
2 bay leaves
1 tsp ginger-garlic paste
1½ tsp coriander powder
1 tsp cummin powder
½ tsp red chilli powder
½ tsp turmeric powder
½ tsp salt
1 tbsp sultanas

Preparation: Wash and drain the meat. Slice the onions fine. Blanch and peel the almonds and chop coarsely. Soak the dried apricots in water for a couple of hours and remove the stones. Soak the saffron, if used, in 2 tsp water. Wash the lime, if used and squeeze out the juice, about 2 tsp.

Method: Heat the oil, burning it if using mustard oil. Lower the heat, put in the whole spices and bay leaves, and fry till they release their fragrance. Add the onions and fry on high heat till beginning to turn golden.

Add the meat, ginger-garlic paste and spice powders. Lower the heat and cook till the meat starts releasing its juices. Raise the heat and cook stirring till it dries. Add ¼ cup water and bhuno a couple of times till the oil separates, adding more water as it dries.

Add the salt and 1-1½ cups water, stir well, and cook under pressure for 8-10 minutes, till the meat is just short of tender.

When the pressure goes down, open the cooker and add the almonds, apricots and sultanas, together with the saffron and lime juice, if used. Simmer uncovered, stirring occasionally, for another 10-15 minutes, reducing the gravy or adding a few tbsp water till it is the consistency you like.

SHABDEGH
Meat with Turnips

A classic of Indian Muslim cookery.

Ingredients for 4-6 servings:

- ¾ kg meat, cut into pieces
- ½ kg turnips
- 2 large onions
- ¾ cup curd
- 3 tbsp oil
- 3-4 cloves
- 5 cm cinnamon, broken into small pieces
- 2 black cardamoms
- 4 green cardamoms
- 1 tsp cummin seeds
- 3-4 bay leaves
- 1½ tsp ginger-garlic paste
- ½ tsp red chilli powder
- ½ tsp garam masala powder
- ½ tsp aamchur
- 1 tsp salt

Preparation: Wash and drain the meat. Peel and wash the turnips, and cut into chunks. Slice the onions. Beat the curd till smooth and blended.

Method: Heat the oil, burning it if using mustard oil. Lower the heat, add the whole spices and bay leaves, and fry for a few moments till fragrant.

Add the meat, onions, ginger-garlic paste, and spice powders. Cook over high heat till dry, stirring often. Bhuno till the oil separates, adding ¼ cup water once or twice as it dries.

Add the curd and continue to stir over high heat till dry. Bhuno again till dry.

Add the salt and 1½ cups water, bring to the boil and cook under pressure for 8-9 minutes, till the meat is ¾ done.

Let the pressure go down, open the cooker and add the turnips. Bring back to the boil and continue cooking till the meat and turnips are tender, about 10-12 minutes, or 2 minutes under pressure.

SAAG GOSHT

Ingredients for 4-5 servings:

½ kg meat, cut into pieces
500 gms spinach
2 large onions
1 tsp cummin powder
1½ tsp coriander powder
½ tsp red chilli powder
½ tsp turmeric powder
1 tsp garam masala powder
2 tsp ginger-garlic paste
1 cup curd
2 tbsp oil
¾ tsp salt

Preparation: Wash the meat and drain well. Wash and chop the spinach as described on p. 109. Slice the onions fine. Mix the spice powders with the ginger-garlic paste, and add water to make a thin paste. Beat the curd till smooth and blended.

Method: Heat the oil, burning it if using mustard oil. Add the onions, and fry, stirring constantly, till just turning golden. Stir in the ginger-garlic-spice paste, and bhuno till the oil separates.

Add the meat, curd and salt, stir well, and continue to cook on high heat stirring constantly till dry. Bhuno once more till the oil separates.

Lower the heat, add the spinach, and cook stirring occasionally till the spinach wilts and gives up its moisture, about 5 minutes. There is so much water in spinach that it may not be necessary to add any more, but if you think there's not enough water to cook under pressure, you can add about ½ cup. Cook under pressure for 10-12 minutes.

DAL GOSHT

Ingredients for 5-6 servings:

½ kg meat, cut into pieces
½ cup chana dal
2 large onions
2 tsp ginger-garlic paste
½ tsp red chilli powder
½ tsp black pepper powder
½ tsp turmeric powder
2 tsp coriander powder

2 tbsp oil
2 bay leaves
3 green cardamoms
5 cloves
10 cm cinnamon, broken into small pieces
1 tsp salt
½ tsp garam masala powder

Preparation: Wash and drain the meat. Wash the dal and soak for an hour or so. Slice the onions fine.

Combine the ginger-garlic paste and the spice powders except garam masala in a small bowl with a little water and mix to the consistency of a thin paste.

Method: Heat the oil in the pressure cooker, burning it if using mustard oil. Lower the heat, add the bay leaves and whole spices, and fry for a few moments till fragrant.

Raise the heat, add the onions and fry till golden. Add the ginger-garlic-spice paste and bhuno till the oil separates.

Drain the dal, lower the heat, add the meat, dal and salt, and cook on low heat till the meat releases its juices, then raise the heat and bhuno again till the oil separates.

The dal absorbs water, so you need more water than for a normal meat curry.

Add water to cover by 2-3 cm, and cook under pressure for 10-12 minutes.

Sprinkle with garam masala and serve.

Variation: You could make **Aloo Gosht** using either of the above 2 recipes. Omit the dal or spinach, and when the meat is bhunoed and ready for the final cooking, add a little more water than you would normally use for a meat curry, and cook it under pressure for about 7 minutes. When the pressure has gone down, open the cooker and add about 3 large potatoes, peeled and cut into medium chunks, then cook under pressure for a further 2 minutes.

HALEEM
Meat with Dal and Broken Wheat

Often cooked by Muslims during Ramzan, and eaten in the evening at the time of breaking the fast, especially in Hyderabad.

Ingredients for 4-6 servings:

300 gms boneless meat
2 tbsp chana dal
2 tbsp split moong dal
2 tbsp masoor dal
¾ cup dalia (broken wheat)
1 medium onion
2 limes
5 tbsp oil
½ tsp ginger-garlic paste
2 tsp coriander powder
1 tsp cummin powder
½ tsp turmeric powder
½ tsp chilli powder
1 bay leaf
1 tsp salt
1 tsp garam masala powder

Preparation: Have the butcher cut the meat in 3-5 cm pieces. Wash and drain the meat. Wash the dals together and soak for about 30 minutes, then drain. Soak the dalia for 30 minutes, then drain. Chop the onion medium fine. Squeeze out the juice from the limes, about 2 tbsp.

Method: Heat the oil, burning it if using mustard oil. Add the onion and fry till the colour starts to change. Add the ginger-garlic paste and continue frying till the onion is golden. Add all the rest of the ingredients, except the lime juice and garam masala, together with 4 cups water. Cook under pressure for 10 minutes.

Let the pressure go down, open the cooker and stir the haleem well, making sure to scrape the base clear of any that's offering to stick. Add 1-2 cups water to loosen it to the consistency of a thin gruel. Bring back to pressure and cook for another 10 minutes.

When the pressure has gone down again, stir well and mash with a potato masher or wooden spoon, to pulverise the meat and integrate it through the dish. Add the lime juice and stir over low heat for a couple of minutes.

Serve sprinkled with the garam masala powder. Notwithstanding that wheat is the principal ingredient, you can serve this with rice or chapatti, or you can eat it with no accompaniment other than a dish of curd.

RAAN MUSALLAM

A whole pot roasted raan is a festive dish. On the other hand, the hassle of carving it at the table may make it seem unsuitable for a large party. Good for a family celebration or a few special guests, this is a simplified version of a north Indian classic.

Ingredients for 5-6 servings:

1 whole haunch (raaṇ), about 1 kg
5-cm piece unripe papaya

Marinade:
2 tbsp curd
2 tbsp bland oil
1 tsp ginger-garlic paste

Gravy:
5 medium onions
1 nutmeg
4 tbsp oil
1-1½ cups curd
2½ tsp coriander powder
1 tsp cummin powder
½ tsp red chilli powder
½ tsp turmeric powder
½ tsp black pepper powder
4 black cardamoms
2 bay leaves
10 cloves
5 cm cinnamon
1½ tsp salt

Preparation: Make sure when buying the meat that it will fit into your pressure cooker. Wash it under the tap, and clean it of any extraneous bits of fat and membrane. Prick all over with a fork or the point of a sharp knife. Wash the papaya, and grate it without peeling as fine as possible. There should be about 2 tsp of grated paste. Beat the curd for the marinade and gravy till smooth and blended. Slice the onions as fine as possible. Grate the nutmeg.

Blend all the ingredients for the marinade in a bowl large enough to accommodate the whole haunch. Add the meat and smear the marinade all over it, rubbing it well in. Cover and leave to marinate for at least 2 hours, or in the fridge for the whole day or overnight. Add the papaya and rub it into the meat *not more than 2 hours before cooking.*

Method: Heat the oil for the gravy in the pressure cooker, burning it if using mustard oil. Add the onions and stir-fry over high heat till rich brown. Add all the other ingredients for the gravy, plus ½ cup water, and stir well to mix. Cook under pressure for 10 minutes.

When the pressure has gone down, add the meat with 1 cup water and cook under pressure for 20 minutes. The gravy should be thick and gooey. If when you open the pressure cooker it seems to be a bit thin, remove the meat, place it on a serving platter or shallow dish, and reduce the gravy by fast boiling for 1-2 minutes.

Spoon the gravy over the meat and serve.

LIVER WITH TOMATO AND ONIONS

Ingredients for 3-4 servings:

½ kg liver, cut into large chunks
1 tbsp malt vinegar
2 large onions
4 medium tomatoes
2 tbsp mustard oil
2 tsp coriander powder
1 tsp cummin powder
½ tsp garam masala powder
½ tsp black pepper powder

½ tsp turmeric powder
1 tsp ginger-garlic paste
2-3 black cardamoms
6 cloves
2 bay leaves
½ tsp salt

Garnish:
8-10 sprigs fresh coriander leaves

Preparation: Wash the liver well. Add the vinegar to 2 cups water, and soak the liver in this for about an hour. Cut the onions into thickish rings. Wash the tomatoes and coriander leaves, and chop roughly.

Method: In a kadhai burn the oil, and let it cool a little. Add all the ingredients except the liver and garnish with 1 cup water, and cook on high heat, stirring often, till the onions and tomatoes have softened, about 5-7 minutes.

Drain the liver and add. Continue cooking on high heat for 5-10 minutes till the liver is tender. Be careful not to overcook, or it becomes tough. If in doubt, cut through one of the larger pieces. There should be no tinge of pink. If the dish seems to be drying up add about ½ cup water.

Garnish with the chopped coriander leaves.

TAMATAR KEEMA

This recipe and the next run contrary to the conventional wisdom that mince must be bhunoed to rid it of its somewhat rank flavour. Bay leaves are the essential ingredient used to cut the rankness.

Ingredients for 3-4 servings:

- 2 large onions
- 2 tbsp oil
- ½ kg mince
- 200 gms/1 tetra pack tomato purée
- 8 cm cinnamon, broken into small pieces
- 2 tsp coriander powder
- ½ tsp black pepper powder
- ½ tsp garam masala powder
- ½ tsp red chilli powder
- 6 cloves
- 6 green cardamoms
- 2 bay leaves
- 1 tsp cummin powder
- ½ tsp salt

Preparation: Chop the onions roughly.

Method: Heat the oil in the pressure cooker, burning it if using mustard oil. Add all the other ingredients and stir well together. Cook under pressure for 12-15 minutes.

Release the pressure, and continue to cook on low heat, stirring occasionally, for another 5-10 minutes, drying it up or adding a few tbsp water till it is the consistency you like.

DAHI AUR HINGWALA KEEMA

Ingredients for 3-4 servings:

½ kg mince
2 tbsp oil, preferably mustard oil
2 cups sourish curd
12 cloves
2 bay leaves
1½ tsp garam masala powder
¼-½ tsp asafoetida powder
½ tsp salt

Method: Burn the mustard oil in the pressure cooker. Add all the other ingredients and stir well. Cook under pressure for 12-15 minutes.

Release the pressure, and continue to cook on low heat, stirring occasionally, for another 5-10 minutes, drying it up or adding a few tbsp water till it is the consistency you like.

KEEMA MATAR

Here's the more conventional way of cooking keema.

Ingredients for 3-4 servings:

2-3 medium onions
1 large tomato *or*
1 cup curd
1½ cups shelled green peas
1½ tbsp oil
3 cm cinnamon
3 green cardamoms
½ tsp cummin seeds
1 tsp ginger-garlic paste
½ tsp red chilli powder
½ tsp turmeric powder
1 tsp coriander powder
½ tsp garam masala powder
2 bay leaves
½ kg mince
1 tsp salt

Garnish:
8-10 sprigs fresh coriander leaves

Preparation: Chop the onions fine. Wash and chop the tomato, or beat the curd till smooth and blended. Defrost the green peas if frozen, or rehydrate dried green peas according to the instructions on the packet. Wash and chop the coriander leaves.

Method: Heat the oil, burning it if using mustard oil. Lower the heat, add the cinnamon and cardamoms and fry for a few seconds till fragrant. Add the cummin seeds and fry till golden and fragrant.

Raise the heat, add the onions and stir-fry till beginning to turn golden. Add the ginger-garlic paste, tomato or curd, spice powders and bay leaves, and fry till the oil separates, stirring all the time.

Add the mince and salt, stir well to mix, lower the heat, cover and cook for a few minutes till the mince gives out its juices. Raise the heat, and cook stirring till it dries and turns brown. Add ¼ cup water, and bhuno again.

When it dries, add ¾ cup water, and cook under pressure for 5-7 minutes. When the pressure goes down, add the green peas and ½ cup water if necessary, and simmer till the green peas are tender.

Garnish with the coriander leaves.

KATCHE KEEME KE KABAB

Regular seekh kababs or shammi kababs are a lot of hassle. These are quick and easy, and no less delicious.

Ingredients for 3-4 servings:

½ kg mince
2 medium onions
A small bunch fresh coriander leaves
4 green chillies
2 tbsp gram flour
2-cm piece unripe papaya
1 tsp black pepper powder
1 tsp cummin powder
1 tsp garam masala powder
1 tsp ginger-garlic paste
1 tsp salt
2 tbsp+1 tbsp bland oil

Preparation: Have the butcher grind the mince fine. Chop the onions as fine as possible. Wash the coriander leaves and chop as fine as possible. Wash the green chillies and chop fine.

Put the gram flour into a small frying pan and roast over low heat, shaking it every now and then, till it turns a shade or two darker and develops a nutty fragrance. Wash the papaya, and grate it without peeling as fine as possible. There should be about ½ tsp of paste.

Put all the ingredients, except the papaya and 1 tbsp oil, into a large bowl and mix well. This is best done kneading with the hands. Set aside for an hour, or all day or overnight in the fridge. Add the papaya *not more than 1 hour before cooking.*

Method: Shape the mixture into balls, the size of large limes, then flatten them between the palms into patties about 1 cm thick. Heat 1 tbsp oil in a large frying pan on medium heat. Reduce the heat and fry the patties on both sides till cooked through, about 3 minutes on each side.

Put a tsp of vinegar into a bowl of water and keep dipping your hands into this while you make koftas or kababs. This prevents the mixture from sticking to your palms.

Note: These kababs are also excellent eaten cold.

Variation: Beat about 2-3 cups creamy curd, not more than slightly sour, till smooth and blended. Stir in ¼ tsp salt, ½ tsp cummin powder, ½ tsp black pepper powder, a small bunch of coriander leaves washed and chopped fine, and a couple of green chillies, washed and chopped fine. Dunk the kababs in this for a kind of non-vegetarian Dahi Bada.

KOFTA

Koftas can be complicated business. This recipe simplifies to the greatest extent possible.

Ingredients for 3-4 servings:

Koftas:
½ kg mince
3 tsp gram flour
1 egg
1 tsp garam masala powder
½ tsp red chilli powder
1 tsp cummin powder
2 tsp coriander powder
1 tsp ginger powder
½ tsp black pepper powder
½ tsp salt

Gravy:
2 large onions
1 cup curd
5 green chillies
3 tbsp oil, preferably mustard oil
12 cloves
6 green cardamoms
4 black cardamoms
2 bay leaves
½ tsp turmeric powder
½ tsp red chilli powder
½ tsp black pepper powder
1 tsp ginger-garlic paste
¼ tsp salt

Garnish:
8-10 sprigs fresh coriander leaves

Preparation: Have the butcher grind the mince as fine as possible. Put the gram flour into a small frying pan and roast over low heat, shaking it every now and then, till it turns a shade darker and developes a nutty fragrance. Slice the onions fine. Beat the curd till smooth and blended. Wash the green chillies and leave whole. Wash the coriander leaves and chop coarsely.

Method: To make the gravy, heat the oil in the pressure cooker, burning it if using mustard oil. Add the onions and stir-fry till well browned. Leave for a few moments to cool. If necessary sprinkle a tbsp of water to prevent the onions cooking and burning further on residual heat.

Put in all the rest of the ingredients for the gravy, except the green chillies, with 3 cups water. Bring to the boil and cook under pressure for about 10 minutes. When the pressure goes down, give it a good stir. The gravy should be smooth and blended and the onions completely integrated.

While the gravy is cooking, make the koftas. Break the egg into a largish bowl and beat lightly. Add all the rest of the ingredients for the koftas and mix together, kneading well with the hands to blend. Now shape the koftas, rolling them between the palms into balls about the size of limes. Place them on a lightly oiled plate.

Pick the koftas up with a slotted spoon and gently lower them into the boiling gravy. Cook uncovered over medium heat, turning the koftas gently with the spoon so that they cook evenly. When they firm up, about 5 minutes, close the cooker, and cook under pressure for 10 minutes.

When the pressure goes down, open the cooker. Add the green chillies, and simmer for 5 minutes. If the gravy seems too thin, reduce it by boiling fast for a few minutes.

Garnish with the coriander leaves.

Note: You could also make koftas using the recipe for Katche Keeme ke Kabab above. The gravy remains the same.

11

Fish

Fish is generally known to be the healthiest form of protein. Even the oils found in many varieties are said to have a beneficial effect on the heart and vascular system. It is rich in vitamins and trace elements that are supposed to be good for the brain. They say that eating fish once a week or so helps to give you a long and healthy life.

In the inland cities, fish is not so plentifully available as meat or chicken. Wherever there is a large population of Bengalis, there is likely to be a fish market or at least a couple of good fish shops. Otherwise, many butchers in upmarket shopping centres keep a few anonymous looking **fillets**—boneless slices—in their refrigerated cabinets, as a sideline. If you trust the vendor, this may be the best option for the novice. You can reckon that if the fish looks OK and smells OK, it is OK.

If you're feeling adventurous, try the fish market, where you'll be confronted with an array of whole fish. Common varieties are singhara, bekti, sole, pomfret, surmai, mackerel, hilsa, katla and rohu. In coastal cities, the variety is even greater.

Check for freshness as indicated by firm flesh, a bright eye and a good bright red colour at the gills. The skin should have a sheen and its markings be pronounced. The smell, though inevitably fishy, should be fresh and mild. If you don't like the smell you won't like the taste—avoid. As always, the way to educate yourself is to find a friendly and helpful vendor and ask questions. But don't betray yourself as a total ignoramus, and never let yourself be persuaded to buy something you have doubts about. In inland cities, it may be as well to avoid buying and cooking fish in very hot weather, or the monsoon.

Fish is more expensive, weight for weight, than meat, but you eat almost everything you buy; the weight of any bones is negligible.

We don't advise that you try cleaning, filleting or skinning fish yourself; these are specialist jobs requiring the proper tools. The fishmonger will clean and cut the fish according to your specifications. Tell him how you plan to cook it—whether in a curry or fried.

If frozen immediately after purchase, fish can be kept for several days. Otherwise, cook it the day you buy it or the following day latest. Before cooking, wash the pieces well, handling them gently, as fish is much more delicate than meat or chicken, and drain in a colander.

Fried fish is just about the quickest and easiest thing ever. Otherwise, prepare almost any kind of masala, not too dry, and cook the fish in it. You could adapt some of our chicken recipes for fish—Murgh Badami for example, or Lal Murgh or Murgh Rizala.

In many Indian cuisines the fish is marinated briefly in salt and turmeric, with or without lime juice. No bhunoing of fish, obviously, its structure is too delicate; and whether you give it a quick preliminary frying over high heat before making the masala and continuing with the dish is entirely a question of your preference. Classic Bengali fish cuisine omits this step, but some Bengalis and others prefer it that way. Our recipe for Maachher Jhol shows how it works, and you can include the procedure in some of the other dishes if you like—but not Dahiwali Machhli, obviously, and not Meen Molee.

You can cook any of our fish curries using frozen prawns, which are readily available in various sizes—small, medium, large and jumbo. Store them in the freezer and defrost according to the instructions on the packet, which will also tell you the cooking times for the various grades.

Most people prefer to eat fish curry with rice rather than roti, and half a kilogram should be enough for four. If you're doing fried or grilled fish with minimal accompaniments, allow a bit more.

MASALA FRIED FISH

Ingredients for 2-3 servings:

½ kg fish fillet
½ tsp salt
½ tsp turmeric powder
½ tsp red chilli powder
1-2 limes
2-3 tbsp oil

Preparation: Have the fishmonger cut the fish into pieces, which shouldn't be very thick—not much more than 1 cm. Wash thoroughly and drain. Mix the salt with the spice powders and rub the mixture into the fish pieces. Set aside for 10-15 minutes. Cut the lime into quarters.

Method: Heat the oil in the frying pan, burning it if using mustard oil. Lower the heat and add the fish pieces in a single layer, being careful not to overfill the pan. Cook over medium heat till the under surface is beginning to brown, probably 4-5 minutes, then turn and cook the other side till similarly ready.

Serve with quarters of lime to squeeze over the fish.

MAACHHER JHOL
Bengali Fish Curry

Ingredients for 3-4 servings:

½ kg fish
½ tsp+½ tsp salt
½ tsp+½ tsp turmeric powder
1 large onion
1 tsp ginger-garlic paste

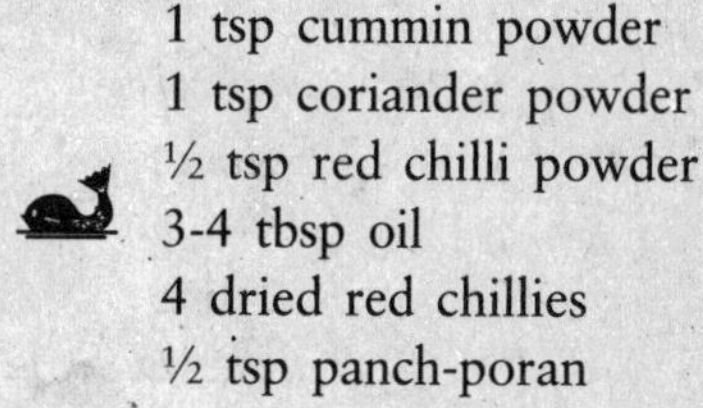

1 tsp cummin powder
1 tsp coriander powder
½ tsp red chilli powder
3-4 tbsp oil
4 dried red chillies
½ tsp panch-poran

Preparation: Have the fishmonger cut the fish into 12-15 convenient-sized chunks. Wash thoroughly and drain. Mix ½ tsp salt and ½ tsp turmeric and rub the mixture into the fish pieces. Set aside for 10-15 minutes.

Chop the onion fine. Put the ginger-garlic paste with ½ tsp turmeric and the cummin, coriander and chilli powders into a small bowl and mix into a paste with a little water.

Method: Heat the oil in a large kadhai, burning it if using mustard oil. Put the fish carefully into the hot oil, 4-5 pieces at a time, and fry, turning once or twice, on medium to high heat till the flesh turns firm and white and is beginning to brown slightly. Remove with a slotted spoon and reserve. You will have to fry your ½ kg in 3 batches or so, each taking about 2-3 minutes.

Pour out and discard half the oil. Return the kadhai to high heat and throw in the red chillies. Fry till plump and black. Lower the heat, put in the panch-poran and cover till the spluttering subsides. Raise the heat, add the onion, and stir-fry till beginning to turn golden. Add the ginger-garlic-spice paste and bhuno till the oil separates.

Lower the heat and stir in 2 cups water and ½ tsp salt. Return the fish to the kadhai and bring to the boil, spooning the gravy over the pieces till they are well coated. Cover, lower the heat and simmer till the fish is ready, probably about 10-15 minutes, depending on the variety of fish and the size of the chunks.

SHORSHE MAACHH
Bengali Fish in Mustard

A simplified version of another Bengali classic. Traditionally made with stone-ground yellow mustard seeds. For this we substitute mustard powder.

Ingredients for 3-4 servings:

½ kg fish
½ tsp+½ tsp turmeric powder
½ tsp+½ tsp salt
2-3 green chillies

1 cup curd
3-4 tsp mustard powder
½ tsp red chilli powder
3 tbsp+½ tbsp mustard oil

Preparation: Have the fishmonger cut the fish into 12-15 convenient-sized chunks. Wash thoroughly and drain. Mix ½ tsp salt and ½ tsp turmeric and rub the mixture into the fish pieces. Set aside for 10-15 minutes.

Wash and slit the green chillies. Beat the curd till smooth and blended.

Put the mustard powder into a biggish bowl. Add the curd a little at a time mixing with the powder till it forms a paste. Add the rest of the curd and all the remaining ingredients except the fish and ½ tbsp mustard oil and mix thoroughly.

Method: Pour the curd mixture into a kadhai and cook on medium heat till it boils. Continue to cook on medium heat stirring occasionally for about 5 minutes, and add the fish. Bring back to the boil, reduce the heat and let it simmer uncovered till the fish is ready and the gravy reduced and somewhat thickened, 12-15 minutes.

Before serving, float ½ tbsp mustard oil on the top of the dish.

Variation: Fry the fish first, as in the recipe for Maachher Jhol (see p. 183).

MAACHHER MALAI KALIA
Bengali Fish in a Creamy Sauce

Ingredients for 3-4 servings:

- ½ kg fish
- ½ tsp + ½ tsp turmeric powder
- ½ tsp + ½ tsp salt
- 2 medium onions
- 3-4 tbsp oil
- 2 dried red chillies
- ½ tsp ginger-garlic paste
- 4 tsp coconut powder
- 2 bay leaves
- ½ tsp sugar
- 1 tsp + ¼ tsp garam masala powder

Preparation: Have the fishmonger cut the fish into 12-15 convenient-sized chunks. Wash thoroughly and drain. Mix ½ tsp salt and ½ tsp turmeric and rub the mixture into the fish pieces. Set aside for 10-15 minutes.

Grate or grind the onions, or chop as fine as possible.

Method: Heat the oil in a kadhai, burning it if using mustard oil. Throw in the red chillies and cook on high heat till plump and black. Lower the heat and add the onions. Stir-fry on low heat for about 5 minutes till soft and translucent but not coloured. Add the ginger-garlic paste and fry stirring for another 2-3 minutes. Add the coconut powder, bay leaves, sugar, ½ tsp turmeric, ½ tsp salt, 1 tsp garam masala, and 1½ cups water, stir well together, bring to the boil and simmer for 2 minutes.

Add the fish, spooning the gravy over the pieces till they are well coated. Bring back to the boil and cook over low heat without covering till the fish is ready, and the gravy medium-thick, 12-15 minutes.

Discard the bay leaves, sprinkle on ¼ tsp garam masala and serve with plain rice.

Variation: Fry the fish first, as in the recipe for Maachher Jhol (see p. 183).

TAMATAR MACHHLI

Ingredients for 3-4 servings:

½ kg fish

Tomato gravy:
3 medium onions
4 large tomatoes
1 tsp ginger-garlic paste
½ tsp red chilli powder
½ tsp turmeric powder
1 tsp coriander powder
2 tbsp oil
1 tsp cummin seeds
½ tsp salt

Garnish:
8-10 sprigs fresh coriander leaves

Preparation: Have the fishmonger cut the fish into 12-15 convenient-sized chunks. Wash thoroughly and drain. Slice the onions. Wash and chop the tomatoes. Wash the coriander leaves and chop coarsely.

Method: Make a tomato gravy as given on p. 102.

Carefully slip the fish into the pan, spooning the gravy over the pieces till they are well coated. Bring to the boil, cover, lower the heat and simmer till the fish is ready, about 10-15 minutes, depending on the variety of fish and the size of the chunks. Garnish with the chopped coriander leaves.

Variations: Fry the fish first, as in the recipe for Maachher Jhol (see p. 183).

- Add ½ tsp ajwain to the chaunk when making the tomato gravy; or add 1 tsp sugar and 2 tsp vinegar for a sweet and sour effect.

MACHHLI KALIA

Ingredients for 3-4 servings:

½ kg fish
½ tsp+½ tsp salt
½ tsp+½ tsp turmeric powder
1 large onion
1 tsp ginger-garlic paste
½ tsp red chilli powder
1 tsp coriander powder

1½ tbsp oil
2 bay leaves
¼ tsp whole black pepper
6-8 cm cinnamon
4 black cardamoms
½ tsp garam masala powder, *optional*

Preparation: Have the fishmonger cut the fish into 12-15 convenient-sized chunks. Wash thoroughly and drain. Mix ½ tsp salt and ½ tsp turmeric and rub the mixture into the fish pieces.

Chop the onion fine. Put the ginger-garlic paste with ½ tsp turmeric and the chilli and coriander powders into a small bowl and mix into a paste with a little water.

Method: Heat the oil, burning it if using mustard oil. Lower the heat, put in the bay leaves and whole spices, and fry for a few moments till fragrant. Raise the heat, add the onion and stir-fry till beginning to turn golden. Add the ginger-garlic-spice paste and bhuno till the oil separates.

Add 1 cup water and ½ tsp salt, stir well and bring to the boil. Add the fish pieces and spoon the gravy over them till well coated. Cover, lower the heat and simmer till the fish is ready, about 10-15 minutes, depending on the variety of fish and the size of the chunks.

Sprinkle with garam masala, if used, and serve.

Variation: Fry the fish first, as in the recipe for Maachher Jhol (see p. 183).

DAHIWALI MACHHLI

Ingredients for 3-4 servings:

½ kg fish
3 medium onions
1-1½ cups creamy curd, a bit sour
½ tsp salt
1 tsp garam masala powder
½ tsp turmeric powder
2 tbsp oil
1½ tsp ginger-garlic paste

Garnish:
8-10 sprigs fresh coriander leaves

Preparation: Have the fishmonger cut the fish into 12-15 convenient-sized chunks. Wash and drain the fish.

Slice the onions. Wash the coriander leaves and chop coarsely.

In a largish bowl beat the curd till smooth and blended and stir in the salt, garam masala and turmeric. Add the fish pieces and toss gently till well coated with curd. Marinate for 30 minutes, or longer in the fridge.

Method: Heat the oil in a kadhai, burning it if using mustard oil. Stir-fry the onions on high heat till just beginning to turn golden. Lower the heat to medium, add the ginger-garlic paste, and stir-fry for a few minutes more till the onions are nicely browned and the aroma of the paste has turned mellow.

Slip the fish and its marinade carefully into the kadhai, spooning the gravy over the pieces till they are well coated. Bring slowly to the boil, cover and simmer till the fish is ready, about 10-15 minutes depending on the kind of fish and the size of the chunks.

Garnish with the chopped coriander and serve.

MEEN MOLEE
Kerala Fish Stew

Ingredients for 3-4 servings:

½ kg fish
4 medium onions
4 green chillies
2 medium tomatoes
2 tbsp bland oil
2 tsp ginger-garlic paste

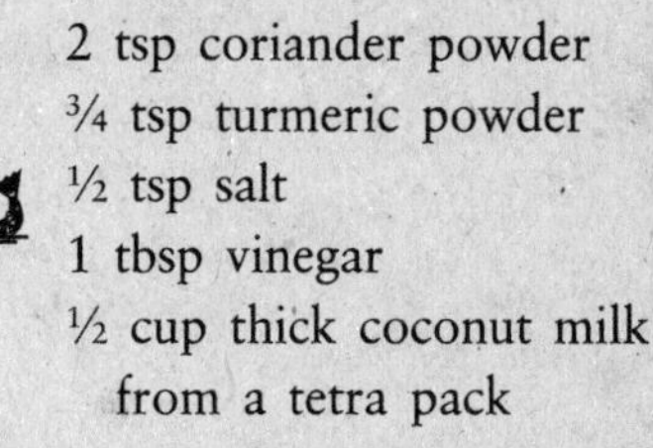

2 tsp coriander powder
¾ tsp turmeric powder
½ tsp salt
1 tbsp vinegar
½ cup thick coconut milk from a tetra pack

Preparation: Have the fishmonger cut the fish into 12-15 convenient-sized chunks. Wash the fish thoroughly and drain.

Slice the onions fine. Wash and slit the chillies. Wash the tomatoes and cut into 8 pieces each.

Method: Heat the oil in a kadhai, add the ginger-garlic paste and stir-fry on medium heat for about a minute. Add the onions and chillies, and continue to stir-fry for 3-4 minutes till the onions are just soft and translucent. Add the spice powders and stir for a minute more. Stir in the salt, vinegar and ½ cup water.

Bring to the boil and slip the fish carefully into the kadhai, spooning the gravy over the pieces till they are well coated. Add the tomatoes, bring to the boil and simmer till the fish is nearly cooked, 8-12 minutes depending on the kind of fish and the size of the chunks. Stir in the coconut milk and simmer a few minutes more till the fish is ready.

12

Chicken

Chicken is reckoned a healthier source of protein than red meat. It is also versatile, being as good a basis for a mayonnaise or aspic dish as for a pulao, curry or casserole.

Chicken is readily available, and can usually be bought dressed—cleaned, skinned and ready to cook. In contrast to Western-style cuisine, the skin is removed for many Indian chicken dishes; the recipes in this book assume skinned chicken.

In the upmarket shopping centres, you may find legs (drumsticks), thighs, wings or the more expensive breasts as cut pieces. Our recipes suggest a kilogram weight, on the basis of the average whole chicken. If you buy a whole chicken, ask the butcher to joint it—cut into pieces—and if he asks how many pieces tell him confidently twelve. If you prefer you can use only thighs, breasts etc; but the bonier pieces add to the flavour.

Well wrapped in plastic, chicken will keep in the chiller of the fridge for three to four days.

Before cooking, chicken like everything else needs to be well washed, and at the same time you can cut out any gobs of fat it may have. Ready-dressed chicken from your upmarket shops will probably be already cleaned of extra fat, but your friendly neighbourhood murghiwala, if that's whom you get it from, may not be so particular. After thorough washing, piece by piece, in two to three changes of water, or under running water, let it drain for a few minutes in a colander.

In most north Indian cooking, the liver is not included in chicken curry-type dishes. You can fry it up separately with an egg for breakfast or a modest lunchtime snack. The gizzard, on the other hand, does go in.

You can't bhuno chicken at the start of cooking, because it's a dry meat. So normally in a curry-type dish, you prepare the masala, then add the chicken last of all and cook without further processing. Alternatively, you marinate the chicken and cook with the marinade in oil for a dry masala dish.

Today's broilers cook in no time. If you're using the pressure cooker, bring it up to pressure, and for a small chicken, or small pieces, take it immediately off the heat, and let the pressure go down. For a larger one, keep it under pressure for only one minute, and then turn off the heat. Not under pressure, it may take anything from fifteen to twenty-five minutes, depending on the size. You can judge that it is done when the meat of the leg is just beginning to come away from the bone.

MURGH NIMBU

A basic recipe for a dry chicken; dead easy.

Ingredients for 4-5 servings:

1 chicken, jointed, about 1 kg	2-3 limes
1 tsp salt	4 tbsp oil *or* ghee
1 tbsp ginger-garlic paste	2 bay leaves
	½ tsp whole black pepper

Preparation: Wash and drain the chicken, putting the liver aside. Mix the salt with the ginger-garlic paste, and smear the chicken pieces with this. Cover and marinate for an hour, or all day or overnight in the fridge. Wash the limes, and squeeze out the juice, 2-3 tbsp.

Method: Heat the oil or ghee in a deep kadhai, burning it if using mustard oil. Let the burnt oil cool for 1-2 minutes, then carefully slip in the chicken and the bay leaves. Stir well to coat with the oil, cover and allow to cook over the lowest possible heat, basting with the oil from time to time.

When half cooked, about 10-15 minutes, depending on the size of the chicken pieces, add the whole black pepper. Continue cooking on low heat till the masala begins to stick to the sides of the kadhai. Then sprinkle 1-2 tbsp water and bhuno till the oil separates.

When the chicken is lightly brown and tender, remove from the heat. Pour the lime juice over it and serve.

SOOKHA MURGH MASALEDAR

A marginally more elaborate version of the above; still very easy.

Ingredients for 4-5 servings:

1 chicken, jointed, about 1 kg
2 tbsp curd
2 tsp ginger-garlic paste
½-1 tsp red chilli powder
1 tsp cummin powder
½ tsp black pepper powder
1 tsp salt
4 tbsp oil *or* ghee
2 bay leaves

Preparation: Wash and drain the chicken, putting the liver aside. In a large bowl beat the curd till smooth and blended. Add the ginger-garlic paste, spice powders and salt. Beat together to mix. Add the chicken pieces and toss in the curd mixture so that they are well coated. Marinate for an hour, or all day or overnight in the fridge.

Method: Heat the oil or ghee in a deep kadhai, burning it if using mustard oil. Let the burnt oil cool for 1-2 minutes, and then carefully slip in the chicken with all the marinade and the bay leaves. Stir well to coat with the oil, cover and cook over low heat, tossing gently and basting a couple of times, till the marinade has dried and the chicken pieces are tender, 15-25 minutes, depending on their size.

If the marinade hasn't dried by the time the chicken is ready, raise the heat and cook, stirring for a few minutes till it dries and the chicken pieces are lightly browned.

SIMPLE CHICKEN CURRY

Ingredients for 4-5 servings:

1 chicken, jointed, about 1 kg
3 medium onions
½ tsp ginger-garlic paste
½ tsp black pepper powder
1 tsp cummin powder
2 tsp coriander powder
½ tsp red chilli powder
½ tsp turmeric powder
2 tbsp oil
10-12 green cardamoms
2 black cardamoms
10-15 cloves
2 bay leaves
1 tsp salt

Preparation: Wash and drain the chicken pieces putting the liver aside. Chop the onions fine. Mix the ginger-garlic paste and the spice powders in a small bowl with about ¼ cup water to a thin paste.

Method: Heat the oil, burning it if using mustard oil. Lower the heat, throw in the whole spices and the bay leaves, and fry for a minute or so till fragrant. Add the onions and fry on high heat, stirring constantly, till golden. Add the mixed spice paste, and stir over medium heat for a few minutes.

Put in the chicken pieces and toss over medium heat for a couple of minutes. Add the salt and ½ cup water, bring slowly to the boil and cook till the chicken is tender, 0-1 minute under pressure, 15-25 minutes without, depending on the size of the chicken pieces.

Reduce the gravy or thin it down with a little water until it is the consistency you like.

Variation: When the chicken is just short of tender, raise the heat and cook for a few minutes to dry the gravy, stirring constantly to prevent it burning. When it is nearly dry, add 4 tbsp of sweet mango chutney. Toss over medium heat till it dries up again.

MURGH TAMATAR

Ingredients for 4-5 servings:

1 chicken, jointed, about 1 kg
3 large onions
2 tbsp bland oil
100 gms/½ tetra pack tomato purée
1 tsp ginger-garlic paste
2 tsp coriander powder
½ tsp garam masala powder
12-15 cm cinnamon *or* 1½ tsp powdered cinnamon
2 black cardamoms
2 bay leaves
10 cloves
½ tsp black pepper powder
1 tsp salt

Preparation: Wash the chicken pieces well, and drain, putting the liver aside. Chop the onions roughly.

Method: Put all the ingredients except the chicken into the pressure cooker with ¼ cup water. Cook under pressure for 10 minutes.

When the pressure has gone down, open the cooker and stir to blend the ingredients. Add the chicken and toss it in the gravy till all the pieces are well coated. Close the cooker and bring it up to pressure again. Cook for 0-1 minute depending on the size of the chicken pieces.

Reduce the gravy or thin it down with a little water till it is the consistency you like.

MURGH SIMLA MIRCH

Ingredients for 4-5 servings:

1 chicken, jointed, about 1 kg
3 large onions
2 large capsicums
2 tbsp bland oil
2 tsp coriander powder
1 tsp cummin powder
½ tsp red chilli powder
1 tsp ginger powder
½ tsp black pepper powder
1 tsp garam masala powder
2 bay leaves
10 cloves
8 green cardamoms
1 tsp salt

Preparation: Wash the chicken pieces well, and drain, putting the liver aside. Chop the onions roughly. Wash, quarter, and de-seed the capsicums, and chop roughly.

Method: Put all the ingredients except the chicken into the pressure cooker with ½ cup water. Cook under pressure for 10 minutes.

When the pressure has gone down, open the cooker and cook on high heat for 3-5 minutes, stirring well to blend the ingredients into a gravy. Add the chicken and toss till all the pieces are well coated. Close the cooker and bring it up to pressure again. Cook for 0-1 minute depending on the size of the chicken pieces.

Reduce the gravy or thin it down with a little water till it is the consistency you like.

MURGH BADAMI

Ingredients for 4-5 servings:

1 chicken, jointed, about 1 kg
2 large onions
½ cup almonds
1½-2 cups curd
6-8 strands saffron
1 lime
2 tbsp oil

6-7 green cardamoms
1 tsp ginger-garlic paste
1 tsp kewra-water, *optional*
½ cup cream, *optional*
1 tsp red chilli powder
1 tsp salt
2 tsp sultanas

Preparation: Wash and drain the chicken and put the liver aside. Slice the onions. Blanch and peel the almonds, and chop coarsely. Beat the curd till smooth and blended. Soak the saffron for a few minutes in 1 tbsp warm water or milk. Wash the lime and squeeze out the juice, about 1 tbsp.

Method: Heat the oil, burning it if using mustard oil. Add the onions and fry on high heat, stirring constantly, till golden. Add all the other ingredients, and bring slowly to the boil, stirring every now and then. Cook till the chicken is tender, 0-1 minute under pressure, 15-25 minutes without, depending on the size of the pieces.

After the pressure goes down, stir for a few minutes over high heat to homogenise the gravy.

MURGH KORMA

Chicken curried in the same masala as used in the classic dish, Murgh Musallam. The operative ingredient that gives it its distinctive flavour is nutmeg.

Ingredients for 4-5 servings:

1 chicken, jointed, about 1 kg	2 tsp coriander powder
2 large onions	1 tsp cummin powder
1 cup curd	2 tbsp oil
2 nutmegs	2-3 black cardamoms
1½ tsp ginger-garlic paste	4-5 cloves
1 tsp red chilli powder	2 bay leaves
	1 tsp salt

Preparation: Wash and drain the chicken and put the liver aside. Slice the onions as fine as possible. Beat the curd till smooth and blended. Grate the nutmegs. Put the ginger-garlic paste and spice powders into a small bowl with about 1 tbsp water, and stir to a paste.

Method: Heat the oil, burning it if using mustard oil. Lower the heat, add the whole spices and bay leaves, and fry for about 30 seconds till fragrant. Add the onions, and cook on high heat till just turning golden. Stir in the ginger-garlic-spice paste, and bhuno till the oil separates.

Stir in the curd, most of the nutmeg powder, and the salt. Add the chicken and toss together so that the chicken is well coated with the masala. Cook till the chicken is tender, 0-1 minute under pressure, 15-25 minutes without, depending on the size of the pieces. After the pressure goes down, stir for a few minutes over high heat to homogenise the gravy.

Before serving, stir in the remaining nutmeg.

LAL MURGH

Ingredients for 4-5 servings:

1 chicken, jointed, about 1 kg
2 large onions
2 tsp kashmiri chilli powder
2 tsp coriander powder
½ tsp turmeric powder
2 tsp ginger-garlic paste
1 cup curd

2 tbsp oil
2 bay leaves
5 cloves
½ tsp whole black pepper
6 cm cinnamon
8-10 green cardamoms
1 tsp salt

Preparation: Wash and drain the chicken and put the liver aside. Chop the onions fine. Combine the spice powders with the ginger-garlic paste, and thin to a medium pasty consistency with about 1 tbsp water. Beat the curd till smooth and blended.

Method: Heat the oil, burning it if using mustard oil. Lower the heat, throw in the bay leaves and whole spices and fry for about 30 seconds till fragrant. Add the onions and stir-fry till just turning golden. Stir in the mixed spice paste, and bhuno a couple of times till the oil separates, adding ¼ cup water as it dries.

Turn the heat down and add the chicken, curd, salt and 1 cup water. Stir well, bring to the boil and cook till the chicken is tender, 0-1 minute under pressure, 15-25 minutes without, depending on the size of the chicken pieces. After the pressure goes down, stir for a few minutes over high heat to homogenise the gravy.

Note: It's the chilli powder, obviously, that makes it *lal*. We have recommended kashmiri chilli powder as it is not so hot and gives a good colour. You can use regular chilli powder if you like your food really hot. If the kashmiri one is not available, use less chilli powder, and have it not so red.

MURGH KHUS-KHUS

The USP of this dish is the poppy seeds, which give it a distinctive and delicious aroma.

Ingredients for 4 servings:

1 chicken, jointed, about 1 kg
2-3 green chillies
1 tbsp poppy seeds
3 tbsp sour curd
2 tsp coriander powder
1 tsp black pepper powder
1 tsp turmeric powder
2 tsp cummin powder
1 tsp salt
2 tbsp oil *or* ghee

Preparation: Wash and drain the chicken and put the liver aside. Wash the chillies and chop. Lightly roast the poppy seeds on the tava or in a small frying pan over low heat, till the colour turns dirty grey, and they give off a wonderful aroma. Cool and grind.

Beat the curd in a large bowl till smooth and blended. Add the poppy seeds with the rest of the spice powders, chillies and salt. Stir and beat till well blended. Add the chicken pieces and toss well so that the pieces are well coated with the curd-spice mixture. Leave to marinate for 1-2 hours, or all day or overnight in the fridge.

Method: Heat the oil or ghee, burning it if using mustard oil. Add the chicken and its marinade, bring slowly to the boil and cook till tender, 0-1 minute under pressure, 15-25 minutes without, depending on the size of the pieces. After the pressure goes down, stir for a few minutes over high heat to homogenise the gravy.

MURGH RIZALA

Large fresh red chillies, available during the winter, are not very hot and give this dish a pleasantly cheerful look.

Ingredients for 4-5 servings:

1 chicken, jointed, about 1 kg
2 large onions
10 large fresh red chillies
1 cup curd
2 tsp ginger-garlic paste
1 tsp garam masala powder
½ tsp red chilli powder
1 tsp salt
2 tbsp oil
2 bay leaves
½ cup milk

Preparation: Wash and drain the chicken and put the liver aside. Slice the onions as fine as possible. Wash the chillies.

Beat the curd in a large bowl till smooth and blended. Add the ginger-garlic paste, spice powders, and salt. Beat well, add the chicken and stir till well coated. Marinate for 2 hours, or all day or overnight in the fridge.

Method: Heat the oil, burning it if using mustard oil. Add the onions and fry on high heat stirring constantly till golden. Add the chicken with its marinade, and bay leaves. Cook over high heat stirring constantly till it dries.

Lower the heat, add the milk and ½ cup water, bring to the boil and cook till the chicken is nearly tender, 0-1 minute under pressure, 12-20 minutes without, depending on the size of the pieces. Add the chillies and cook till the chicken is ready and the chillies al dente.

13

Eggs

Eggs! The answer to the reluctant cook's prayer; the rescue-kit for many a culinary emergency; the indispensable fallback for those occasions when there is nothing much else in the larder, and no time to cook anyway. Never be without them.

Eggs are no doubt an essential ingredient in cakes, puddings, mousses, soufflés, some sauces, meatballs and probably much else, but they also lend themselves to simple and speedy dishes of which they are the only or main ingredient. Soft-boiled, hard-boiled, poached, scrambled, bhujia, fried, omelette, most of them capable of an infinite number of variations—when all you need to do is toast a couple of slices of bread and in ten minutes you have an adequate, even a comforting meal.

Eggs aren't standardised in India, so when you buy them you can't specify the size. In lists of ingredients, you may assume that medium-sized eggs, 55-60 gms in weight, are meant. If it so happens that you're working with unusually small or large ones, use one or two more or less than asked for, especially in recipes where eggs are only one of several ingredients and relative proportions matter.

Reasonably fresh eggs will keep in the fridge for a week or more.

The use of eggs in cooking depends on the ability of both yolk and white to set. The white has another remarkable property, in that, when vigorously beaten, uncooked, it swells like a balloon—actually like an infinite number of balloons, as air is incorporated into its jelly-like protein. If you beat the white and leave it, the air will gradually leak out and the white will revert to its previous state. But if you expose the aerated white to heat, usually after incorporating sugar or some other substance, you get exciting things like meringues, soufflés and sponge cakes—for all of which you need an oven, unfortunately. You can also use gelatine to set the whites and achieve a similar effect without heating; that's a cold mousse or soufflé.

To separate the yolk and the white, wash the egg and dry it. Hold it over a bowl and break it carefully with a sharp tap from a knife around the equator. Gently pull the two halves apart, holding back the yolk in one of the half-shells and letting the white overflow into the bowl. Tilt the half-shell to transfer the yolk into the other one, encouraging the remains of the white to escape into the bowl. Repeat this a couple of times till there is practically no white adhering to the yolk, then drop the yolk into another bowl. A little white among the yolks does no harm, but yolk should not get into the whites, because the whites won't beat up satisfactorily if even a trace of yolk has leaked into them. The fresher the egg, the stronger the membrane which holds the yolk together and the less likely it is to break.

To beat the whites, use an electric or hand-beater, or a wire whisk. Use a large enough bowl, because with the air you beat in the volume increases dramatically. As you beat, you at first notice the formation of bubbles. As more air is incorporated the bubbles get smaller and more numerous till you have a white froth. Continue beating, and the froth begins to stand up in soft, and eventually in stiff peaks.

HARD-BOILED EGGS

No problem. Put as many as you want in a pan of convenient size, cover with tap water, put on the heat, bring up to the boil, and boil for 7-9 minutes depending on the size. They can't overcook, so short of forgetting them on the heat for so long that the water boils dry, you can't go very far wrong.

To peel a hard-boiled egg, tap it gently all over with the back of a teaspoon. The shell will crack and is easy to remove. Try to do this as soon as possible after boiling the egg. If it cools through, the shell tends to stick to the white.

ŒUFS MOLLETS

There seems to be no term in English for eggs boiled between hard and soft. Three-quarters boiled, perhaps? Proceed as for soft-boiled eggs, adjusting the time by 1-2 minutes more, according to the size of the egg. Some may like them like this for breakfast and œufs mollets are ideal for making egg sandwiches. Peel as described for hard-boiled eggs, only be careful to handle them gently as they are still a good deal softer.

SOFT-BOILED OR HALF-BOILED EGGS

You have a choice of two methods, each of which has its advantages and its drawbacks.

Method 1: Boil the water, then lower the egg gently into it and cook for 3½-5 minutes depending on the size of the egg and the degree of softness you like. If you cook a medium-sized egg for 4 minutes, the white will be firm, and the yolk runny or only just beginning to coagulate at the edges.

The advantage of this method is that it's cut and dried; in a couple of attempts, you know exactly how long to cook your egg to get it exactly as you like it.

The drawback is that the shock of the boiling water may crack the eggshell, and the egg will leak out into the water in an unappetizing way, especially if you've only just brought the egg out of the fridge; but who ever remembered to take it out the night before?

An egg that stands up on end when you put it in water is less likely to be fresh and more likely to crack than one which lies on its side.

Method 2: Put the egg into the pan, cover with tap water, bring up to the boil, and boil for 2-3 minutes, depending on the size of the egg. The drawback is that it starts cooking well before the water boils, so it's impossible to give precise instructions as to time; a couple of attempts and you'll get it as you want it. The advantage is that this way they're less likely to crack.

Eggs cook at well under boiling point, and continue to cook on residual heat even after the gas is turned off, so never leave them in the water beyond the specified cooking time, unless you want them hard.

FRIED EGGS

Heat ½ tbsp bland oil in a frying pan till fairly hot but not smoking, turn down the heat and immediately break the egg into the pan. The underside will set on contact with the hot metal. As the egg begins to cook through, gently detach it from the pan by sliding a thin spatula under it, to make sure it isn't sticking.

Cook on low to medium heat till it is to your liking. If you like the underside brown and crisp, raise the heat a bit. To ensure more even cooking, you can spoon a little of the hot oil over the egg, or cover the pan.

If you like the yolk well set, turn the egg over carefully with the spatula, being careful not to break the yolk and cook till it is done to your liking. Remove it from the pan with the spatula, and serve with, or on top of, hot buttered toast.

To make fried eggs a bit more interesting, for 2 eggs crush a clove of garlic with salt, and cook gently in the oil along with ½ tsp lime juice, till the garlic just begins to turn golden. Add the eggs to the pan and fry as above. Garnish with a little dried mint rubbed between the palms and sprinkled over the eggs. This is a west Asian recipe.

POACHED EGGS

Poaching means cooking in water just below boiling point. To poach well, an egg should be really fresh, otherwise the white spreads through the water before it sets.

Add enough water to fill a medium-sized pan up to a depth of 5 cm. Add 1 tsp vinegar or a good pinch of salt (this is to keep the white from spreading), and bring it to the boil.

Break the egg into a saucer. When the water boils, lower the heat, and using a fork, stir it vigorously in one direction till you have a little whirlpool. Slip the egg from the saucer into the vortex of the whirlpool. (This also helps to prevent the white from spreading.) Cook on low heat till the water shows signs of boiling again (probably just a minute or so) then turn off the heat. Cover, and let it continue cooking on residual heat till it seems ready, with the white nicely set and the yolk just a bit wobbly. Total cooking time is 2-3 minutes, depending on the size of the egg. When the egg is ready, take it out carefully with a slotted spoon, draining off the water as you do so.

The best way to eat a poached egg is on hot buttered toast— a breakfast fit for the gods.

To make a more substantial dish, serve poached eggs on a bed of mashed potatoes or puréed spinach. You could even make a purée of leftover spinach and use a couple of poached eggs to stretch it.

Or you could go to town like the Parsis, who are great eaters of eggs, and have an interesting technique of cooking eggs on a bed of pre-cooked vegetables, or even mince.

BHAJI PER EEDA
Eggs on Leafy Greens

Ingredients for 3-4 servings:

½ kg cholai *or* spinach
2 medium onions
3 green chillies
2 medium tomatoes
A medium bunch fresh coriander leaves

1 tbsp bland oil
1 tsp ginger-garlic paste
½ tsp turmeric powder
1 tsp salt
6-8 eggs

Preparation: Prepare the cholai or spinach as described on p. 109, and chop. Slice the onions. Wash the green chillies and chop fine. Wash and chop the tomatoes and the coriander leaves.

Method: Heat the oil in a large frying pan and stir-fry the onions till light brown. Add the chillies, ginger-garlic paste and turmeric and fry for a minute till the oil separates. Stir in the tomatoes, coriander leaves and half the salt. Simmer on low heat for a few minutes till the tomatoes give up their juice.

Mix in the cholai or spinach, and cook covered on low heat till tender. If the mixture seems very moist, raise the heat and cook stirring for a few minutes till it dries.

Spread the mixture evenly in the pan, make depressions in it, break the eggs one by one into a saucer and slide them into the depressions. Sprinkle lightly with the remaining salt. Cover the pan with an inverted lid and pour boiling water into the lid. Cook on low heat till the eggs are set, about 20 minutes.

Serve with plain bread, toast or chapatti.

Variations: **Keema per Eeda (Eggs on Mince)**—Instead of the green vegetable use 250 gms mince. Add to the browned onions, along with 2 tsp cummin powder, and stir-fry till well browned. Add the remaining ingredients as above, plus 2 tbsp malt vinegar and 1 tsp sugar, and simmer, stirring occasionally, adding a little water if necessary, till mince is done, about 20 minutes. Add the eggs and continue as above.

- **Tamatar per Eeda (Eggs on Tomatoes)**—Same idea, only instead of green vegetables or mince, increase the amount of tomatoes to 1 kg for your 6-8 eggs. Simmer the tomatoes till thick, about 30 minutes or more, and before adding the eggs stir in 1-2 tbsp malt vinegar and ½ tsp sugar.

- You can cook eggs like this over almost any vegetable, as long as the consistency is such as to provide an even base for them.

OMELETTE

Ingredients for 1 serving:

2 eggs
¼ tsp salt
¼ tsp black pepper powder
1 tbsp milk *or* cream, *optional*
1-2 tsp bland oil

Method: Break the eggs into a bowl, add salt, pepper and milk or cream, if used (it lightens the texture). Beat together till yolks and whites are more or less homogenised.

Heat the oil in a medium to large frying pan, and swirl the pan to coat the base and sides. It should be good and hot, though not actually smoking. Drop in a few drops of the egg mixture to test. If it sizzles and sets immediately, you're probably OK.

Keeping the heat high, pour the egg mixture into the pan, when the underside will set immediately on contact with the hot metal. With a thin spatula, lift the sides, tilting the pan so that the liquid on top dribbles down to set in its turn. When there is no more loose liquid left to flow (though the topside is still a bit wet and uncooked), turn the heat down and use the spatula to fold the omelette in half. The inside cooks in its own heat.

> *In dishes where the eggs are broken and beaten together (e.g. omelette, scrambled eggs, or caramel custard), you must take precautions in case there is a rotten egg hiding among the good ones which may contaminate the whole lot. Break each egg separately into a cup or saucer, and don't incorporate it with the rest until you've ascertained that it's OK. It takes only a glance to be sure—but remember the golden rule: if in doubt, chuck it out.*

For those who like it lightly cooked and still slightly juicy inside, lift it out of the frying pan and onto a plate immediately.

For anyone who likes it dry throughout, leave it in the pan for a further 15 seconds or so before removing.

The whole process, from pouring the beaten eggs into the pan to removing the omelette, shouldn't take more than 1 minute.

Serve immediately—it gets leathery if kept waiting.

Variation: **Omelette aux Fines Herbes (Omelette with Herbs)**—Stir chopped herbs into the beaten egg. Try coriander, mint, basil, dill, even curry leaves. Parsley, if available, is ideal.

STUFFED OMELETTE

Prepare your stuffing first, and then cook the omelette as given above. Before folding the omelette, put 1 tbsp of stuffing down the centre. If this is cold, leave the folded omelette on low heat for a minute or so before serving.

Suggested Stuffings:

Mushrooms: chopped small, and fried for a couple of minutes on gentle heat in a little oil or butter with salt and pepper to taste.

Chicken liver: chopped small, and fried for 5 minutes on gentle heat in a little oil or butter with salt and pepper to taste.

Tomato masala: tomatoes cooked in a little oil with onion and/or garlic and/or green herbs and possibly ½ tsp cummin seeds. Cook till mushy.

Leftover chicken, meat or vegetables: strip the meat off chicken pieces, chop the meat from a raan or pot roast or throw in any leftover vegetable or mince.

SWEET OMELETTE

Eggs are neutral in taste, and become savoury or sweet according to what you add to them. Substitute 1-2 tsp powdered sugar in place of the salt and pepper in the omelette mixture. Spread 1-2 tbsp of warmed jam, marmalade or honey, or some fresh or tinned fruit, medium-diced before folding. Sprinkle a little sugar over the top when serving.

SOUFFLÉ OMELETTE

Put a little oil in the pan and heat it as for a regular omelette.

Separate the yolks and the whites of 2 eggs as described on p. 203. Season the yolks with salt and pepper and beat lightly.

Beat the whites till standing in soft peaks. If you beat them till the stiff-peak stage, your omelette will split when you fold it.

Combine the yolks with the whites, using a gentle 'folding' motion to minimise the leakage of air, till you have a delicately golden coloured froth. Pour this froth into the pan, and level off the top with a spatula. Cook on medium to low heat for about 5 minutes, till the underside is well set.

Fold the omelette in half, cook for 30 seconds more, and slide it out on to a hot plate. Serve immediately, or it will collapse and you might have saved yourself the bother of beating the whites.

Variation: You can stuff the soufflé omelette and you can also make a sweet soufflé omelette, as in the recipe above.

SPANISH OMELETTE

A more substantial version of the stuffed omelette and a useful method of using up small or leftover amounts of foodstuffs.

Heat a bit more oil than for a regular omelette (try 1 tbsp), and on medium heat fry up any combination of the following: onions, tomatoes, capsicum, potatoes, french beans, green peas, or leftover cooked vegetables, meat or chicken, all chopped or sliced as appropriate.

When all this is cooked, beat up your eggs in a bowl, as for a regular omelette, season with salt and pepper, and pour it over the vegetables in the pan. Stir well to mix, and cook on low heat till the eggs are set, about 10-15 minutes, depending on the number of eggs.

To brown the top of the omelette, slide a knife or spatula around the edges to detach it from the pan. Take the pan off the heat and cover with a large plate or flat lid, lubricated with ½ tsp bland oil. Quickly invert the pan so that the omelette drops out on to the plate. Now slide it back into the pan so that the base is on top, and cook for another minute or two.

Fold in half if you can, otherwise just slide the whole thing out onto a dish.

As a rough guide to quantities, 4-5 eggs and enough vegetables, etc to cover the base of a 20-cm frying pan will make a substantial meal for 2 hungry people.

EGGAH

The West Asian variant of the omelette is even more substantial than the Spanish omelette; it is almost like a cake, in which the eggs serve more as a binding for the other elements than as the principal ingredient. It's actually served cut into wedges like a cake.

Eggah can be eaten cold as well as hot, which increases its usefulness as an all-purpose dish. Cut into small pieces, it becomes finger food or an hors d'oeuvre. Medium slices are ideal for a picnic or a packed lunch at the office. Hot or cold, it can be an attractive and unusual main dish for a party, served perhaps with curd and a variety of salads.

AUBERGINE EGGAH

West Asian Omelette with Aubergines

Ingredients for 4-6 servings:

6 eggs
1 tsp salt
1 tsp black pepper powder
250 gms aubergines
1 medium onion
2 cloves garlic
2 small tomatoes
2 tbsp oil *or* butter

Garnish:
8-10 sprigs fresh coriander leaves *or* parsley

Preparation: Beat the eggs and stir in the salt and pepper. Wash the aubergines, and cube them evenly (the long thin ones can be sliced into rounds). Chop the onion fine. Crush the garlic. Wash and chop the tomatoes and coriander or parsley.

Method: Heat the oil or butter in a large heavy frying pan, and fry the onion and garlic on medium heat till the onion is soft and just turning golden.

Add the aubergines and stir-fry till soft and lightly coloured. Stir in the tomatoes and cook till soft and disintegrated. Take the pan off the heat and let it cool a bit.

Add the egg mixture and stir gently together till well mixed. Return to the heat, cover and cook over the lowest possible heat till the eggs are set, about 15 minutes.

Turn it over by inverting it onto a plate and sliding it back into the pan, as described for Spanish Omelette (see p. 213). Cook for a further 5 minutes.

Eggah can also be cooked in the oven. Preheat the oven to 160°C. Pour the egg and vegetable mixture into a well-greased ovenproof dish, cover and cook for 45-60 minutes, till done. Remove the lid after 30 minutes to allow the top to brown.

Turn it out carefully onto a plate, garnish with the parsley or coriander and serve as a main dish with salads and curd.

Variations: **Bread and Courgette Eggah**—Substitute sliced courgette (you can use toori) for the aubergines, and to the egg mixture add 3 slices of white bread, crusts removed, soaked in a little milk, then squeezed dry and crumbled.

- **Spinach Eggah**—Substitute ½ kg spinach, prepared as described on p. 109, for the aubergines. Stew in a little oil in a kadhai with 1 clove crushed garlic till cooked. Dry it as much as possible over high heat, stirring all the time, and drain off any surplus liquid. Allow to cool a bit, and blend with the egg, to which you have added ½ tsp grated nutmeg.

- **Meat Eggah**—Substitute ½ kg mince for the aubergines. Fry a large finely chopped onion in 1-2 tbsp oil till golden, add the mince, and stir-fry over high heat till it dries and browns. Stir in 1 tsp cummin powder, and ½ tsp garam masala powder and remove from the heat. Strain off any surplus fat through a strainer. Add the mince to the egg mixture together with a peeled and grated potato (optional).

SCRAMBLED EGGS

When you cook beaten eggs on high heat, they solidify into omelette or bhujia. If you put them on gentle heat, they become soft and creamy; it is this property that is the basis of scrambled eggs. But there's a catch. If having heated them gradually you let them become too hot, they curdle into a semi-solid mass and a whey-like liquid, which isn't, as far as we know, good for anything. This happens way below boiling point, so you have to take care.

Ingredients for 2 servings:

4 eggs
½ cup milk *or* cream
½ tsp salt
½ tsp black pepper powder
½ tbsp bland oil

Preparation: Break the eggs into a bowl, add milk or cream, salt and pepper, and beat lightly till yolk and white are more or less homogenised.

Method: Use an ordinary pan or kadhai, but not too large. The egg should fill it to a depth of at least 3 cm. Put the oil into the pan. There should be just enough oil to lubricate the pan and prevent the egg sticking. Swirl it around to coat the base and sides.

Heat to medium, turn the heat to low and pour in the eggs. They will solidify slightly on contact with the warm base of the pan. Stir and scrape well to detach the solidified matter and permit the liquid to come in contact with the base. Keep stirring; if you don't, the solid part at the base will burn. It may seem a bit slow, but in a few minutes most of the liquid will have coagulated into a semi-homogenous creamy mass. When it seems still just a little more liquid than you'd want to eat it, turn off the heat, cover the pan and leave it for about 2 minutes. The cooking will be completed on residual heat and the eggs should be just the right texture—creamy and delectable.

Cold scrambled egg makes very successful sandwiches. It also combines well with cooked prawns or shrimps for party canapés.

Pile the eggs on hot buttered toast and serve immediately.

Variations: Add some chopped herbs as in Omelette aux Fines Herbes (see p. 211) to your beaten eggs.

- Use a bit more oil, and soften some onion, then add tomato and/or mushroom and cook till soft; only be sure that the pan isn't very hot when you pour in the beaten eggs.

- In a version of scrambled eggs popular in west Asia, crush a couple of cloves of garlic and fry slowly in rather more oil or butter than suggested above, till just golden. Pour in the eggs and cook as above, with 1 tbsp of vinegar for every 2 eggs, added as they begin to thicken.

- For Parsi-style scrambled eggs, known as **Akoori,** fry 2 medium onions, sliced, in 1 tbsp oil till just golden. Add 3 cloves garlic, and a minute later 2 green chillies, 1 medium tomato and 8-10 sprigs fresh coriander leaves, all chopped fairly small. Stir together over medium heat for 1 minute and pour in the beaten eggs. Cook on low heat stirring all the time as given for scrambled eggs. Serve them with toast or chapatti, or as a snack on salted biscuits.

PIPERADE
Scrambled Eggs with Tomato and Capsicum

Another, particularly delicious, variation on the scrambled egg theme.

Ingredients for 2-3 servings:

6 eggs
½ tsp salt
½ tsp black pepper powder
2 medium onions
3 medium capsicums
3 medium tomatoes
1 tbsp bland oil

Preparation: Break the eggs into a bowl and beat lightly to blend the yolks and the whites. Stir in the salt and pepper.

Slice the onions fine. Wash, de-seed and slice the capsicums into thin strips. Wash the tomatoes and chop fine.

Method: Heat the oil till medium-hot in a pan or kadhai, add the onions, cover and cook over low to medium heat till soft, wilted and translucent, but not brown. Add the capsicums and tomatoes, cover and continue to cook on low heat till the capsicums are soft and the tomatoes disintegrated and mushy. Raise the heat and stir till the mixture has dried up a bit.

Pour in the eggs, and cook on low heat stirring all the time as given for scrambled eggs.

Serve immediately with hot buttered toast, or even better, garlic bread.

EGG BHUJIA

The Indian way of cooking beaten eggs.

Ingredients for 3-5 servings:

6-8 eggs	½ tsp salt
1 tsp cummin powder *and/* *or* 1 tsp coriander powder	2 green chillies
	1 tbsp bland oil

Preparation: Beat the eggs as for omelette. Season with the spice powders and salt. Wash the green chillies, chop and stir into the eggs.

Method: Heat the oil in a frying pan till hot but not quite smoking. Pour the eggs into the pan and cook on high heat, stirring constantly. The constant stirring breaks up the egg. Cook till the egg has solidified and is beginning to brown.

Serve with chapatti or paratha, or toast and butter.

Variation: To make a more interesting dish, slice a medium onion and soften it in the oil by frying it on medium heat till pale gold. Add a couple of chopped, medium tomatoes, and 8-10 sprigs of green coriander. Raise the heat and cook stirring for 2-3 minutes till the tomatoes are soft and mushy and beginning to dry up. Add the seasoned eggs and proceed as above.

INSTANT EGG CURRY WITH TOMATO

A simple-minded dish, which can be assembled in 15 minutes; useful in an emergency.

Ingredients for 4-6 servings:

6-8 eggs
1 tbsp bland oil
1 tsp ginger-garlic paste
10-12 cloves
200 gms/1 tetra pack tomato purée
2 black cardamoms
1 tsp coriander powder
1 tsp cummin powder
½ tsp black pepper powder
½ tsp salt
½ tsp + ½ tsp garam masala powder

Garnish:
10-12 sprigs fresh coriander leaves

Preparation: Hard-boil the eggs as given on p. 204. Peel and cut in half lengthwise. Wash the coriander leaves and chop coarsely.

Method: Heat the oil in a medium-sized frying pan or kadhai. Add the ginger-garlic paste and stir-fry over medium heat for a couple of minutes.

Stir in all the other ingredients except the eggs, garnish and ½ tsp garam masala. Add ½ cup water, bring to the boil and simmer over low heat, stirring occasionally, till the gravy reduces to a consistency a little thicker than that of the unprocessed tomato purée.

Remove the black cardamoms and decant the gravy into a shallow serving dish. Put in the eggs, yolk side up and sprinkle the remaining ½ tsp garam masala over them.

Garnish with the chopped coriander leaves.

Variation: Substitute for the tomato purée 3 large onions sliced fine, and cooked to a pulp in the pressure cooker (see p. 28), with 2 tsp tamarind pulp, thinned with a little water.

14

Salads, Raitas and Relishes

All sorts of vegetables can be cut up and mixed, uncooked, with herbs, lime juice and a just a hint of chopped onion (or more; but the flavour of raw onion in more than minuscule quantities tends to linger on the breath), to make a **salad** that gives freshness to any meal in any cuisine.

For Indian food, the most basic salad is **kachumbar,** a combination of **tomato, cucumber** and **onion,** with the possible addition of some whole or chopped **green chillies.** Wash, peel if necessary, chop or slice all the ingredients, mix them together or arrange artistically; sprinkle over a little salt and a squeeze of lime juice. Chill and serve.

To crisp onion and take away some of its pungent 'onioniness', cut in paper-thin rings, put into a small bowl with cold water and a cube or two of ice, cover and leave in the fridge for half an hour. Drain and pat the onion dry with kitchen paper or a clean cloth, scatter on top of your sliced cucumber and tomato.

A nice substitute for cucumber at the beginning of summer, is **kakdi.** It doesn't need peeling. Just wash and cut into rounds. Kakdi goes surprisingly well with **dill**, during the short period when their seasons overlap. Cut the kakdi and chop the dill, mix together, and add salt and a squeeze of lime juice.

Another good variation on the salad theme is **capsicum.** Goes well with cucumber or kakdi as well as with tomato. All of these make good **raitas**, too.

KHEERA KA RAITA

Ingredients for 4-5 servings:

2 cups creamy curd	1 medium cucumber
½ small onion	¼ tsp salt
3-4 sprigs mint, *optional*	¼ tsp red chilli powder

Preparation: Beat the curd till smooth and blended. Chop the onion as fine as possible. Wash the mint, if used, strip the leaves from the stalks and chop them. Wash and peel the cucumber, cut lengthwise into quarters, cut out and discard the seeds and dice.

Method: Add the onion, mint, if used, and salt to the curd and stir well. Gently fold in the cucumber.

Turn into a serving bowl and chill. Sprinkle with chilli powder and serve.

Variations: Substitute chopped tomato or diced boiled potato for the cucumber.

- Substitute coriander leaves for the mint.
- Omit the herb; instead add one medium capsicum, chopped.
- Omit the chopped onion.

AKHROT KA RAITA

A speciality of Kashmir, where they use green walnuts.

Ingredients for 4-5 servings:

2 cups creamy curd
½ tsp salt
A small bunch fresh coriander leaves
1 spring onion *or* ½ small onion
1 green chilli
¾ cup shelled walnuts

Preparation: Beat the curd with salt till smooth and blended. Wash and chop the coriander leaves and spring onion or onion fine. Wash, de-seed and chop the green chilli. Chop the walnuts fairly small.

Method: Stir all the ingredients except walnuts into the curd. Fold in the walnuts, chill and serve.

ALOO KA RAITA

Ingredients for 4-5 servings:

1½ cups creamy curd
2-3 medium potatoes
1 tbsp bland oil
1 tsp cummin seeds
½ tsp salt
½ tsp black pepper powder
½ tsp red chilli powder

Garnish:
8-10 sprigs fresh coriander leaves

Preparation: Beat the curd till smooth and blended. Wash the potatoes, boil, peel and cut them into medium dice. Wash and chop the coriander leaves.

Method: Heat the oil and fry the cummin seeds, letting them sizzle for 3-4 seconds. Add the potatoes, salt, pepper and chilli powder. Stir together for 4-5 minutes.

Remove from the heat and allow to cool for a few minutes, then add to the curd. Stir lightly to mix.

Garnish with the coriander leaves and serve at room temperature.

CARROT SALAD

Ingredients for 4-5 servings:

3-4 medium carrots
½ tsp salt
½ lime

1 tbsp bland oil
1 tsp mustard seeds

Preparation: Wash and scrape the carrots. Grate coarsely and toss in a bowl with salt. Squeeze out the juice from the lime, 1-2 tsp.

Method: Heat the oil in a small kadhai or frying pan, add the mustard seeds and cover till the spluttering subsides. Pour over the carrots.

Sprinkle in the lime juice and toss all together. Serve at room temperature.

Variation: Make it a raita by stirring 1 cup creamy curd, beaten till smooth, into the salted carrot. Baghar with mustard seeds as above, and omit the lime juice.

CUCUMBER AND MOONG DAL SALAD

Ingredients for 4-5 servings:

½ cup husked moong dal
2 small cucumbers
A small bunch fresh coriander leaves
3-4 limes

A small sprig curry leaves
½ tsp salt
½ tbsp bland oil
1 whole dried red chilli
½ tsp mustard seeds

Preparation: Pick through the moong, wash in several changes of water, and soak for several hours (in the fridge during the summer or monsoon seasons). Rinse well and drain before using. Peel the cucumbers, cut lengthwise into quarters, cut out and discard the seeds, and cut into medium dice. Wash the coriander leaves and chop fine. Wash and halve the limes and squeeze out the juice, about ¼ cup. Wash the curry leaves and strip them off the stem.

Method: Put the moong, cucumber, coriander leaves, lime juice and salt into a bowl and toss together to mix.

Heat the oil in a small kadhai or frying pan. Put in the red chilli and fry on high heat till black and plump. Lower the heat, add the mustard seeds and cover till the spluttering subsides. Add the curry leaves. Turn the baghar out immediately into the salad, and stir in.

Serve at room temperature.

PALAK RAITA

Ingredients for 4-5 servings:

½ kg spinach
1 medium onion
2-3 green chillies
1 dried red chilli
1 cup curd
8-10 fresh curry leaves
1 tbsp oil
1 tsp cummin seeds
1 tsp husked urad dal
½ tsp salt

Preparation: Pick through, wash, drain and chop the spinach as given on p. 109. Chop the onion fine. Wash the green chillies and chop fine. Break the red chilli into 2-3 pieces. Beat the curd till smooth and blended. Wash the curry leaves and strip them off the stem.

Method: Heat the oil, burning it if using mustard oil. Throw in the red chilli and fry till it turns black. Add the cummin seeds and urad dal. As soon as the dal turns reddish, put in the onion and green chillies, and stir-fry till the onion turns golden.

Lower the heat, add the curry leaves and put in the spinach, which will immediately start to wilt and reduce in bulk as it releases its moisture. Stir, cover and cook on low heat till the spinach is tender.

Sprinkle in the salt, turn up the heat and cook stirring till the excess water evaporates. Let it cool, then stir in the curd.

Serve chilled or at room temperature.

Variations: Omit the curd, double the quantities of the other ingredients, and cook this as a vegetable dish rather than a raita. Alternatively, you could use any of the recipes for spinach given in the vegetable chapter, and mix with the curd for a slightly different raita.

- **A simpler raita**—Cook ½ kg spinach in a chaunk of 1 medium onion and 2 cloves garlic, chopped fine. Stir in 1 cup curd, beaten till smooth, and give it a baghar of ½ tsp mustard seeds and ¼ tsp asafoetida powder in 1 tbsp oil.

ALOO KA BHARTA

Ingredients for 3-4 servings:

4-5 medium potatoes
1 small onion
A small bunch fresh coriander leaves
1-2 green chillies
1 tsp cummin powder
½ tsp salt
1-2 tbsp oil

Preparation: Peel and wash the potatoes and cut into chunks. Chop the onion as fine as possible. Wash and chop the coriander leaves. Wash the green chillies and chop as fine as possible.

Method: Boil the potatoes till good and soft. Mash with a potato masher or fork. Mix in all the other ingredients except the oil, then add enough oil to bind into a semi-sold mass.

Serve at room temperature with Khichdi (see p. 50), or use it for stuffing parathas.

Note: You can use unburnt mustard oil; its strong flavour is rather good in this dish.

Variation: Fry the onions in the oil till golden and add both oil and onions to the mashed potato with the remaining ingredients.

BAINGAN KA BHARTA, BIHARI-STYLE

The USP of this bharta is the finish with raw mustard oil.

Ingredients for 4-5 servings:

2 large round aubergines
1 small onion
2-3 green chillies
1 tsp cummin powder
½ tsp salt
1½-2 tbsp mustard oil

Garnish:
8-10 sprigs fresh coriander leaves

Preparation: Wash the aubergines. Chop the onion as fine as possible. Wash the green chillies and chop as fine as possible. Wash the coriander leaves and chop coarsely.

Method: Roast the aubergines over low heat, either over a direct flame, or preferably on the tava, over which you can invert a large pan. Keep turning them so that they cook evenly, and be sure that they are cooked through. It takes forever on the tava—over an hour for large aubergines. But needs little or no attention, except to turn them once in a while. If the skin burns and splits and some juice oozes out, it's no matter.

When the aubergines are good and soft, remove from the tava and place on a trivet over a plate, piercing the skin in 1-2 places to let the juice drain out.

Let them cool a bit, then peel them carefully and mash the pulp. Add the onion, green chillies, cummin powder, salt and mustard oil, and mix well together.

Garnish with the coriander leaves, and serve at room temperature.

Variation: You can make **Baingan ke Bharte ka Raita** to the same basic recipe, omitting the mustard oil and the garnish of coriander leaves. Beat 1½-2 cups thick curd and fold into the seasoned aubergine. Give it a baghar with 1 tbsp bland oil, 1 tsp mustard seeds and 10-12 curry leaves.

BAINGAN AUR DAHI

Ingredients for 4-5 servings:

½ kg aubergines
½ tsp red chilli powder
½ tsp turmeric powder
½ tsp+½ tsp salt
2 cups curd

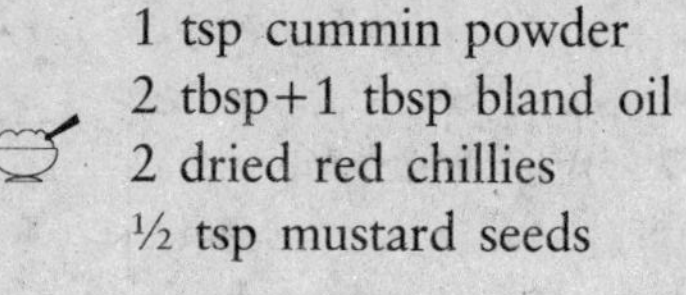

1 tsp cummin powder
2 tbsp+1 tbsp bland oil
2 dried red chillies
½ tsp mustard seeds

Preparation: Use whichever kind of aubergines you find convenient. Wash, and cut them into medium slices. Mix the chilli powder, turmeric and ½ tsp salt, and rub over both sides of the aubergine slices. Beat the curd, adding the cummin powder and ½ tsp salt, till smooth and blended.

Method: Fry the aubergines in 2 tbsp oil over medium heat till just turning brown. Add more oil if needed. As you take the slices out of the pan, place them on a plate lined with kitchen paper to blot up the excess oil. Put the curd mixture into a serving bowl, and carefully dunk the fried aubergine slices in it.

Heat 1 tbsp oil. Add the red chillies and fry till plump and black. Add the mustard seeds and cover till the spluttering subsides, then pour the mixture over the aubergines and curd.

HARA DHANIA KI CHUTNEY

Ingredients for ½ cup chutney:

A medium bunch fresh coriander leaves
1 green chilli
1-2 cloves garlic
½ lime
1 tsp cummin powder
½ tsp black pepper powder
¼ tsp salt

Preparation: Wash the coriander leaves thoroughly, discarding roots and coarse lower stems and any wilted or discoloured leaves. Wash the green chilli and chop roughly. Chop the garlic roughly. Wash the lime and squeeze out the juice, about 1 tsp.

Method: Put all the ingredients together in the electric blender and give them a whirl till thoroughly blended. Chill and serve.

DAHI AUR PUDINA KI CHUTNEY

Ingredients for 1 cup chutney:

A small bunch fresh mint leaves
½ cup creamy curd
½ tsp cumin powder
¼ tsp red chilli powder
½ tsp sugar
¼ tsp salt

Preparation: Wash the mint thoroughly, discarding any wilted or discoloured leaves, and strip the leaves off the stems.

Method: Put all the ingredients in the electric blender and give them a whirl till thoroughly blended. Chill before serving.

15

Desserts

Most reluctant cooks are probably content to settle for fruit to round off a good meal, or if they have a sweet tooth to make for the nearest sweet shop and buy rasgollas or gulab jamuns. Even these can be given a bit more zing with practically no effort at all. Offer **cream** to slurp over the **gulab jamuns**, or dissolve a few strands of **saffron** in a cup of warm milk and pour over the **rasgollas**.

Cream is a useful standby. Even the humble **banana** peeled and sliced into a bowl of cream acquires a certain class, and the addition of a spoonful of honey lifts it into the gourmet category. Try the same with **mangoes** if you get tired of having them plain, though the addition of honey would probably be superfluous. If you're really desperate, you can serve **tinned fruit**—pineapple, peaches, cherries or mixed—with cream.

When you buy **melon** or **papaya**, taste it ahead of serving. If you find that it falls far short in flavour of what its tempting exterior promised, you can improve the taste with lime juice and sugar.

Then there is a mixture of fresh fruits in a Fruit Salad, or lightly cooked fruit in a compote, or simply stewed fresh or dry fruit.

However, it may happen that once in a way you feel like going to town; so we also offer a selection of easy-to-do Western and Indian-style desserts.

For a start, you should know how to make **sugar syrup** and **caramel syrup**, both used in a variety of sweet dishes.

SUGAR SYRUP

Ingredients for ¾ cup syrup:

4 tbsp sugar
½ cup water

Optional ingredients:
1-2 limes
1-2 tbsp rum *or* brandy
1 tsp powdered cinnamon

Preparation: Wash and halve the limes, if used, and squeeze out the juice, 1-2 tbsp.

Method: Put the sugar and water into a small heavy-bottomed pan, and place on low heat stirring occasionally. If it seems to be about to boil and the sugar hasn't yet dissolved, take it off the heat for a while. When you're sure the sugar is well dissolved, bring it to the boil, taking care that it doesn't froth up and boil over, and simmer for 5 minutes. Cool and stir in the optional ingredients.

It's important that the sugar should have dissolved before the syrup comes to the boil, otherwise it tends to re-crystallise when it cools. This rule holds good for making jam or squash, or any other sugar-based item that is to be preserved.

CARAMEL SYRUP

Ingredients for ¾ cup syrup:

As for the previous recipe

Method: Put the sugar into a small heavy-bottomed pan. Place it on low heat and let the sugar melt and caramelise, using a pakad to shake the pan every now and then. It takes about 5 minutes—keep an eagle eye on it to be sure it doesn't burn.

When the sugar has melted and browned nicely, take it off the heat and let it cool for a few minutes, when the caramel will solidify. Add the water, return to the heat and bring it up to the boil on low heat, stirring occasionally till the caramel dissolves. Cool, and stir in the optional ingredients.

FRUIT SALAD

It takes time and care but, as the finale for a special party, the result is worth it.

Ingredients for 4-6 servings:

About 1½ kg selection of fruit, according to season
¾ cup sugar

Optional ingredients:
1-2 limes
2 tbsp brandy *or* rum
1 tsp powdered cinnamon

Preparation: Choose ripe but firm fruit. Pomegranates are available most of the year, and their seeds add an intriguing crunchiness, as well as dots of colour. Chickoo is a boring enough fruit by itself, but blends well with other fruits in a Fruit Salad. For preference use crisp apples, not very sweet—Golden Delicious are good.

Wash the limes, if used, and squeeze out the juice, 1-2 tbsp.

Make a plain or caramel syrup with the sugar and ½ cup water, and let it cool.

Wash, peel and cut the different fruits according to their nature, removing all seeds, pith, etc, and drop the pieces into the syrup.

Don't cut the fruit into very tiny pieces, as these will tend to go mushy. Bananas, for example, might be cut in rounds about 1 cm thick.

Cut fresh pineapple into bite-sized chunks, or cheat by using tinned pineapple (it's the only tinned fruit we'd recommend for this or any other purpose).

Peaches should be peeled by blanching them for 30 seconds in boiling water, and slipping off the skins.

If you use oranges, you really need to take the trouble to peel each individual segment.

Method: After assembling the fruit salad, toss gently together, taste for sweetness and flavour, and add as much of the optional ingredients as you think fit.

Chill for several hours and toss again gently before serving, to blend the juices. Serve with cream.

Note: It can be a very pretty dish, so choose fruits with contrasting colours. A mixture of bananas, apples and pears, for instance, would look very pallid and boring. Watermelon, however, should not be added, in spite of its gorgeous colour, as it gives off so much water that the whole salad would become watery.

APPLE COMPOTE

Ingredients for 4-6 servings:

1 kg crisp apples, preferably Golden Delicious
1 cup sugar

Optional ingredients:
1-2 limes
3-4 cloves
2 tbsp brandy *or* rum
1 tsp powdered cinnamon

Preparation: Make a sugar syrup with the sugar and ½ cup water (see p. 233).

Wash the apples, peel and cut into quarters lengthwise. Cut each quarter into 2-3 slices, and drop into the hot syrup immediately. Wash the limes, if used, and squeeze out the juice, 1-2 tbsp.

Method: Add the cloves, if used, to the apples in the syrup. Bring slowly to the boil and simmer for a couple of minutes. Cover the pan, remove from the heat, and allow to stand for about 15 minutes. The apples should be tender, but not mushy.

When it is cool, lift the apples out with a slotted spoon and place gently in a serving dish.

Bring the syrup back to the boil, and simmer for a few minutes if necessary to reduce. It should have a slightly thick, viscous consistency. Remove the cloves and add any or all of the optional ingredients. Let the syrup cool slightly and pour it over the apples. Chill before serving.

Variation: You can make **Pear Compote, Peach Compote, Apricot Compote** and **Guava Compote** in the same way. Apricots need not be peeled, and guavas need to have the seedy part removed.

STEWED APPLES OR PEARS

Even easier than compote, and some people like it better.

Ingredients for 2-3 servings:

½ kg apples *or* pears
Sugar to taste, depending on the tartness of the fruit
½-1 cup water
4-5 cloves *or* 3 cm cinnamon, *optional*

Preparation: The fruit should be of a tart, crisp variety. Peel, core and slice.

Method: Place the fruit in a pan with the sugar and water and optional spice. Bring slowly to the boil, and simmer till tender and slightly mushy.

Cool and chill. Serve with or without cream.

STEWED APRICOTS

Ingredients for 3-4 servings:

250 gms dried apricots

Sugar, *optional, depending on the sweetness of the apricots*

Preparation: Wash the apricots carefully to remove any grit, etc, that may be sticking to them. Put them in a pan with optional sugar and boiling water to cover. Leave to soak for 20-30 minutes.

Method: Bring apricots slowly to the boil. This may be enough to make them tender, otherwise simmer for a couple of minutes. Cool and chill.

Serve with or without cream.

FRUIT FOOL

Stewed or fresh fruit, puréed and combined with an approximately equal quantity of thick cream. Easy and delicious.

CHOCOLATE MOUSSE

Rich, heavy and delicious; and dead easy.

Ingredients for 4 servings:

100-125 gms dark chocolate
4 eggs
4 tsp sugar, *optional, if chocolate is not sweet enough*

Preparation: Break the chocolate into squares, put them in a mixing bowl with the sugar, if used, and set the bowl over a pan of simmering water. Stir occasionally with a wooden spoon till well melted. Separate the yolks and whites of the eggs as given on p. 203.

Method: Beat and stir the yolks one at a time into the melted chocolate, using a wooden spoon. Each yolk must be completely blended in before the next is added, otherwise the mousse will taste disagreeably eggy. The first yolk will turn the mixture stiffish, but as the rest go in it will loosen up and become glossy.

Beat the egg whites till they stands in stiff peaks, as given on p. 203. Add to the chocolate mixture, using a gentle folding motion to blend the 2 elements together without causing the egg whites to collapse. Quickly spoon the mousse into a serving dish and put in the fridge to set, which may take 1-2 hours.

Serve with cream.

Note: Don't make less than the amount suggested.

BANANA FLAMBÉ

A spectacular finale to a festive dinner; quite easy to do.

Ingredients for 4 servings:

2 limes
30-40 gms butter
2-3 tbsp sugar

4 bananas
2 tbsp brandy *or* rum

Preparation: Wash the limes and squeeze out the juice, about 2 tbsp.

Method: Use a shallow fireproof serving dish if you have such a thing, otherwise a frying pan. Into this put the lime juice, butter and sugar and cook, stirring often, over low heat till the sugar begins to caramelise and turn colour. It should be no more than golden, and the mixture should still be fairly runny.

Peel the bananas and cut in half across, then slit each piece down the middle. Add to the dish, spooning the syrup over them till well coated and cook till slightly softened, about 1 minute each side. (You could do it in advance to this point, and 5 minutes before it's to be served, nip out to the kitchen and put it on low heat to reheat.)

Switch off most of the lights in the dining area, or get a collaborator to do it for you. Sprinkle the brandy or rum over the hot bananas, and immediately put a match to it. It will burn with a flickering blue flame for approximately 30 seconds. Quickly pick up the dish and carry it to the table, and graciously accept the applause of your admiring guests.

Serve with cream.

Note for non-drinkers: It's the alcohol that burns, so the residue of brandy or rum, left when the flame dies down, is completely non-alcoholic.

Variation: Non-drinkers who don't believe the last statement, or who don't keep brandy or rum in their kitchen cabinet, can substitute apricot jam for the liquor. Cook the bananas as above with butter, sugar and lime juice in a large frying pan. To serve, lift out of the pan into a shallow serving dish. Put 1-2 tbsp apricot jam into the pan, and stir over low heat for a minute or so, till well blended. Pour the jam sauce over the bananas and serve.

BLANCMANGE

Sweetened flavoured milk, thickened with cornflour. Simple-minded and dead easy, a strangely comforting nursery-style dessert.

Ingredients for 4-5 servings:

½ litre milk	2 limes
1 tbsp cornflour	2 tbsp sugar

Preparation: Put the cornflour into a cup or small bowl, add a little milk and stir till you have a smooth cream of pouring consistency. Wash the limes and squeeze out the juice, about 2 tbsp.

Method: Bring the rest of the milk carefully to the boil. Remove from the heat, and slowly pour in the cornflour mixture, stirring all the time. It will start thickening immediately.

Return to the heat and bring slowly back to the boil, stirring all the time. When it boils, take it off the heat and stir in the sugar. Let it cool, stirring every now and then to prevent the formation of a skin. As it cools, it will thicken further.

When it is cool, stir in the lime juice. Decant it into a serving dish, and put into the fridge to chill.

Note: The quantity of cornflour given in the recipe will give you a fairly solid blancmange. If you want a lighter consistency, reduce the amount.

Variations: **Coffee Blancmange**—Omit the lime juice and substitute 1-2 tsp instant coffee powder, stirred in after you remove the thickened milk from the heat.

- **Chocolate Blancmange**—Omit the lime juice and substitute 30 gms or so of dark chocolate, grated and dissolved in the milk as it comes to the boil; or alternatively 2 tsp cocoa powder worked to a paste with a little milk or water, stirred into the milk as it comes to the boil.

- **Butterscotch Pudding**—Start by making caramel as given for caramel syrup on p. 234. When the sugar has browned well, pour in the milk. The addition of cold liquid will turn the caramel hard, but it will soften and dissolve as you heat it, stirring occasionally, over medium heat. Bring up to the boil and continue as above.

CARAMEL CUSTARD

Ingredients for 4-6 servings:

4 tbsp sugar or to taste
3 eggs
2½ cups milk, preferably full-cream

Method: Put half the sugar in a small heavy-bottomed pan without handles. Place it on low heat and let the sugar melt and caramelise, using a pakad to shake the pan every now and then, about 5 minutes. Keep an eagle eye on it to be sure it doesn't burn.

When the sugar has melted and browned nicely, take the pan off the heat and, holding it carefully with the pakad, tilt it all ways to coat the inside with caramel. Carry on tilting it till the caramel cools and turns viscous and refuses to run any more. Stand it upside down on a plate, and let it cool for a few minutes. It is now a caramelised mould.

Crack the eggs into a bowl, and beat them up with the rest of the sugar. Heat the milk almost to boiling, and pour slowly on to the sugar-and-yolk mixture, beating all the time.

Pour the custard into the caramelised mould, cover it tightly, and place on a trivet either in the pressure cooker, or in another large pan. Cook under pressure for 15 minutes, or steam in the pan with water coming halfway up the sides of the mould for 30 minutes. Don't worry if it still seems a bit wobbly, it'll firm up as it cools.

Let it cool, then chill. To turn it out, cover the open top of the mould with the serving dish, and quickly turn it over so that the mould is bottom-up. The custard should drop into the dish with a satisfying plop, and you then lift the mould off gently.

MISHTI DOI

An integral part of Bengali culture. Best made with date palm jaggery, but other sweeteners can be substituted.

Ingredients for 3-4 servings:

1 litre full-cream milk
200 gms date palm jaggery

2 tsp curd as starter

Method: Boil the milk carefully, and simmer till reduced to between ½ and ⅔ of its volume. Crumble the jaggery and add to the milk, stirring till it dissolves. When the milk has cooled sufficiently, use the starter to make curd as given on p. 21, setting it in the dish in which it is to be served.

> *Don't on any account try to make Mishti Doi (or any other milk-based dish) using ordinary jaggery. The milk will split (curdle) immediately.*

Note: Sweetened milk doesn't set so readily as plain milk. You should have it on the hot side, so that when the starter has been mixed in and the curd put to set you can barely keep your finger in it for the standard count of 10.

Variation: Date palm jaggery may not be readily available all year round, all over the country. You can substitute sugar, preferably brown sugar; or you can caramelise the milk. Make caramel as given for caramel syrup (see p. 234), and let it cool a bit. Instead of adding water; pour in the hot boiled-down milk. (Take care, if you add the milk to hot caramel it will boil up with alarming violence.) Return to low heat and simmer for a few minutes till the caramel is well dissolved. Either way, cool the milk and proceed as above.

BHAPA DOI

Another Bengali classic.

Ingredients for 4-6 servings:

2½ cups creamy curd | 1 tin/400 gms sweetened condensed milk

Preparation: Beat the curd till smooth and blended. Add the condensed milk, stirring and folding to blend well with the curd, and pour into a heatproof serving bowl. Cover the bowl tightly.

Method: Put about 3 cm of water in the pressure cooker, or quarter-fill a large pan with water, and place the bowl with the curd mixture on a trivet in the water. If in the pressure cooker, cook under pressure for 10 minutes, otherwise bring the water to the boil and steam for 20-30 minutes. To test, pierce with a knife. It should come out clean.

Let it cool, and put it in the fridge to chill.

Variation: Lal Dahi—exactly the same recipe, but cook in the oven preheated to 150° C for 20-30 minutes.

KHEER

Ingredients for 4-5 servings:

½ cup basmati rice
4 green cardamoms *or* 8-10 strands saffron
1 litre full-cream milk
4 tbsp sugar
1 tbsp sultanas
1 tsp rose-water *or* kewra-water, *optional*

Decoration:
12 almonds, *optional*

Preparation: Wash and soak the rice in water for at least 30 minutes. Crush the cardamoms in a small mortar if you have one, or use a rolling pin. Discard the skins, and crush the seeds to a coarse powder. Alternatively, soak the saffron in ¼ cup warm milk. Blanch and peel the almonds. Cut them lengthwise into thin slivers.

Method: Bring the milk carefully to the boil in a heavy-bottomed pan, adding the soaked saffron, if used. Let it simmer, taking care not to let it boil over, till reduced to about ⅔ its original volume.

Add the rice and continue to simmer, stirring occasionally, till it is good and soft, and the milk has thickened slightly. Add the sugar and stir till dissolved. Stir in the cardamoms, if used, and sultanas.

Decant the kheer into a serving dish. It will thicken further as it cools. Put the dish into the fridge, and sprinkle on the almonds and rose-water or kewra-water, if used, before serving.

Variation: **Phirni** is kheer made with crushed rice. The same ingredients, except that cardamom isn't normally used. Soak and crush the rice according to the instructions on p. 38. To the rice powder, add ½ cup additional cold milk, a little at a time, till you have a thin runny paste. Gradually pour this into the reduced simmering milk, stirring all the time. Simmer, stirring often, till the phirni has thickened slightly, and the grains of rice powder have softened till they are barely perceptible. Carry on as above.

SEWAI KI PHIRNI

Ingredients for 4-6 servings:

1 litre full-cream milk
4 tbsp sugar
½ cup roasted vermicelli

8-10 strands saffron, *optional*

Decoration:
12 almonds, *optional*

Preparation: Soak the saffron, if used, in ¼ cup warm milk. Blanch and peel the almonds, if used, and cut lengthwise into thin slivers.

Method: Bring the milk carefully to the boil in a heavy-bottomed pan. Let it simmer, taking care not to let it boil over, till reduced to about ⅔ its original volume.

Add the sugar and stir till dissolved. Then add the vermicelli and cook for about 5 minutes on low heat, stirring all the time. Be careful to stir gently, so that the vermicelli doesn't disintegrate.

Stir in the saffron, if used, and decant into a serving dish. It will set as it cools. Put the dish into the fridge, and sprinkle on the almonds, if used, before serving.

SOOJI KA HALVA

Ingredients for 6-8 servings:

6 green cardamoms
4 tbsp almonds, cashew nuts *or* walnut kernels
8-10 strands saffron
2 tbsp sultanas

1 cup sugar
4 cups water, *or* 2 cups water+2 cups milk
1 cup+¼ cup ghee *or* bland oil
1½ cups semolina

Preparation: Crush the cardamoms in a small mortar if you have one, or use a rolling pin. Discard the skins and crush the seeds to a coarse powder. Blanch and peel the almonds, if used. Roughly chop the nuts of choice. Soak the saffron in 1 tbsp warm water.

Method: Make a syrup with the sugar and water as given on p. 233. If using milk, allow the syrup to cool and then stir in the milk.

Heat 1 cup ghee in a heavy frying pan or kadhai over medium to low heat, add the semolina and fry, stirring constantly, till it is golden, about 8-10 minutes. Add the syrup, cardamom seed powder, nuts, saffron and sultanas. Lower the heat, and cook, stirring constantly, till the mixture leaves the sides of the pan, about 5-10 minutes.

Stir in ¼ cup ghee and serve hot.

Note: It coagulates when cold, so if you have to reheat it, stir in 1-2 tbsp milk and mash with a fork to break up the lumps, before reheating on low heat.

MEETHA TUKRA

Just the thing for those with a sweet tooth. Rich and delicious and surprisingly easy.

Ingredients for 4-6 servings:

Syrup:
1 cup sugar
1½ cups water
A few drops kewra-water
8-10 strands saffron

Tukras:
6 slices white bread
3 tbsp bland oil
½ cup thin cream *or*
2 cups milk

Decoration:
2 sheets silver leaf *or*
4-5 almonds

Preparation: Cut the crusts off the bread, and cut each slice in half. Boil the milk, if used, and reduce it to ½ cup. Blanch and peel the almonds, if used, and cut lengthwise into fine slivers.

Method: Make the syrup with sugar and water as given on p. 233. Remove from the heat and stir in the kewra-water and saffron. Pour into a shallow dish and let it cool to lukewarm.

To make the tukras, heat the oil to medium hot and fry the slices of bread in batches depending on the size of your frying pan. Fry till golden; take care not to over-brown them. As they get ready, carefully lift them out of the pan with a slotted spoon, and place them in the syrup.

As each batch absorbs the syrup, lift it out and place on a flat fireproof platter. When all the bread slices are arranged on the platter, pour on any remaining syrup. Place the platter on very low heat, on top of the tava if necessary, and simmer till the syrup has nearly dried.

Pour the cream or milk over the bread and continue simmering till almost all the liquid has been absorbed. It should be barely moist. Remove from the heat and allow it to cool.

Decorate with the almonds or silver leaf.

Note: Meetha Tukra can be made a day in advance and kept in the fridge. Take the dish out well before serving, to let it reach room temperature. Sprinkle with an additional tbsp each of syrup and cream to refresh. Decorate and serve.

16

Beverages

MASALA CHAI

Ingredients for 2 cups:

1-2 tsp tea leaves
½ cup milk
Sugar to taste
2 cups water

Any of the following:
2-cm piece ginger
1-2 green cardamoms
¼ tsp fennel seeds

Preparation: Peel and wash the ginger. Gently bash the ginger or cardamoms to bruise.

Method: Put the water and optional ingredient in a pan and bring up to the boil. As it approaches the boil put in the tea leaves and milk. Bring back to the boil and when it boils remove it immediately from the heat and cover it. Leave it to infuse for 2-2½ minutes.

Put sugar to taste into the cups, stir the tea again. Strain into the cups and drink hot.

Note: The amount of tea leaves you use will vary according to their quality as well as the taste of the drinkers.

LASSI

Ingredients for 1 tall glass:

¾ cup curd
¾ cup water
1 tsp sugar
or ¼ tsp salt

Optional seasoning for salt lassi:
¼ tsp black pepper powder
or ½ tsp cummin powder

Method: Beat the curd till smooth and blended. Add the water together with the sugar, or salt and seasoning, and beat and stir to mix.

Chill and pour into the glass over ice cubes.

SATTUA PANI

Sattu is powdered roasted chana dal and is readily available in most grocery stores.

Ingredients for 1 tall glass:

½ lime
1½ tbsp sattu
¼ tsp red chilli powder
1½ cups water

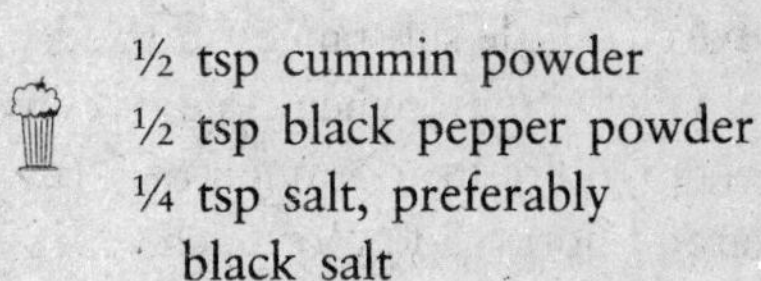

½ tsp cummin powder
½ tsp black pepper powder
¼ tsp salt, preferably black salt

Preparation: Squeeze out the juice from the lime, about ½ tbsp.

Method: Put all the ingredients into the blender and give it a whirl.

Chill and pour into the glass over ice cubes.

MILK SHAKE

Milk, sugar, fruit *and/or* flavourings

1 tsp sattu *or* pre-cooked oats per cup of milk, *optional*

Method: There is no hard-and-fast recipe. Put the milk, boiled and cooled if necessary, with sugar and fruit or flavourings to taste into a blender. Give it a whirl, taste, adjust the sugar and flavourings, whirl again, pour onto ice in a large mug or glass and drink.

Flavourings could be cocoa, instant coffee, jam or marmalade if good and tangy, or even lemon or lime juice, or a tbsp of Lime Squash. (It's only when they are heated together that lime juice curdles milk.)

Use bananas, peeled and cut in chunks, with a little lime juice if you like; or ripe mangoes, peeled and sliced. You won't get good value from very delicately flavoured fruits like papaya or melon, which is too watery anyhow. Apricots in season might be good, if you can be bothered to peel them.

You could even use some stewed fruit—apple or dried apricots—left over from the previous night's sweet dish, perhaps.

The optional sattu or oats, besides subtly changing the flavour, gives it a little substance, and adds to the virtues of this simple drink as a pick-me-up, when tired or convalescent; or even in the morning when you're in too much of a rush to have a proper breakfast. Be careful not to add too much, or it will make the drink stodgy. Sattu is better than oats, as it blends more smoothly. If using oats, try soaking them in the milk for 30 minutes before whirling in the blender.

JEERA PANI

Ingredients for 4-5 glasses:

2 tsp tamarind paste
5 cups water
1½ tsp salt
2 tsp cummin powder

½ tsp. red chilli powder
1 tsp garam masala powder
Sugar *or* jaggery
to taste

Preparation: Thin down the tamarind paste by working in a little water till it's thin enough to mix with the rest of the water.

Method: Combine all the ingredients. Stir well, check the seasoning and chill before serving.

LIME SQUASH

Ingredients to make ½ litre of concentrate:

1 cup lime juice
2 cups sugar

1 cup water

Preparation: You should get a cup of juice from 8-10 limes, depending on their quality. Wash and halve the limes and squeeze them first. Measure the juice and calculate the amount of the sugar and water according to the proportions given.

Method: Make a syrup with the sugar and water as described on p. 233. Bring it to the boil and simmer for a couple of minutes.

Allow the syrup to cool, pour the lime juice into it through a strainer, stir well, pour into a bottle and refrigerate.

Dilute with water as you would a commercial squash. It will keep for at least a couple of weeks in the fridge.

PANNA

Supposed to be the best possible preventive and remedy for heat stroke during the searing days of the north Indian summer, when the loo, the hot dry wind, threatens to dehydrate you completely.

Ingredients to make 4 tall glasses:

4 unripe mangoes, about ½ kg
1 cup sugar *or* to taste

½ tsp salt
½-1 tsp cummin powder *or* to taste

Method: Prepare a syrup with the sugar and water as given on p. 233. Bring up to the boil, simmer for a couple of minutes and cool.

Put the washed mangoes in a separator on the trivet in the pressure cooker, and cook under pressure for 5 minutes. When the pressure goes down, lift out the separator and let the mangoes cool.

Separate the pulp from the stones and the skin, and give it a whirl in the blender with the other ingredients.

Dilute to taste with chilled water, and serve poured over ice.

TANGARITA

Mix equal quantities of tomato juice and unsweetened orange juice in a jug. Add salt and pepper to taste, stir well and pour onto ice in glasses. Garnish with mint, basil, dill or coriander leaves, in that order of preference, washed and coarsely chopped, or not, as you like.

17

Videshi

Here is a small miscellaneous selection of simple recipes from Europe and west Asia, all of which have been successfully tried in an Indian kitchen. Several of them use **flour (refined flour/maida)**, to thicken a sauce, etc. This technique, though not used in most Indian cuisines, is basic to Western cookery. It's well worth learning, and not very difficult once you get the hang of it. However, in contrast to most of the Indian-style recipes, you have to be careful about quantities. Not necessarily to the last gram or millilitre; but you must stick more or less to the suggested proportions. If the proportions of oil, flour and liquid are not OK, the finished result will be too runny, or too oily, or too stodgy. If you do it often enough, naturally you'll develop an accurate judgment; but in the beginning you'll have to resign yourself to weighing and measuring.

The preferred oil for most Mediterranean dishes, especially salads, is olive oil, but this is prohibitively expensive. Use best quality bland oil, never mustard, coconut, sesame, etc, for all videshi dishes.

WHITE SAUCE

Ingredients for 2 cups:

1½ cups milk *or* stock
30-40 gms butter *or*
1½ tbsp bland oil
1 rounded tbsp flour

Salt, pepper *or* other seasoning/flavouring

Method: Heat the milk or stock till almost boiling.

Heat the butter or oil on medium heat for 1-2 minutes. It shouldn't be too hot. The butter, if that's what you're using, should be melted and sizzling gently, but nowhere near turning brown.

Lower the heat and stir the flour into the butter or oil. Using a wooden spoon, work it in till the two ingredients are well blended together into what is known as a **roux.** It should be the consistency of a rather dry paste. Cook, stirring all the time, for a couple of minutes to get rid of the raw flour taste.

Remove the pan from the heat and leave for a minute or two till it stops sizzling. Immediately pour in the hot liquid, and stir well, taking care to scrape up all the roux from the edges. It will start to thicken. Return the pan to medium heat, and bring up to the boil stirring all the time. Lower the heat, and stir the sauce for another minute or two.

Any flour-thickened sauce, soup, etc, continues to thicken even after it is cooked, and as it cools it thickens even more. So you're usually safe to add more rather than less liquid and make it a bit thinner than you want the finished product. However, you can thin it down at a later stage, if necessary, by stirring in more liquid as the sauce simmers, or thicken it by boiling it down over medium heat, stirring all the time to ensure that it doesn't stick and burn.

Made good and thick, this sauce is the basis of several elements in Western cuisine, like soufflés; and the same technique is used to thicken meat and chicken dishes and soups.

Actually, there is a short-cut method of making this sauce, which may not quite please the purist, but the result of which is all but indistinguishable from the classic method.

Half-fill a shaker or screw-top jar of about 500 ml capacity (a 500-gm **jam jar** is fine) with cold or warm (NOT hot) liquid. Add the flour to this liquid, close the jar firmly and shake vigorously using an up and down motion. The flour and the liquid should blend completely. Heat the rest of the liquid, along with the butter or oil. When the mixture boils, pour in the liquid-flour blend slowly, stirring all the time, and cook, still stirring, for a minute or two.

You can also use the jam jar method for thickening soups, stews, etc.

CABBAGE WITH NUTMEG

Although there's little truth in the myth that the British exist entirely on boiled food, it is nevertheless undeniable that British cuisine is less than inventive when it comes to dealing with vegetables. Boiled, and served as a side dish, they are often accompanied by a white sauce made from the water they were boiled in. This recipe is an unusual take on that principle. You could serve it with Meat Loaf, Irish Stew or Pot Roast.

Ingredients for 4-5 servings as a side dish:

1 small cabbage, about ½ kg
1 tbsp bland oil *or*
25 gms butter
1 tbsp flour
½-1 cup milk
1 nutmeg
½ tsp salt

Preparation: Prepare and cut the cabbage as given on p. 118. Grate the nutmeg.

Method: Heat 2 cups water in a pan, and when it boils, add the cabbage. Bring back to the boil on high heat, cover, lower the heat and simmer till the cabbage is al dente, not more than 5 minutes. Drain, using a strainer, reserving both cabbage and cooking water.

Make a white sauce as in the previous recipe, using the hot cabbage water. If too thick, thin it down with a little milk, as much as necessary to give a medium consistency—too thin is preferable to too thick—and cook stirring for a couple of minutes till it seems just right. Stir in the nutmeg and the salt.

You can cook in advance to this point. At the time of serving, reheat the sauce, stirring often so that that it doesn't stick, and fold in the cooked cabbage. Bring to the boil stirring all the time, and serve immediately.

CHICKEN FRICASSÉE

A bland and easy chicken dish, good at any time but particularly suitable for convalescents, or those getting over a stomach upset.

Ingredients for 4-5 servings:

1 chicken, jointed, about 1 kg	10 cm cinnamon
2 medium onions	1 tbsp bland oil
2 black cardamoms	1 level tbsp flour
4-5 cloves	½ tsp salt
	½ tsp black pepper powder

Preparation: Wash and drain the chicken, putting aside the liver. Slice the onions.

Method: Put the chicken in a pan or pressure cooker along with the whole spices and about 2 cups water. Bring up to the boil, and cook till the chicken is very tender, 1-2 minutes under pressure, 25-30 minutes without.

Using a slotted spoon take the chicken out of the stock and set aside. Strain the stock and reserve, discarding the spices. Degrease (see p. 65) if necessary. When the chicken has cooled a bit, take the meat off the bones.

Heat the oil in another pan and add the onions. Cover and cook on low heat till they are soft and translucent. Add the flour, and stir it in till it has blended thoroughly with the oil to form a roux. Fry stirring all the time on low heat for 1-2 minutes. Add the stock to make a sauce as given on p. 258. If it seems thicker that you'd like it, add some milk.

Add the chicken pieces, salt and pepper, bring back to the boil and cook for 1-2 minutes.

MEAT LOAF

Usually cooked in the oven, this easy and useful dish can also be steamed in the pressure cooker.

Ingredients for 3-4 servings:

Loaf mix:
- 2 slices white bread
- 1-2 onions
- 1 egg
- 1-2 tbsp milk
- ½ kg mince
- ½-1 tsp black pepper powder
- ½ tsp salt
- 1-2 tsp bland oil

Any or all of the following seasonings:
- 2 cloves garlic
- 1-2 meat stock cubes
- 1½ tbsp tomato purée or tomato sauce
- 2 tsp Worcestershire sauce
- 1 tsp mustard powder

Preparation: Cut the crusts off the slices of bread and discard. Chop the onions as fine as possible. Crush or chop the garlic, if used, as fine as possible. Crumble the stock cubes.

Method: Beat the egg in a large bowl, and crumble the 2 slices of bread over it. Mash, adding as little milk as necessary to achieve a pulpy consistency. Add all the other ingredients except the oil, and mix and knead till well blended. This is best done with your hands. The mixture will be moist, but should be stiff enough to hold its shape when moulded.

Using the oil, grease a large piece of aluminium foil. Turn the mince mixture out into the centre of this, and mould it into a loaf shape. Bring up the sides of the foil and fold down to make a parcel. Wrap the parcel in one more layer of foil.

Put the parcel in a separator of the pressure cooker, and place it on the trivet in the cooker. Put water in the pressure cooker to a depth of about 5 cm, close the cooker and cook under pressure for 40-45 minutes.

When the parcel is unwrapped, the meat loaf will look unattractively pallid and moist. To dry the surface, either place it on the trivet on the tava, covered with a large enough pan, and dry off over low heat for 15-20 minutes; or fry in hot oil in a large frying pan over high heat till all the surfaces are nicely browned, 5-10 minutes.

Serve hot or cold. Good for sandwiches and packed lunches.

Variation: If you do happen to have an oven, preheat it to 180°C. Pack the mince mixture into a greased loaf tin or rectangular fireproof dish, and cover with a lid or greased foil. Bake for 1-1½ hours, till the loaf starts to come away from the sides of the tin.

IRISH STEW

A classic of British cookery. Simple-minded it may be, with only three main ingredients, but these somehow combine into a supremely satisfying dish.

Ingredients for 5-6 servings:

½ kg meat, preferably chops
3-5 medium potatoes
1-2 large onions
1 tsp salt
½ tsp black pepper powder

Preparation: Wash and drain the meat. Peel, wash and slice the potatoes thick. Slice the onions medium-thick.

Method: Put all the ingredients into a pan with just enough water to cover. Cook over the lowest possible heat till the meat is tender and the potatoes have disintegrated, to thicken the gravy. It can also be cooked in the pressure cooker for 8-10 minutes, then simmered without pressure for another 15 minutes or so.

Variation: If you have an oven, use exactly the same ingredients to make **Lancashire Hot Pot.** Slice the onions and potatoes fine, and arrange the ingredients in layers in a greased ovenproof dish or casserole, sprinkling the salt and pepper between each layer and finishing with a layer of potatoes. No water. Cover the casserole and put it in the oven preheated to 150°C and leave it for at least 2 hours, longer won't hurt. Thirty minutes before the meal, raise the temperature to 180°C and remove the lid to brown the top layer of potatoes.

CRUMB-FRIED FISH

Ingredients for 2-3 servings:

½ kg fish fillet
½ cup crisp breadcrumbs
1-2 limes
1 egg

½ tsp salt
½ tsp pepper
2-3 tbsp bland oil

Preparation: Have the fishmonger cut the fish into pieces, which shouldn't be very thick—not much more than 1 cm. Wash it thoroughly and drain.

To prepare the breadcrumbs you need to have either rusks, which you can buy in any provision shop, or bread slices dried through in a slow oven, or in the sun covered with a thin muslin cloth. Put the broken rusks or dried bread into the grinder, and give it a whirl to reduce it to crumbs.

Cut the lime into quarters.

Method: Beat the egg in a shallow dish, along with the salt and pepper. Spread the breadcrumbs on a plate.

Put the oil in the frying pan over medium heat. Leave it for 3-4 minutes to heat.

Lay the fish pieces in the egg, first one side then the other, and then in the breadcrumbs to cover both sides.

Put the fish into the oil in a single layer, being careful not to overfill the pan. Cook over medium heat till the under surface is beginning to brown, probably 4-5 minutes, then turn and cook the other side till similarly ready.

Serve with quarters of lime to squeeze over the fish.

SPAGHETTI BOLOGNESE

A simplified version of the Italian classic.

Ingredients for 3-4 servings:

4 medium onions
8-10 cloves garlic *or*
1 tsp garlic paste
6 medium tomatoes
1 nutmeg
2 tbsp+1 tbsp bland oil
½ kg mince
1 tsp+2 tsp+¼ tsp salt
½ tsp black pepper powder
2 bay leaves
1 tbsp flour
400-500 gms pasta

To serve:
Grated Parmesan cheese, *optional*

Preparation: Slice the onions, crush the garlic cloves, if used, wash and roughly chop the tomatoes. Grate the nutmeg.

Method: Heat 2 tbsp oil in a heavy-bottomed pan. Add the mince, stir to break it up, and stir-fry on high heat till brown and dry. Stir in the onions and the garlic.

Lower the heat, cover the pan, and cook for a few minutes to let the onions sweat out their moisture and soften. Open the pan, raise the heat and cook, stirring constantly, till it dries up again and looks brown and smells savoury.

Lower the heat, add the tomatoes, nutmeg, 1 tsp salt, pepper, and bay leaves. Stir well, bring to the boil, cover and simmer till the tomatoes are cooked and blended, about 30 minutes. Stir occasionally to make sure it isn't sticking. Alternatively, cook under pressure for 8-10 minutes, and then without pressure on low heat for 5-10 minutes more, stirring occasionally.

Put 1 cup cold water into a jam jar or shaker to half-fill it, add the flour, close the lid firmly, and shake vigorously. Stir in the flour-and-water blend into the sauce, pouring it in slowly. Continue to stir till it comes back to the boil, and simmer for another 5 minutes stirring occasionally.

Meanwhile cook the pasta. Follow the directions on the packet, or use the following method:

Half-fill a jumbo-sized pan with water and 2 tsp salt. Bring to the boil, and then put in the pasta. Don't worry about the long thin variety, if that's what you're using, not fitting into the pan. As soon as one end goes into the water, it becomes pliable and can be manoeuvred in without difficulty. Bring back to the boil, but keep a careful eye on it, as the starch in the pasta makes it liable to froth up and boil over. Lower the heat and cook till al dente. When you think it's just about done, test it by taking out a piece and eating it. It should be tender but firm, with just a little bite to it.

Have a large colander ready in the sink and turn the pasta into this to drain. Give the colander a shake to get rid of excess water, and slip the pasta into a serving dish. Sprinkle over 1 tbsp oil, ¼ tsp salt and some more pepper, and get the dish to the table as quickly as possible, as pasta loses heat very fast.

Serve the pasta and sauce separately. Hand around the Parmesan cheese, if you like it, to be sprinkled on individual servings according to taste.

Note: There is quite a variety of pasta available in the provision shops of the metropolitan cities. Choose whichever you like, except lasagne. The Chinese-style egg noodles that may be available in even the smaller bazaars are perfectly acceptable, and much cheaper than imported pasta.

SPAGHETTI ALLA MARINARA

An almost instant pasta dish; working time not more than 10 minutes flat.

Ingredients for 3-4 servings:

4 medium tomatoes
6 cloves garlic
A small bunch mint, basil, dill, coriander *or* any other fresh herb
1 tbsp oil
½ tsp salt
½ tsp black pepper powder
400-500 gms pasta

Preparation: Wash the tomatoes and quarter, or chop roughly. Cut the garlic cloves in half if very large. Wash and coarsely chop the herb.

Method: Heat the oil in a kadhai or frying pan, and add the garlic. Fry for a minute or so on high heat till golden. Add the tomatoes, salt and pepper.

Lower the heat, cover and cook for about 5 minutes till the tomatoes are soft and giving up their juice, but still just holding their shape. Stir in the herb, and serve with pasta cooked as described in the recipe for Spaghetti Bolognese above.

JELLIED CHICKEN

A delicious and simple cold dish; ideal for a lunch party on a summer Sunday.

Ingredients for 4-5 servings:

1 chicken, jointed, about 1 kg	2 tbsp bland oil
2-3 limes	½ tsp black pepper powder
6-8 strands saffron *or* ¼ tsp turmeric powder	2-3 green cardamoms
	2 bay leaves
	1 tsp salt

Preparation: Wash the chicken and drain. Wash the limes and squeeze out the juice, about ½ cup. Soak the saffron, if used, in the lime juice for about 30 minutes.

Method: Put all the ingredients except the chicken into a heavy-bottomed pan, along with ½ cup water, and bring up to the boil.

Add the chicken pieces, toss to mix, cover tightly and cook over the lowest possible heat till the chicken is tender, about 30 minutes. Check every now and then, and add another ½ cup water as it dries.

When the chicken is cooked, take the pan off the heat and let it cool. Carefully take the chicken meat off the bone, and arrange in a serving dish. Strain the cooking liquid over it, and chill in the fridge. The liquid will set into a pale yellow jelly.

Serve with an assortment of salads.

POT ROAST

Ingredients for 4-6 servings:

1 whole haunch (raan), about 1 kg
12-15 cloves garlic
1-2 limes
1 tbsp+3 tbsp bland oil
1 tsp salt
1 tsp black pepper powder
12-15 cloves
2 bay leaves
1½ tsp flour for gravy, if served hot

Preparation: Make sure when buying the haunch that it will fit into your pressure cooker. Wash it under the tap, and clean it of any extraneous bits of fat and membrane.

Cut each garlic clove into 2-3 slivers. Wash the limes, and squeeze out the juice into a bowl, about 1 tbsp. Add 1 tbsp oil, the salt and the pepper, and blend together as best you can.

With the point of a sharp knife pierce the meat all over to a depth of about 1 cm, and insert the garlic slivers and the cloves into the slits. Rub the oil and juice mixture over the meat, and leave to marinate for several hours, or overnight or all day in the fridge. If convenient, baste every now and then with the juice.

Method: Heat 3 tbsp oil in the pressure cooker, swirling it around so that the sides as well as the base are well coated. When the oil is hot, but short of smoking, put in the meat, reserving the surplus juice of the marinade. Cook over high heat turning often, till well browned on all sides, about 10-15 minutes. As some of the juice is forced out of the meat, it will coagulate at the base. Keep scraping it as best you can to prevent it from burning.

When the meat is well browned, remove it from the cooker, and pour off the hot oil through a wire strainer into a small metal bowl and reserve. Put a trivet in the cooker and place the meat on top of this. Add the bay leaves, reserved marinade and 1½ cups boiling water. Cook under pressure for 20 minutes.

Test if done. Pierce with the point of a sharp knife. It should slide in and out easily and the juice which runs out should be clear.

The meat may also show signs of shrinking away from the bone. If it still doesn't seem cooked, close the cooker and cook under pressure for another 5 minutes or so. Remove the roast to a serving platter and keep hot.

To make the gravy, remove the trivet from the cooker, pour off the cooking liquid into a small bowl, and return about ½ tbsp of the reserved oil to the cooker. Thicken with the flour, stirring over low heat to make a roux (see p. 258). Take the cooker off the heat, and stir in the hot cooking liquid. Return to the heat and cook stirring constantly for a few minutes till smooth and blended. Add a little more water if it seems too thick.

This roast is as good cold as hot. If it is to be eaten cold, avoid making the gravy and instead boil down the cooking liquid till it is reduced to about ½ cup. It will congeal as it cools and can be eaten along with the cold meat as a relish. This makes a good sandwich for a packed lunch.

TUNISIAN MEAT CASSEROLE WITH APRICOTS

In North Africa and Iran, they have a wonderful way of cooking meat with fruit. Here are a couple of examples.

Ingredients for 3-4 servings:

½ kg meat, cut into pieces
200 gms dried apricots
2 large onions
3 cloves garlic
2 limes, *optional*
1 tbsp bland oil
½ tsp cummin powder
1 tsp powdered cinnamon
4 cloves
2 bay leaves
½ tsp black pepper powder
½ tsp salt

Preparation: Wash and drain the meat. Wash the apricots thoroughly. Add cold water just to cover and soak for a couple of hours. Slice the onions fine. Crush the garlic. Wash the limes, if used, and squeeze out the juice, about 2 tbsp.

Method: Heat the oil till just short of smoking. Add the meat and cook stirring over high heat till well browned.

Stir in the onions and garlic, cover the pan, lower the heat and cook till the onions are limp and moist. Raise the heat and cook stirring frequently till the onions are beginning to brown and the dish smells savoury.

Add the rest of the ingredients except the apricots and lime juice, together with 1 cup water, and cook under pressure till the meat is nearly done, about 8-10 minutes, depending on the quality of the meat.

Mix in the apricots with as much of the soaking water as you need for the gravy to have the consistency you like, and simmer without pressure till the apricots are tender and the meat is done. Check seasoning, and add the lime juice if it seems too sweet.

Serve with plain rice, or preferably chilau (see p. 45).

Variation: Add the apricots along with the onions and cook with the meat. They will naturally soften till they become integrated with the gravy rather than remaining a separate entity. In this case, soak the apricots a bit longer and remove the stones before adding them to the pan.

APPLE KHORESH

Although the preceding recipe is from Tunisia, and this one from Iran, they are essentially the same, only with the substitution of apples for apricots. Use a crisp slightly tart variety—Golden Delicious for preference. Wash, peel, core and cut 3 medium apples into largish pieces. Fry them gently in oil or butter for a few minutes till lightly coloured. Cook the meat according to the previous recipe, adding the apples near the end of the cooking time, and cook till soft but not mushy (unless you'd prefer them that way).

Since the Iranian Khoresh is conceived of as a sauce rather than a solid dish, use more water (2-2½ cups), and cook the meat till very tender.

MEAT AND FRUIT POLO
Persian Meat and Fruit Pulao

This is actually what in India would be called a biryani rather than a pulao.

Cook meat and fruit according to the recipe for Tunisian Meat Casserole with Apricots or Apple Khoresh, in any of their variations given above, keeping it a bit dry. Reduce the gravy if necessary by boiling it fast.

Prepare and boil the rice as given for chilau (see p. 45), till ¾ cooked.

Put 1 tbsp bland oil into a large heavy-bottomed pan and place on medium heat, swirling it well around to coat the sides of the pan. Arrange the meat and rice in layers in the pan, starting and finishing with a layer of rice. Cover with a tight-fitting lid around which you have tied a clean cloth to absorb the steam.

Cook on low heat without stirring for 15-20 minutes.

SPINACH SALAD

Ingredients for 5-6 servings as a side dish:

1 kg spinach
1 cup creamy curd
1-2 cloves garlic

½ tbsp bland oil
½ tsp salt
½ tsp black pepper powder

Preparation: Prepare the spinach as given on p. 109. Beat the curd till smooth and blended. Crush the garlic.

Method: Heat the oil in a large pan or kadhai, swirling it well around the sides. Add the spinach by handfuls, as it wilts and loses bulk, till you can get it all in. Cook uncovered on low heat till tender. Raise the heat and cook stirring for a few minutes till nearly dry. Leave to cool.

Blend the garlic, salt and pepper into the beaten curd. Fold the curd mixture into the spinach. If you like, you can avoid mixing them thoroughly, so that you get an attractive dappled or marbled effect.

Turn out into a serving dish and chill.

TOMATO AND AUBERGINE SAUCE

Ingredients for 2-3 cups:

250 gms aubergines
4 large tomatoes
2 large onions
6-8 cloves garlic
3 tbsp bland oil

½ tsp salt
½ tsp black pepper powder
A small bunch fresh mint, dill, basil *or* coriander leaves, *optional*

Preparation: Use any type of aubergines. The long thin ones may be most convenient to handle. Wash them and cut into medium dice or rounds, without peeling. Wash the tomatoes and chop fine. Slice the onions fine. Crush the garlic. Wash and chop the green herb, if used.

Method: Heat the oil in a kadhai. Add the onions and garlic, cover and stew on low heat till soft and translucent. Raise the heat and stir-fry till starting to turn brown.

Add the aubergines and continue to stir-fry till they begin to soften. Stir in the tomatoes, salt, pepper and herb, if used, bring to the boil, cover and simmer over low heat for at least 30 minutes. As the juice from the tomatoes dries, give it a stir every now and then to prevent it sticking and burning.

Serve as a sauce with a substantial ingredient like **pasta,** cooked as in Spaghetti Bolognese (p. 266). You could also serve with **chickpeas (kabuli chana), lobia, rajma** or even **chana dal**—cooked without masala according to the times recommended in the chapter on dal, and with the water drained off (use minimum water).

Failing all else, have it with plain rice, or boiled potatoes. A little curd on the side goes very well, and there you have your simple one-dish meal.

Variation: Substitute capsicum for the aubergine, and halve the quantity of oil. This changes the character of the sauce entirely.

RICE SALAD

Ingredients for 4-5 servings:

2 cups long-grain rice
2 limes
3-4 spring onions *or*
1 small regular onion
A small bunch fresh mint, basil, parsley *or* coriander leaves
3 medium tomatoes
2 tbsp salad oil
1 tsp salt
½ tsp black pepper powder

Optional ingredients:
1 tin tuna fish
Black *or* green olives
1 medium cucumber
Raw vegetables, e.g. carrot, cabbage to make ½ cup after preparation
Vegetables for boiling, e.g. french beans, beetroot, cauliflower to make ½ cup after preparation

Preparation: Wash the rice and soak for about 30 minutes. Wash the limes and squeeze out the juice, about 2 tbsp. Chop the spring onions or onion fine. Wash and chop the green herbs and the tomatoes.

Of the optional ingredients, open the tin of tuna, drain out and discard the oil, turn the fish out onto a plate and shred medium-small. Halve the olives and stone if necessary. Wash and peel the cucumber, cut lengthwise in quarters, cut out and discard the seeds and dice the flesh. Wash, peel and grate the carrot. Cut the cabbage into small pieces.

Wash, trim and dice the french beans and beetroot. Cut the cauliflower into florets and wash. Boil these three vegetables lightly in minimum water, till al dente.

Method: Boil the rice according to one of the recipes on p. 38-39, and let it cool a bit. You can use leftover rice out of the fridge, but the tastes blend better if mixed when the rice is still warm. Add the chopped onion, herbs, lime juice, salad oil, salt and pepper to the warm rice, and toss together till well mixed. Taste and add a little more salt, pepper, lime juice and/or oil as required.

Add all the rest of the ingredients, and toss together till well mixed. Chill.

TAHINA CREAM

A west Asian classic. From Iraq to Greece, tahina (sesame seed paste) is a basic ingredient for all sorts of exciting dishes, and is available readymade. With a grinder, it is not difficult to make it at home.

Ingredients to make 1 cup:

Tahina paste:
1 cup sesame seeds
1-1½ tbsp good-quality salad oil, preferably olive oil

Seasonings:
2 limes
1 clove garlic
¼ tsp salt
1 tsp cummin powder, *optional*

Garnish:
8-10 sprigs parsley *or* coriander leaves, *optional*

Preparation: Roast the sesame seeds on a tava, or in a small heavy-bottomed frying pan, over medium to low heat. Shake them gently every now and then, and within a couple of minutes they will start to crackle and change colour. Keep on shaking till they are a more or less uniform golden brown, then remove from the heat, and leave a few seconds longer till the base of the tava cools.

Wash the limes and squeeze out the juice, about 2 tbsp. Crush the garlic. Wash and chop the herbs.

Method: To make the tahina paste, grind the roasted seeds, turn out into a small bowl, and stir in the oil a little at a time till you have a medium-consistency paste.

To make tahina cream, add the lime juice, garlic, salt, and cummin powder, if used, gradually to the tahina, tasting till the blend of flavours is to your liking. If necessary, gradually beat in a few tbsp of cold water, till the consistency is that of a light cream.

Serve in a bowl or on a plate, garnished with the chopped herbs. Eat with bread as a spread or dip.

Variations: Use good-quality mild malt vinegar instead of lime juice.

- Stir in a larger quantity of chopped parsley or coriander.
- Blend with an equal quantity of creamy curd.
- To make **Teradot,** stir in 100 gms walnut kernels, pounded or ground till well disintegrated but not yet reduced to a paste.

HUMMUS-BI-TAHINA
West Asian Chickpea and Sesame Dip

Possibly the most widely used application of tahina. Puréed chickpeas (kabuli chana) blended with tahina and seasoned with lime and garlic. Inspired.

Ingredients for 2 cups:

1 cup chickpeas
2 limes
1-2 cloves garlic
8-10 sprigs fresh parsley *or* coriander leaves, *optional*
½ tsp salt

Tahina paste made with ¾ cup sesame seeds and 1 tbsp oil

Garnish, optional:
2 tsp good-quality salad oil, preferably olive oil

Preparation: Wash and soak the chickpeas as given on p. 92, and cook under pressure till soft. Allow to cool. Wash the limes and squeeze out the juice, about 2 tbsp. Crush the garlic. Wash and chop the herb, if used.

Method: Put half the chickpeas into the goblet attachment of the blender with enough of the water in which it was cooked, and give it a whirl till reduced to a purée. Add the rest, with more of the water if it seems too thick, and repeat.

Turn out into a bowl and stir in the lime juice, garlic, herb, if used, and salt. Best to add them gradually and keep tasting till you get it to your liking. Add the tahina, and stir well to blend.

Turn into a serving bowl and dribble the oil over it. Eat with bread or biscuits as a spread or dip.

Variation: Make **Chickpea Cream**, using the above recipe minus the tahina, adding 1 tsp cummin powder and 1 tbsp salad oil. Try blending in ½-1 cup of well-beaten creamy curd.

LENTIL OR BEAN SALAD

Ingredients for 3-4 servings:

1½ cups whole urad, masoor, rajma *or* lobia
1-2 cloves garlic *or* ½ small onion
2 limes

A small bunch fresh coriander leaves
2 tbsp salad oil
1 tsp salt
1 tsp black pepper powder
1 tsp cummin powder

Preparation: Wash the dal or beans. Dal needs to soak for minimum 1 hour, and beans for several hours or overnight.

Crush the garlic or chop the onion. Wash the limes, and squeeze out the juice, about 2 tbsp. Wash the coriander leaves and chop coarsely.

Method: Drain the dal or beans, wash and cook in the pressure cooker, using rather less water than you would to cook a dal dish. Your urad will take about 20 minutes, masoor or rajma 10 minutes and lobia 5-6 minutes.

Using a slotted spoon, remove the dal or beans from the water. Set the pressure cooker back on the heat and boil the water till thickened and reduced to ½ cup or so. Pour over the dal or beans.

Mix all the ingredients except the coriander into the dal or beans while still fairly hot. Cool and add the coriander, mixing some of it in and sprinkling the rest on top for a garnish.

Chill lightly and serve.

Variation: **Lentil or Bean and Tomato Salad:** Fry 2 chopped onions in 1 tbsp oil till golden. Add 3 chopped tomatoes and cook stirring for a few minutes on high heat till the juice runs. Add the dal or beans and continue as above omitting the raw garlic or onion in the final assembly.

CURD DIP

Use as a dip, or sandwich filling, or spread on savoury biscuits.

Ingredients for 2 cups:

2½ cups curd
½ small onion or to taste
½ tsp salt

Any or all of the following seasonings:
A small bunch coriander leaves, mint, basil *or* dill

1-2 cloves garlic
1 tsp cummin powder
1-2 tbsp mayonnaise *or* 1 tbsp french dressing
1 tbsp tomato sauce
1 tsp mustard paste
½-1 tsp black pepper powder

Preparation: Thicken the curd by hanging it as given on p. 22. Chop the onion as fine as possible. Wash and chop the green herb. Chop the garlic fine, or crush it.

Method: Stir and fold all the ingredients together.

Note: Best not to make an awful lot at a time. This dip keeps in the fridge, no doubt, in the sense that it doesn't go bad; but it may turn unpleasantly sour within 2-3 days.

18

Packed Lunches

The first thing that comes to mind, obviously, is **sandwiches**. The important thing about sandwiches is that they should be **well filled.** There's nothing more miserable than two slices of bread stuck together with just a scrape of something in between. Start with a generous spreading of **butter** on both slices of bread. (Have the butter fairly soft before you start spreading.) The filling should be moist, but not too thin or it'll tend to leak at the sides.

For an **egg sandwich**, use **Scrambled Eggs** (p. 216), or **Œufs Mollets** (p. 204), well mashed and seasoned with salt and pepper. For someone who doesn't like half-cooked eggs, use **Hard-boiled Eggs** (p. 204), softened with butter, or thin **Omelettes** (p. 210).

Cut slices from a **Meat Loaf** (p. 262), **Raan Musallam** (p. 170) or **Pot Roast** (p. 270), moistening them with plenty of the masala or gravy, for a **meat sandwich.**

When making **Pish-pash** (p. 44) or **Chicken Fricassée** (p. 261), save a couple of pieces of boiled chicken; take the meat off the bone, shred, season with salt and pepper, and moisten with a little stock or mayonnaise for a **chicken sandwich.** Or use any leftover chicken curry, taking the meat off the bones, shredding it and loosening with some of the gravy.

Mash tinned **sardines** or **tuna** (discarding most of the oil), mix with a little creamy curd or mayonnaise, salt and pepper to taste, and there's your **fish sandwich.**

Clap some leftover dry vegetable between your two slices for a **vegetable sandwich.**

Slices of tomato and/or cucumber, with or without a little shredded cabbage, well seasoned with salt and pepper and perhaps a dash of mayonnaise for **salad sandwiches.**

Hummus-bi-tahina, or any of its variations (p. 280) make good sandwiches; but be sure to make the hummus on the thick side. Same goes for **Curd Dip** (p. 282), another tasty sandwich (but better not in hot weather, the curd will go sour).

Your friendly neighbourhood provision shop will certainly stock several varieties of **processed cheese**, which you can use for sandwiches if you like that sort of thing. In the metropolitan cities you can also buy different kinds of **genuine cheese**, Indian and foreign, in the upmarket shopping areas—at a price. Not perhaps for every day, but a nice treat once in a way when you're feeling affluent.

And remember, for virtually any sandwich, a bit of **green herb—coriander, mint, basil** or **dill**—chopped fine and mixed into the filling, will definitely add freshness and zing. A teaspoonful of **mayonnaise** is also a pleasant addition to most sandwiches.

For variety's sake, you could try **toasting** your sandwiches. There are sandwich toasters available in the market which come with directions for use, with which you can toast any of the above.

Apart from sandwiches, almost anything that can be eaten cold, can be packed for an office or picnic lunch, or to eat in a train. **Thayir Shadam** (p. 42), set in a secure container with a well fitting lid, is ideal for the purpose. **Katche Keeme ke Kabab** (p. 176) are excellent cold, and so is **Eggah** (p. 214). **Rice Salad** (p. 277), or **Lentil or Bean Salad** (p. 281), the version with or without tomatoes. **Sprouts** (p. 97), cooked or in a salad.

Some dryish vegetable dishes aren't bad cold: **Sookhi Gobhi** (p. 117), for example, or **Mirchwali Gobhi** (p. 116); **Bund Gobhi ki Subzi** (p. 101); **Toori ki Subzi** (p. 128); **Panch-poran ka Palak** (p. 111) or **Palak Mughlai** (p. 113), or even **Palak Raita** (p. 227) (but in hot weather the curd might tend to turn sour out of the fridge). **Baingan Masaledar–1** (p. 124) is surprisingly good eaten cold. And of course **Baingan ka Bharta,** or **Baingan ke Bharte ka Raita** (p. 229)—with the same caveat as for the Palak Raita. Cook a bit extra when you're making supper the day before, and put some aside. A couple of rotis or a little rice, and there's your lunch.

Stuffed Parathas (p. 60): you could make them the night before and crisp them on the tava in the morning before packing them. A spoonful of **pickle** or (when it's not very hot) a little **curd** packed in a screw-top jar would help.

Into making **soups**? Carry some in a thermos flask, either hot or cold depending on the season; have some savoury crunchy biscuits—say cream crackers, sandwiched together in pairs with plenty of butter—for a contrast in texture.

19

Suggestions for Simplified Eating

It's not necessary to eat the full conventional dal-subzi-rice or -roti meal every day, with or without a non-vegetarian item. A few of our recipes can be regarded as literally one-dish meals, e.g.

- **Haleem** (p. 168)
- **Pish-pash** (p. 44)
- **Upama** (p. 142)
- **Thayir Shadam** (p. 42)—especially if you happen to be feeling a bit fragile
- **Irish Stew** (p. 264)
- **Lancashire Hotpot** (p. 264)
- **Spaghetti Bolognese** (p. 266)
- **Spaghetti alla Marinara** (p. 268).

Others require minimal accompaniments. Almost any egg dish can be served with toast and butter or with roti in the case of

- **Egg Bhujia** (p. 219)
- The Parsi **Akoori** (p. 217) and **Eeda dishes** (p. 208).

If you're pushed, rice dishes like

- **Meat** or **Chicken Pulao** (p. 48)
- **Khichdi** (p. 50)

can be eaten with just curd and pickle.

Meat and vegetable dishes like

- **Shabdegh** (p. 164)
- **Aloo Gosht** (p. 167)
- **Dal Gosht** (p. 166)
- **Saag Gosht** (p. 165)

can be served by themselves with just rice or roti.

Likewise

- **Dal with vegetables** (p. 89)
- **Choley** (p. 92), with **Pooris** (p. 56)
- **Rajma/Lobia aur Tamatar;** (p. 91)
- **Kadhi-chaval** (p. 94)—a marriage made in heaven.

For snack-lunches or brunches at weekends, we suggest, in addition to a possible selection from the above list

- **Hummus-bi-tahina** (p. 280), served with toast or cream crackers
- **Rice Salad** (p. 277)
- **Chicken Fricassée** (p. 261) with rice
- **Meat Loaf** (p. 262), hot or cold, with boiled potatoes and perhaps some green salad
- **Stuffed Parathas** (p. 60) with curd and optional pickle
- Any **thick soup,** with **Sippets** (p. 64) or toast.

Glossary-cum-Index of Ingredients and Culinary Terms

Page numbers where given refer to further definitions or essential information about the term concerned.

Hindi names and terms used in this book, which are more commonly understood than the English equivalent, if any:

Index of Recipes